Real-Life BPMN

3rd edition

II

Jakob Freund
Bernd Rücker

Real-Life BPMN

3rd edition

Using BPMN, CMMN and DMN to analyze, improve, and automate processes in your company

Jakob Freund, Bernd Rücker
Founders of Camunda
www.camunda.com

This third edition in English is based on the successful fifth German edition.
Also available in Spanish.

Editing for the English-language edition of this book was provided by James Venis of Lakewood, Colorado, USA, with assistance from Kristen Hannum (1st edition), Jalynn Venis (2nd edition) and James Simmonds (3rd edition).
www.jvenis.net

Copyright 2016 Jakob Freund and Bernd Rücker.
All rights reserved.
ISBN-10: 1541163443
ISBN-13: 978-1541163447

Contents

Preface		XI
1	**Introduction**	**1**
1.1	Business process management	1
	1.1.1 Definition	1
	1.1.2 BPM in practice	1
	1.1.3 Camunda BPM life cycle	2
	1.1.4 Process automation	4
1.2	The BPM standards trio	6
	1.2.1 BPMN for structured workflows	6
	1.2.2 CMMN for unstructured case processing	7
	1.2.3 DMN for rule-based decisions	9
	1.2.4 An example of interaction	10
1.3	Can BPMN bridge the gap?	15
	1.3.1 The dilemma	15
	1.3.2 The customers of a process model	16
1.4	A method framework for BPMN	17
	1.4.1 The Camunda house	18
	1.4.2 The great misunderstanding	19
Preface		1
2	**The notation in detail**	**23**
2.1	Understanding BPMN	23
	2.1.1 Things BPMN does *not* do	23
	2.1.2 A map: The basic elements of BPMN	24
	2.1.3 Perspectives in process analysis	25
	2.1.4 Models, instances, tokens, and correlations	26

	2.1.5	Symbols and attributes	26
2.2		Simple tasks and none events	27
2.3		Design process paths with gateways	28
	2.3.1	Data-based exclusive gateway	28
	2.3.2	Parallel gateway	30
	2.3.3	Data-based inclusive gateway	33
	2.3.4	Default flow and getting stuck	36
	2.3.5	Complex gateway	36
2.4		Design process paths without gateways	38
2.5		Lanes	40
2.6		Events	43
	2.6.1	Relevance in BPMN	43
	2.6.2	Message events	47
	2.6.3	Timer events	49
	2.6.4	Error events	51
	2.6.5	Conditional	51
	2.6.6	Signal events	52
	2.6.7	Terminate events	53
	2.6.8	Link events	54
	2.6.9	Compensation events	54
	2.6.10	Multiple events	56
	2.6.11	Parallel events	57
	2.6.12	Escalation events	58
	2.6.13	Cancel events	58
	2.6.14	Event-based gateway	58
	2.6.15	Event-based parallel gateway	61
2.7		Special tasks	61
	2.7.1	Typification	61
	2.7.2	Markers	63
	2.7.3	Global tasks and call activity	66
2.8		Subprocesses	66
	2.8.1	Encapsulate complexity	66
	2.8.2	Modularization and reuse	69
	2.8.3	Attached events	71
	2.8.4	Markers	72
	2.8.5	Transactions	74
	2.8.6	Event subprocesses	76
2.9		Pools and message flows	78

	2.9.1	The conductor and the orchestra	78
	2.9.2	Rules for application	80
	2.9.3	The art of collaboration	81
	2.9.4	Collapse pools	83
	2.9.5	Multiple instance pools	84
2.10	Data		85
2.11	Artifacts		87
	2.11.1	Annotations and groups	87
	2.11.2	Custom artifacts	88
2.12	Comparison with other notations		88
	2.12.1	Extended event-driven process chain (eEPC)	89
	2.12.2	UML activity diagram	89
	2.12.3	ibo sequence plan	91
	2.12.4	Key figures and probabilities	91
2.13	Choreographies and conversations		94

3 Strategic process models — 97

3.1	About this chapter		97
	3.1.1	Purpose and benefit	97
	3.1.2	Model requirements	98
	3.1.3	Procedure	99
3.2	Case example: Recruiting process		101
3.3	Restricting the symbol set		102
	3.3.1	Pools and lanes	102
	3.3.2	Tasks and subprocesses	105
	3.3.3	Gateways	106
	3.3.4	Events and event-based gateway	106
	3.3.5	Data and artifacts	109
	3.3.6	Custom artifacts	110
	3.3.7	Hide and reveal symbols	111
3.4	Process analysis on the strategic level		112
3.5	Conversations and choreographies		114

4 Operational process models — 117

4.1	About this chapter		117
	4.1.1	Purpose and benefit	117
	4.1.2	Model requirements	118
	4.1.3	Procedure	118
4.2	From the strategic level to the operational level		120

4.3	Processes of the participants	122
4.4	Preparing for process automation	125
	4.4.1 Designing for support by a workflow engine	125
	4.4.2 Required processes of the workflow engine	127
	4.4.3 Further requirements	129
	4.4.4 Technical implementation beyond the workflow engine	130
	4.4.5 Technical implementation without workflow engine	132
4.5	Hands-on tips for the operational level	134
	4.5.1 From the happy path to the bitter truth	134
	4.5.2 The true benefit of subprocesses	139
	4.5.3 The limits of formalization	140
	4.5.4 Taking business decisions out of processes	141

5 CMMN - Introduction and overview **145**

5.1	Understanding CMMN	145
	5.1.1 CMMN or BPMN?	146
	5.1.2 Introduction example	147
	5.1.3 Life cycle in CMMN	148
	5.1.4 User interfaces of case management systems	149
5.2	Notation elements	151
	5.2.1 Cases and tasks	151
	5.2.2 Types of tasks	152
	5.2.3 Sentries	153
	5.2.4 Manual activation rule	154
	5.2.5 Repetition rule	155
	5.2.6 Required rule	155
	5.2.7 Auto complete	156
	5.2.8 Milestones	157
	5.2.9 Stages	158
	5.2.10 Exit criterion	159
	5.2.11 Modeling without do-it tasks	160
	5.2.12 Events	160
	5.2.13 Case file items	161
	5.2.14 Conditions	162
	5.2.15 Non-blocking tasks	163
	5.2.16 Discretionary tasks	163
5.3	Linking BPMN and CMMN	165

6	DMN - Introduction and overview	167
6.1	Understanding DMN	167
6.2	Notation elements	168
	6.2.1 Decision tables	168
	6.2.2 Expressions in decision tables	171
	6.2.3 Hit policy	174
	6.2.4 Advanced FEEL	177
	6.2.5 Decision requirements	179
6.3	Practical tips	181
	6.3.1 Linking BPMN and DMN	181
	6.3.2 Decisions with a decision flow	182
	6.3.3 Linking CMMN and DMN	185
	6.3.4 The life cycle of decisions	186

7	Automation	189
7.1	Purpose and benefit	189
7.2	Basics	190
	7.2.1 Model execution with model execution engines	190
	7.2.2 Executing the BPMN, CMMN, and DMN standards	192
	7.2.3 Alternative automation languages	192
	7.2.4 When is it worth using a workflow or case engine?	193
	7.2.5 When is it worth using a decision engine?	195
	7.2.6 Decision and workflow engines in interaction	195
7.3	Automating technical process flows	197
	7.3.1 Model requirements	197
	7.3.2 Procedure	197
	7.3.3 The executable process model	198
7.4	Practical tips	201
	7.4.1 The zero code trap	201
	7.4.2 The myth of engine interchangeability	202
	7.4.3 Modeling or programming	203
	7.4.4 Overcoming technical challenges	204
	7.4.5 Acceptance criteria when introducing a BPM platform	207

8	Introducing BPMN on a broad base	211
8.1	Goals	211
8.2	Roles	213
	8.2.1 Of gurus, followers, and unbelievers	213
	8.2.2 Anchoring in the organization	214

		8.2.3	Training of BPMN gurus	215
	8.3	Methods		216
		8.3.1	Range of symbols	217
		8.3.2	Naming conventions	218
		8.3.3	Layout	219
		8.3.4	Modeling alternatives	219
		8.3.5	Design patterns	220
	8.4	Tools		222
		8.4.1	Definition of your own BPM stack	222
		8.4.2	The BPMN modeling tool	224
		8.4.3	Camunda BPM: An open source BPM platform	224
		8.4.4	It can't always be software	225
	8.5	Meta-processes		228
	8.6	Practical example: Process documentation at Energie Südbayern		229
		8.6.1	Energie Südbayern company profile	229
		8.6.2	Starting point and assignment	229
		8.6.3	Project development	229
		8.6.4	Conclusion	230

9 Tips to get started — **231**

9.1 Develop your own style — 231
9.2 Find fellow sufferers — 232
9.3 Get started — 232

Bibliography — **233**

Preface

■ Preface to the 3rd edition

Well – a lot has happened...

This succinct statement was actually only supposed to be a placeholder for the preface that we still had to write. But it is actually a perfect summary:

- BPMN has now firmly been established and was "honored" with an ISO standard in 2013.
- In March 2014, OMG, the institution which developed BPMN, adopted their new CMMN standard which is a very good complement to BPMN for representing unstructured business processes.
- In September 2015, the very same OMG performed yet another feat by adopting the DMN standard which deals with modeling and automating decisions and is also an excellent complement to BPMN.

This is reason enough to publish the third edition of our practical guide in order to provide a compact description of both of these latest additions. We have already integrated both CMMN and DMN into our own software product Camunda BPM and have thus created the technological basis for using all three standards individually or in combination. This has already occurred several times and therefore, seven years after first putting our practical experience with BPMN to paper, we are now able to share our first practical experiences of CMMN and DMN with you.

In addition to this, we have included several selective updates and improvements. The chapter on automation in particular has been completely revised as we have now come to understand so much better what information is relevant to this book through countless practical projects. To make space for new content we have deleted all examples related to BPMN-XML since nobody ever read them anyway.

And we have renamed two terms:

In previous editions we called a software that was able to technically execute BPMN models a *process engine*. In this edition you will note that we instead use the term *workflow engine*. Here we are acknowledging that BPMN is an instrument which is very well suited to modeling and automating clearly structured processes. It is however less suited to unstructured processes which cannot always be described as an unambiguous process diagram. We give some examples of this in section 1.2.2 on page 7, among others. Such unstructured processes are however understood by us as being *business processes* which we will deal with in order to move our company forward. This is why we no longer speak of a *process engine* when we mean the execution of structured processes but instead refer to a *workflow engine*.

We have also done away with the term *rule engine*. As mentioned above, there is now the DMN standard and the *D* stands for *Decision*. This reveals a shift in paradigm which we deem to be very useful. Ask yourself the following question: Is it more important to you to stick to the rules or to take the right decisions? Well there you go.

Of course it may be necessary to stick to rules and this therefore also determines certain decisions. But focusing on the idea of taking the *right decision* is in our opinion a better idea. On the technical level as well, a *decision engine*, i.e. software which executes the decision models, may work differently to a *rule engine*. We believe that the future belongs to *Business Decision Management* and that both at business and technical levels the methods, standards and technologies that go along with it are a wiser choice.

Finally, we were not able to resist the temptation of patting ourselves on the back: When we wrote the first version of this book in 2009 we also explored the limits of BPMN. We realized that BPMN was less suitable for unstructured activities, and that here solutions in the area of *case management* would be necessary. We furthermore foresaw that the combination of BPMN with the topic of *business rules* represented one of the greatest potentials for business process management as a whole. Seven years down the line there is now a CMMN standard for case management and a DMN standard which in our view represents an improvement of the business rule approach. Both of these standards are designed to be combined with BPMN, and therefore we were able to take the same passages which previously referred to the limits of BPMN and complete them by adding these new solution approaches.

So there you have it.

We would now as always like to wish you great success in working with BPMN, CMMN and DMN, and of course we hope you enjoy reading this book!

Jakob Freund and Bernd Rücker
November 2016

■ Preface to the 2nd edition

"Ah, here are Mr. Freund and Mr. Rücker. Gentlemen, it's a pleasure to finally meet you! You know, I'm a real fan of your book. I especially like your method framework —it helped us a lot."

"We're glad to hear it, though we've changed that section in the new edition."

"Really? That's a shame. I liked the pyramid."

"It's a house now."

"Okay, that's reasonable. Every house has a basement —that's where we keep the IT Department. Meanwhile, up at the top, that's where you'll find me. I have a great view and, after all, I *am* the boss here!"

"Well, that's not really what we had in mind. Instead..."

"Hogwash! Anyhow, why the change?"

"Because the pyramid sometimes led to misunderstandings. For example, some people thought that *executable* process models always were refined versions of their *operational* process models."

"But that's exactly what they are! This is how our projects work, you see: The Business Department, guided by management, of course, creates an operational process model. That's the specification we send down to the basement —I mean, to the IT Department. They make it executable. It's easy for them; they just need to refine the operational model to make it executable!"

"So tell us, how well do these projects work?"

"Well, of course there are problems here and there, misunderstandings, delays, and so on. But that's just the way it is with IT. You just have to keep the pressure on!"

"What you're describing is one of the more inept approaches. That's why we changed from the pyramid to the house."

"Well excuse me! Do you have any other better ideas?"

"We do, actually. You'll find them in section 1.4.1 on page 18 of this new edition."

"Very well, I'll take a look at that. Any other news?"

"Sure. We've corrected a few mistakes, applied some improvements, and we've updated many topics to make them more current."

"More current topics? Can you give an example?"

"Among other things, we re-evaluated the relevance of the BPEL standard."

"The what?"

"Exactly."

"Is there any news about BPMN software tools?"

"Thank you for that question! Since the last edition, we have become a BPMN tool vendor. In section 8.4.2 on page 224, we describe the Camunda BPM platform and our latest project: bpmn.io."

"Excuse me, are you really advertising your software here? Is that even legal? I'm disgusted!"

"But it helps to describe it all with a specific example. Otherwise, it just remains abstract theory. Besides, Camunda BPM and bpmn.io are open-source projects."

"Oh, so I don't have to pay for it? Like free beer? That's great!"

"Well, that's not entirely how open source works..."

"Pah, you and your preaching again! Instead of listening to your rambling, I'll go read your book. At least that won't contradict me the whole time!"

"Enjoy!"

Jakob Freund and Bernd Rücker
September 2014

■ Preface to the 1st edition

This is a book about Business Process Management (BPM) and Business Process Model and Notation (BPMN). Truth be told, there are several BPMN books on the market, and some of them are quite good. So why should you care about this one?

This book distills the BPMN project experience that we have accumulated while running Camunda, our consulting company in Berlin, Germany. Our firm specializes in BPM. During the past five years, we have applied BPMN in practically every one of more than 250 customer engagements. These were big businesses, small companies, and public institutions.

In 2009, we published the first edition of our "BPMN Hands-On Guide." According to Amazon.de, it is still the highest-ranked book on BPMN in German. We are honored by the number of five-star-ratings that readers have awarded that book. And if you read their reviews, you see that what they like best about it are the real-life examples and the vivid language. (Most German books on this topic suffer from being abstract, and the writing is uninspired.)

We joined the Object Management Group (OMG) in 2009, and we helped to finalize BPMN 2.0. We also contributed chapters to the *BPMN 2.0 by Example* tutorial that the OMG provides to beginners. These interactions showed us that, even outside of Germany, few people have applied BPMN as often, as deeply, or as broadly as have we. We decided to translate our book into English, and we gave it a cooler-sounding title than *Hands-On Guide*.

We hope you'll enjoy reading this book. Even more, we hope that you will find lots of help in it —great examples, meaningful tips and suggestions, and patterns that can lead you to solutions for your own real-life BPMN challenges.

You hear people bashing BPMN once in a while with arguments that are more or less pointless. You also hear valid critiques and useful suggestions. The good news is that we have a global community of people driving BPM generally and BPMN in particular, and we thank every one of them for contributing to a standard that, while not perfect, is definitely a big step in the right direction.

Our special thanks goes to Bruce Silver, whose own book, *BPMN Method & Style*, is one of those quite good BPMN books on the market, and to James Venis, our editor for this English-language version. If you enjoy reading it, most of your praise should go to him.

Jakob Freund and Bernd Rücker
October 2012

1 Introduction

1.1 Business process management

This book is about Business Process Model and Notation (BPMN 2.0). To understand why BPMN was invented, we need first to understand business process management (BPM).

1.1.1 Definition

Experts use different definitions for business process management. We use the definition given by the European Association of BPM (EABPM) in its reference work, *BPM Common Body of Knowledge* [Eur09]:

> Business process management (BPM) is a systemic approach for capturing, designing, executing, documenting, measuring, monitoring, and controlling both automated and non-automated processes to meet the objectives and business strategies of a company. BPM embraces the conscious, comprehensive, and increasingly technology-enabled definition, improvement, innovation, and maintenance of end-to-end processes. Through this systemic and conscious management of processes, companies achieve better results faster and more flexibly.
>
> Through BPM, processes can be aligned with the business strategy, and so help to improve company performance as a whole thanks to the optimization of processes within business divisions or even beyond company borders.

What *end-to-end process* really means is *from start to finish*. The goal is to understand and thus to assess and improve an entire process —not just its components. We find the EABPM's definition helpful because it treats automated and non-automated processes as both equally important and equally subject to the power of BPM. This understanding is essential to applying BPM successfully because it is rarely sufficient to improve only organizational procedures or the supporting technologies; most often we must improve both the procedures and the technology cooperatively.

1.1.2 BPM in practice

As consultants who specialize in BPM, our new projects almost always involve one of the following three scenarios:

1. The client wants to improve a process using Information Technology (IT).
2. The client wants current processes documented.
3. The client wants to introduce entirely new processes.

A vast majority of the time, we encounter the first scenario: the client seeks to improve a process with IT. The motivation often is a desire to improve efficiency, for example, to use software to eliminate manual keying or re-keying of data. A client may want to implement IT-based monitoring and analysis of routine processes based on key performance indicators (KPIs).

The second scenario, documenting processes, usually comes about because the client needs the documentation to guide the work of the people involved. Another rationale is that the documentation is mandated by regulation or required to obtain certification such as ISO 9000.

The third scenario happens least often. We find that when companies want to introduce entirely new processes, it is usually because they are being forced to adapt to changed market conditions, develop new channels of distribution, or introduce new products.

In public announcements companies may speak in generalities: they have an interest in exploring BPM or they want to increase their process orientation. In practice, especially in large organizations, the argument for BPM is usually well-defined and specific, but it can take two forms:

1. There is an acute reason for using BPM. The project concerns essential processes that need to be created, improved, or documented.
2. The reason for BPM is *strategic*. There will be no direct or immediate benefit, and the project likely was initiated by some manager trying to advance his or her career.

As you can imagine, serious people don't greet the second argument with enthusiasm. It is our own experience, however, which makes us advocate for this view strongly: BPM, process management, or whatever you want to call it, is not an end in itself.

We always recommend introducing BPM in steps. Each step should yield a practical, measurable benefit that justifies the time and effort that it took to accomplish. Once the justification of the first step is established, take the next step. You may think that this approach produces solutions isolated from each other, but what we mean to emphasize here is the controlled nature of the approach. Each step contributes to the big picture: the company's process orientation. A hiker may use a map and a compass to guide his or her steps. Likewise, when you introduce BPM, you should use a good procedure model and common sense as your guides.

1.1.3 Camunda BPM life cycle

Procedure models always seem to be either too simple or too complex. The overly-simple ones contain only the most painfully obvious elements. They may be useful for marketing presentations, but not much else. On the other hand, overly complex models work so hard at anticipating every contingency that they trap the user like a fly in amber. They are unrealistically rigid. Still, without a model, we wouldn't have our map to orient ourselves.

After examining the simple BPM life cycle, which is the most well-established BPM procedure model, we refined it according to our experience. We wanted to create a relatively

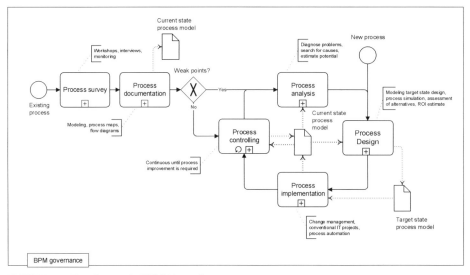

FIGURE 1.1 The Camunda BPM life cycle.

lightweight model without too many restrictions. We thought this would be more practical than the brightly colored marketing materials we see so often at conferences and in meetings. We call ours the *Camunda BPM life cycle*. See it in figure 1.1.

We intend the Camunda BPM life cycle to describe one process at a time. Any process can run through the life cycle independently of any other process, and the process can be at a different stage each time it repeats. The cycle triggers when one of the following situations arises:

- An existing process is to be documented or improved.
- A new process is to be introduced.

We have to start by examining an existing process. The *process discovery* clearly differentiates the subject process from other processes both upstream and downstream. The discovery reveals the output generated by the subject process as well as the importance of that output for the client. We use e.g. workshops or one-on-one interviews to identify not only what needs to be accomplished, but also who needs to be involved, and which IT systems.

We document the findings from the process discovery in a current state process model. This *process documentation* may include many different charts and descriptions; it usually has multiple flow charts. A systematic examination of the current state process clearly identifies weak points and their causes.

We conduct *process analysis* either because first-time documentation or continuous process control has revealed a weakness of a process that cannot be remedied easily.

The causes of weak points identified by a process analysis become the starting point for another *process design*. If necessary, different process designs can be evaluated by means of the process simulation. We also conduct a process design when introducing a new process. The result in either case is a target state process model.

In reality, we normally want to *implement* the target state process model as a change in business or organizational procedures as well as an IT project. Change management, especially process communication, plays a decisive role in successful organizational change. For the IT implementation, the process can be automated or software can be developed, adapted, or procured. The result of the process implementation is a current state process corresponding to the target state process model that, conveniently, has already been documented.

In most cases, we find all the stages from process discovery to process implementation to be necessary. Because *process monitoring* takes place continuously, however, it reveals more about the ongoing operation of the process.

The most important tasks of process control are the continuous monitoring of individual process instances and the analysis of key data so that weak points can be recognized as quickly as possible. Problems with individual entities require direct remedies, and so do structural problems if that's possible. If necessary, the current state process model has to be adjusted.

If the structural causes of the problems are unclear or complex, this calls for an improvement project that —once again —starts with a systematic process analysis of the weak points. The decision to initiate such a project lies with the process owner and anyone else who depends on the process. It is common to regard continuous process control as something that follows process implementation, though it may be better to have it follow the initial documentation. This is especially true when doubt exists about the necessity of the improvement.

Given the importance of the process model within the BPM life cycle, you can imagine the importance of a modeling standard such as BPMN. Yet you may also notice that process modeling is *not* a stage in the Camunda BPM life cycle. That's because process modeling is a method that affects *all* stages, especially process documentation and process design. As consultants, we constantly encounter people who try to insert process modeling as a stage at the same level as current state documentation. We think that's a misconception.

The BPM life cycle describes a simple way to achieve continuous improvement. Applying it requires coordination of the *triad*: The responsible parties, the applied methods, and the supporting software tools. Getting the triad moving toward a common goal is the task of BPM governance, which has authority over all processes and all BPM projects in an organization.

The EABPM's definition of BPM used the term *process automation*, and we've also used that term in describing the Camunda BPM life cycle. BPMN was developed to automate processes better. Even if you are not an IT expert, you need to understand what process automation means because it will help you to grasp how BPMN builds bridges between business and technology.

1.1.4 Process automation

Here's a simple process: A potential bank customer mails a paper credit application, which ends up on the desk of a bank accountant. The accountant examines the application, then checks the potential customer's creditworthiness through the web site of a credit rating agency. The results are positive, so the accountant records the application in a special software —let's call it *BankSoft* —and then forwards the documents to a manager for approval.

Here's the same process automated: A potential bank customer mails a paper credit application. At the bank, a clerk scans the application into electronic form. Software known as a *workflow engine* takes over the document and routes it to the bank accountant's virtual task list. The accountant accesses the task list, perhaps through the bank's web site or an email program like Microsoft Outlook, examines the application on screen, then clicks a button. The workflow engine accesses the credit rating agency, transfers the pertinent details, and receives the report. Since the report is positive, the engine passes the information to BankSoft, and it creates an approval task in the manager's task list.

Whether this example represents optimal processing is not the point. It's here only to illustrate the following principles of process automation:

- Process automation does *not* necessarily mean that the entire process is fully automated.
- The central component of process automation is the *workflow engine*, which executes an executable process model.
- The workflow engine *controls* the process by informing humans of tasks that they need to do, and it handles the result of what the people do. (This is human workflow management.) It also communicates with internal and external IT systems. (This is service orchestration.)
- The workflow engine *decides* which tasks or service calls take place or not, under what conditions, and according to the result of the task execution or service call. Thus the people involved still can influence the operational sequence of an automated process.

Figure 1.2 illustrates these principles.

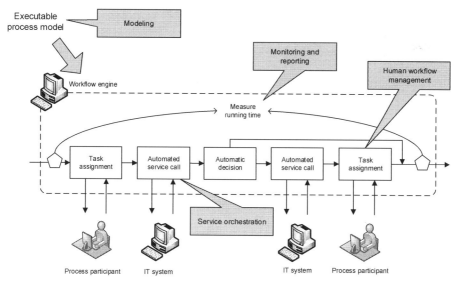

FIGURE 1.2 Process automation with a workflow engine.

If you think that process automation is just a kind of software development, you are right. The workflow engine is the compiler or interpreter, and the executable process model is the program code. A workflow engine is the mechanism of choice where process automation is concerned.

- The workflow engine specializes in representing process logic. The services it provides would have required extensive programming in the past; using a workflow engine now can make you considerably more productive than before. (Or perhaps productivity is not an issue for you, and so you develop your own spreadsheet, word-processing, and drawing programs!)
- A workflow engine combines workflow management with application integration. This makes it a powerful tool for implementing all kinds of processes from start to end, regardless of other applications or the geography of people in the process. In some BPM software solutions, we can add a separate Enterprise Service Bus (ESB) or other components to the workflow engine to make the whole more versatile.
- As the workflow engine controls the process, it tracks everything. It always knows the current stage of the process and how long each task took to complete. Because the workflow engine monitors key performance indicators directly, it provides a means to analyze performance as well. This offers huge potential for successful process control.

The three features above would themselves justify using a workflow engine, but there is a fourth justification: The workflow engine works on the basis of an executable process model. In the best cases, this model can be developed —or at least understood —by someone who is not a technician. This promotes genuinely good communication between business and IT, and it can even result in process documentation that corresponds to reality.

■ 1.2 The BPM standards trio

Our focus in this book is on BPMN as a standard for modeling and automating processes. Two more recent standards relate closely to BPMN, and they complement BPMN well. These are Case Management Model and Notation (CMMN) for managing unstructured activities and Decision Model and Notation (DMN) for managing decisions.

In this section, we provide an overview of all three standards, and then we describe both how they interlink and how they can be used in combination.

1.2.1 BPMN for structured workflows

Initially, BPMN stood for *Business Process Modeling Notation.* The first version was developed predominantly by Stephen A. White from IBM before it was published in 2004 by Business Process Management Initiative (BPMI). From the outset, the aim was to provide a standardized graphical process notation that also could be used for process automation. In 2005, Object Management Group (OMG) took over BPMI along with the further development of BPMN. OMG is an important institution in the world of IT. It is known especially for its Unified Modeling Language (UML), a modeling standard for software design. The merger of BPMI with OMG was also the beginning of a global triumph for BPMN, as it provided incentive for many companies to switch.

In February 2011, OMG released the current version, BPMN version 2.0. We were able to play a part in that. Version 2.0 came with a new definition of BPMN: *Business Process Model and Notation*, because not only did version 2.0 define the notation but also the so-called *formal metamodel*. Then in September 2013, BPMN was published as an ISO standard by the International Organization for Standardization (ISO) under ISO/IEC 19510:2013.

By now you may be wondering what this mysterious BPMN is in a material sense. BPMN is a specification. It exists in the form of a PDF document that you can download free from the OMG [Obj09] website. Whereas the specification document for BPMN version 1.2 was about 320 pages, version 2.0 has expanded to 500 pages. The documents define all the BPMN symbols, their meanings, and the rules on combining them.

With version 1.2, BPMN had not yet defined all the technical attributes necessary for direct execution of BPMN models in workflow engines. This led to several unfortunate attempts to convert ("map") BPMN models to BPEL models (see section 7.2.3 on page 192). BPMN version 2.0, however, made direct execution possible. That's an important factor in terms of the use of BPMN models. Another important factor is standardization, which offers the following advantages:

- You become more independent from certain BPM tools when you do not have to learn a new notation every time you change tools. Today more than 100 BPMN tools exist; many of them are free.
- There's a good chance that your partners in other companies (customers, suppliers, consultants, and so on) are familiar with BPMN and can therefore understand your process models quickly.
- When hiring new staff, it's likelier that more of them already can read or generate your BPMN process models.
- When universities and private companies invest time and money to develop additional solutions based on BPMN, this is to your benefit as well. Our BPMN framework, which we present later, is an example of this commitment —we never would have developed it if BPMN were not a standard.

Although BPMN focuses on business processes, there is an important limitation: There are some processes that are poorly suited to modeling or automation in BPMN. These are the *unstructured processes*; processes that do not always take place in a predictable and repeatable way. An example of an unstructured process is that of a doctor coming upon the scene of an accident with injuries. She is unlikely to work through a BPMN diagram but instead will quickly plunge in, making decisions based on her knowledge and experience, of course, but also in reaction to the chaos of the scene. We could draw other examples from practically every sector or industry, though many are less obvious. This is why the CMMN standard now exists alongside BPMN.

1.2.2 CMMN for unstructured case processing

CMMN is short for *Case Management Model and Notation*. OMG published CMMN version 1.0 in March 2014. In March 2016, OMG published version 1.1, a so-called beta version. We foresee that CMMN version 1.1 will be adopted with no major changes, which is why we describe it in this book.

To help understand the motivation behind CMMN, imagine that you are hosting a workshop to design a business process. You have a room full of people who have a stake in the process, and your mutual goal is to come up with a BPMN process model. You start with a manageable circle of participants, and you ask them what the first task should be.

The answer to your question depends, they tell you, and they proceed to pepper you with an entire list of conditions. It seems that you will have to model the evaluation of conditions first, and you'll use a gateway with many possible paths leading out of it.

During the course of the meeting, participants also point out the frequent need to jump back within the process and to repeat a previous task. While it is easy enough to represent such jumps in BPMN, if they have to be represented for more than half of the tasks, your model quickly starts to resemble a bowl of spaghetti. There are two ways out of this mess:

1. You explain that they will have to start working in a more structured manner, with fewer exceptions, deviations, backtracks, and the like. This will limit their flexibility when acting within the process, which may frustrate employees and customers alike. On the other hand, the process will become predictable, repeatable, and it will be less dependent on the implicit knowledge of the humans controlling the process.

2. You accept that every case may be different, and that this process cannot be structured homogeneously. You need to ensure that the people working on cases have enough latitude to make use of all their knowledge and experience. Case processing cannot be represented as a BPMN process; you need an alternative way to model it. This is where CMMN comes in.

Typical applications of the CMMN standard include:

- Dealing with exceptional situations, for example, customer complaints
- Complex evaluations, for example, suspicion of fraud in claims settlements
- Creative activities, for example, designing new products

CMMN can model these types of case processing visually, and the models can be carried out in a CMMN-compatible case engine. The result will be IT-supported case management as described in section 5.1.4 on page 149 from the user's point of view.

At first, CMMN diagrams appear similar to BPMN diagrams. That's hardly surprising, as both standards deal with activities and both standards are published by OMG. The most striking difference is the sequence flows, which are first presented in section 2.2 on page 27. Sequence flows, an essential building block of BPMN, are missing entirely from CMMN.

The lack of sequential flow in CMMN reveals a fundamental difference in basic design. BPMN assumes a clear order, a basic sequence in which the tasks are expected to be carried out. The existence of process branches, backflows, and reactions to events don't undermine the essential nature of a process defined as a series. The opposite is true of CMMN. The lack of flow sequences implies more jumping between and among tasks, with decisions about what happens next left up to the person in charge of the process, the so-called *knowledge worker*. There can be exceptions in CMMN in the form of pre-defined conditions for orders or tasks, but pre-defined conditions are the exception —so to speak —in CMMN, whereas in BPMN they are the rule.

In the real world, an entire process seldom fits a completely structured or unstructured pattern. More commonly, there are some structured parts within a process —and these can be captured in BPMN —as well as some unstructured parts for which you will need CMMN. That is why it makes sense to combine the standards as we discuss in section 1.2.4 on page 10.

1.2.3 DMN for rule-based decisions

DMN is short for *Decision Model and Notation*. Like BPMN and CMMN, it is administered by OMG. DMN is the newest of the three standards. Version 1.0 was released in September 2015. By June 2016, version 1.1 had been adopted, and that's the version to which we refer in this book.

A *decision* in the DMN sense means deriving a result (*output*) from given facts (*input*) on the basis of defined logic (*decision logic*).

Unlike BPMN and CMMN, DMN is not about activities or processes. DMN works in an operationally similar fashion: decisions can be modeled by a business user and then executed by a decision engine. Another similarity to BPMN and CMMN is that the DMN standard specification contains both a written description of the notation and an XML-based formal metamodel.

The DMN standard offers different ways to model decisions. The most popular way is the *decision table* described in section 6.2.1 on page 168. Within decision tables you must define the specific conditions needed to determine a result. The definition has to be understandable and implementable on a technical level —BPMN users will recognize how this corresponds to BPMN —and it is why we use a formal language called Friendly Enough Expression Language (FEEL). FEEL is part of the DMN standard, and we introduce it in section 6.2.4 on page 177.

Often, complex decisions are made up of comparatively simple decisions. The Decision Requirements Diagrams (DRDs) described in section 6.2.5 on page 179 help us to dissect complex decisions into their components and make them clearer.

Similar to BPMN and CMMN, the value of DMN peaks when modeled decisions are executed by a compatible decision engine. This offers the following advantages:

* **Transparency:** Everyone can easily understand how decisions are being made. This knowledge is no longer buried either in the heads of certain employees nor in barely intelligible application source code.
* **Traceability:** Every decision can be logged automatically by the decision engine. It is possible to trace why certain decisions were made.
* **Flexibility:** The decision logic can be adapted more readily. It does not have to be rolled out accompanied by lengthy training or documentation; it can just be deployed. In this regard, DMN is slightly superior to BPMN because changing BPMN diagrams intended for execution by a process engine can be too risky for a non-programmer. (This may be hard to appreciate —after all, how hard can it be to add, move, or delete a few symbols? True, but the technical process is only one part of an entire application architecture that can be affected by the unintended consequences of small changes.) Something similar can happen with a DMN decision table, but the consequences are more easily recognizable and, unlike in BPMN, there are no technical attributes behind the symbols that have to be maintained. It is thus more easily possible for the business department to design or adapt software solutions independently of IT.

Activities and decisions are closely entwined in business processes. BPMN version 2.0 defined a *business rule task* more than four years before the first version of DMN. Even then it was assumed that when completing processes, rules would be assessed constantly as part of making decisions. The term *decision management* was not common at that time, however; we spoke instead of *business rule management*, which explains the description of that task type in BPMN. CMMN version 1.1 introduced the concept of a *decision task*, which in meaning and modeling is equivalent to BPMN's business rule task.

In the next section, we examine how BPMN and CMMN can be combined with DMN through these task types.

1.2.4 An example of interaction

Our scenario for demonstrating the three standards comes from the insurance industry. It is simplified, but it represents the kinds of real-life situations we have encountered repeatedly. Note that the models used here are more than theoretical constructs or documentation only; they are executable by engines, one of which is our own product, Camunda BPM. Camunda BPM allows you both to model and to execute models in all three standards: BPMN, CMMN, and DMN.

If you have no experience with BPMN, CMMN, or DMN, the following may seem like a forced march through notational language you don't yet know. To help, we have added cross references to the sections of the book in which we detail the notational elements.

Let's get started.

Suppose you want to take out car insurance. Nowadays, your first stop is the Internet, where you compare offers and decide on a provider. You visit the website of your chosen insurance company —in this case, the fictitious *Camundanzia Insurance*. You complete an application form (see figure 1.3) with the following data:

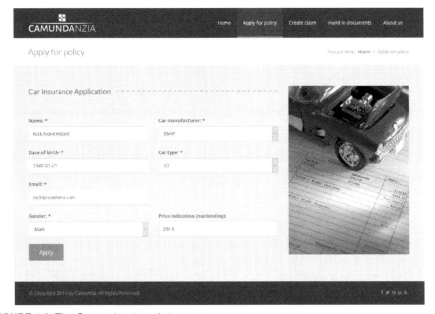

FIGURE 1.3 The Camundanzia website.

- Your date of birth is January 1, 1980. At the time we wrote this, you were 36.
- The manufacturer of your vehicle is BMW.
- The vehicle model is X3.

You click to submit the form, and lean back, eagerly awaiting your insurance policy.

The data from the form immediately creates an instance of a business process at Camundanzia, which has been modeled in BPMN and is technically implemented in Camunda BPM (see figure 1.4). We can tell this from looking at the starting event *application received*. The BPMN-compatible workflow engine first mentioned in section 1.1.4 on page 4 now goes to work.

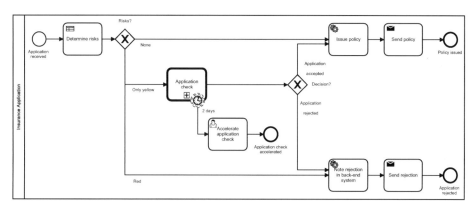

FIGURE 1.4 Request processing in BPMN.

The process starts with the *determine risks* business rule task. On the model side, this task is linked to the DMN decision table *risk assessment* (see figure 1.5) that is now carried out by the decision engine. The decision engine evaluates the input values for applicant age, vehicle manufacturer, and car model. The workflow model transferred these values to the decision engine when the business rule task was carried out.

Risk assessment					
C	Age	Vehicle manufacturer	Vehicle type	Risk	Risk rating
1	<= 21	-	-	"Beginner"	"yellow"
2	<= 25	"Porsche"	"911"	"Too young and fast"	"red"
3	<= 30	"BMW"	-	"Young and fast"	"yellow"
4	-	"Porsche"	"911"	"Pointless speeding"	"yellow"
5	-	"BMW"	"X3"	"High value vehicle"	"yellow"

FIGURE 1.5 Risk assessment in DMN.

Because you said you drive a BMW X3, rule number 5 applies regardless of your age. This rule states that any driver of a high-value vehicle gets a *yellow* risk rating.

The decision engine feeds two output values —one for the vehicle and one for the risk rating— back to the workflow engine, which continues to execute the process. In the following step we encounter an XOR gateway (see section 2.3.1 on page 28), which decides how the process should continue based on the risk assessment.

If no risks had been recognized, the gateway would have selected the path labeled *none*. This would have led to the *issue policy* service task (see section 2.7 on page 61). The workflow engine would have called Camundanzia's backend system through an interface, and the backend system would have generated a document. In turn, the document would have been fed back to the workflow engine. The next step would have been the *send policy* task, which would have forwarded the document to you.

Your risk, however, fell into the *yellow* category. The XOR gateway activates the *application check* call activity (see section 2.8.2 on page 69). This call activity is linked to a CMMN model (see figure 1.6) within the attributes of the BPMN model, and the CMMN model now instantiates in the case engine. The workflow engine waits for the case engine to report completion. The workflow engine is patient, but because of the attached time event (see section 2.6.3 on page 49), after two days of waiting it will launch an escalation. It will initiate a user task (see section 2.7 on page 61) called *accelerate application assessment*. The user task could be assigned, for instance, to the team leader of the knowledge worker who was responsible for this application assessment.

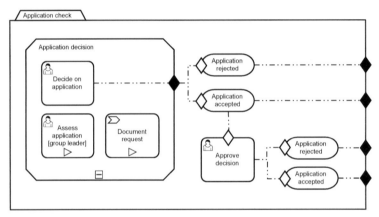

FIGURE 1.6 Application check in CMMN.

Let's assume that the knowledge worker, meaning the office clerk with the expert knowledge, processes the case immediately. He asks himself: "Should this applicant be insured despite the high value of this vehicle?" In addition to the obligatory *decide on application* task that he has to process, the clerk can choose to:

- Request further documents: The clerk can launch the *request documents* process task (see section 5.2.2 on page 152), which in turn is linked to a separate BPMN process model.
- Ask for a second opinion: The clerk can launch the user task *assess application*, which assigns the task to his team leader.

The steps above can be carried out in any order and multiple times, or they can be skipped and the application decided upon immediately. That decision is up to the office clerk. In figure 1.7 on the next page, we see what the clerk's task form looks like. The options available to him are shown on the right side.

If the clerk accepts the request, then the sentry (see section 5.2.3 on page 153), represented as a small diamond, shows that the decision has to be authorized by another person. The

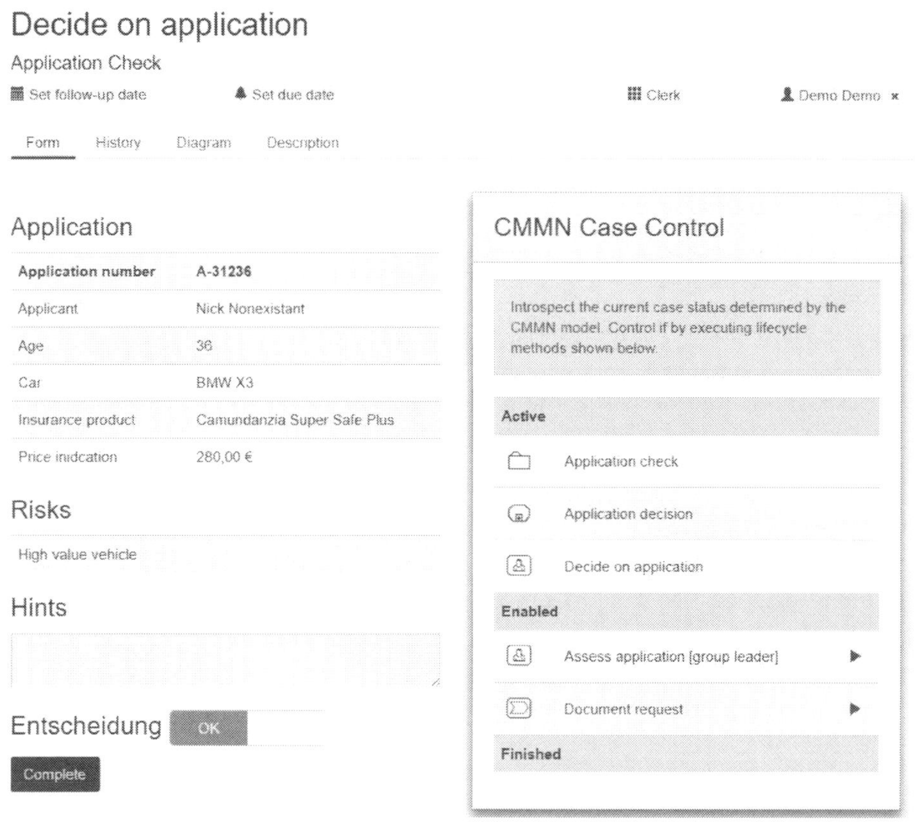

FIGURE 1.7 Office clerk's task form when deciding on the application.

circumstances that make authorization necessary may have been stored as an expression in the sentry, or they may have been defined in a separate DMN decision table referenced by the sentry. In either case, the case engine automatically determines if the *approve decision* user task has to be carried out.

If the end result is to accept the application, the CMMN case completes in that state. Now the BPMN process continues, that is, the workflow engine reaches the XOR gateway *decision* and selects the path *application accepted*. Now the possibility described above becomes reality: the service task retrieves the insurance policy from the back-end system, and the send task sends it to the applicant by email.

Perhaps only half an hour has elapsed since you sent your application for car insurance. You spent it idly snoozing at your desk, didn't you? But your reverie ends when a new email arrives. You are thrilled at the speed with which Camundanzia was able to issue your insurance policy.

This concludes our example. We hope it was enlightening. If you like, you can get a snazzy poster of this example at http://camunda.com/poster. We will gladly send it to you free of charge.

As you can see, each of the three BPM standards has a role to play, but they also overlap. Two questions we get often about this are:

- Decisions on the basis of business rules can be represented in BPMN by gateways, so why do we need decision tables? We answer this question in section 4.5.4 on page 141.
- In BPMN, ad hoc subprocesses exist (see section 2.8.4 on page 72). Was this not developed specifically for the use case that CMMN is now supposed to handle? We deal with this question in section 4.5.3 on page 140.

There is another tricky topic: The difficulty of achieving a high degree of structure during process harmonization. The people involved may conclude that the process *must* preserve their flexibility to act. Perhaps they fear that BPMN will become too restrictive, and so they are quick to sidestep to CMMN as an alternative. They hope to remain flexible but still enjoy all the benefits of process improvement. That's a fallacy! The connection between clearly defined process structures and process improvement is not negotiable. To lean on CMMN in preference to BPMN is to risk giving up:

- Transparency: CMMN diagrams reveal less about how the business process was processed, that is, under what circumstances which activities were carried out. The decisions, after all, are being left up to the knowledge worker. Consequently, the company remains comparatively dependent on the knowledge worker.
- Efficiency: Knowledge workers have special knowledge and experience acquired over time. This means that they are expensive and hard to replace —or to replicate as business volume increases. How can you envision full automation of the process under such conditions? The scalability of the business model is therefore capped.
- (Structural) flexibility: If processes need to be modified, CMMN can simply be adapted. If a knowledge worker is expected to work differently than in the past, however, he or she will have to be informed and persuaded. This is cumbersome and, in a sense, makes the structure less flexible. Yes, you can argue that the point of CMMN is to provide knowledge workers great flexibility to make autonomous decisions, but the trade-off in comparison to using BPMN is that it will require more time and effort to influence the decision-making behaviors of the company. If market conditions shift more quickly than the ability or willingness of knowledge workers to change their habits, it could be problematic.

Are we now arguing against CMMN? No. CMMN rests on sound thinking, and it is extremely valuable when used well. The point we are striving to make is that it is a mistake to use CMMN simply as the path of least resistance, when it seems otherwise too hard to develop a clearly defined process structure with BPMN. We don't want to create what in software development is called *technical debt* —something that makes life easier in the short term but creates more intransigent and costlier problems in the future.

Our recommendation therefore, and basically our rule of thumb, is to make a serious initial attempt to define the desired process in BPMN. For those parts of the process in which you can't achieve a clear process structure and you need to give the knowledge workers lots of leeway, consider CMMN.

In other words, use as much BPMN as *possible* and only as much CMMN as *necessary*.

1.3 Can BPMN bridge the gap?

1.3.1 The dilemma

First, BPMN provides a set of symbols. Second, it implies a methodology that expresses itself as rules for combining the symbols graphically. Third, the symbol definitions and the rules for applying them is called syntax. Fourth, the meaning of the symbols and constructs that you can model with the symbols is called semantics.

Unfortunately, just knowing the BPMN symbols is not enough for you to create useful process models. Since 2007, we have used BPMN extensively and often, and you can believe that we have suffered terribly! Mainly, we suffered because we always aimed for models with correct syntax and consistent semantics —in other words, unambiguous models. Others took the easy way out by saying: "Our process model is not really syntactically correct, and it's not really unambiguous. But that doesn't matter because the main thing is that the consumer understands it!" This attitude backfires because:

- When you apply BPMN in a syntactically incorrect way, you lose all benefits of standardization. After all, what do you need a standard for if the models all look different in the end? Many BPMN tools won't even enable syntactically incorrect modeling.
- Semantic inaccuracies or inconsistencies always create the risk that your model will be misinterpreted. This risk is particularly high if you create an inconsistent target state process model and then send it to IT to implement.

If you want to supply your process model directly to the workflow engine, you must make your model correct, precise, and consistent. At that point, you still have to reconcile two contradictory objectives:

1. Different consumers must understand and accept the process model. Making the model easy to comprehend helps to reach agreement.
2. Because the process model has to meet the requirements of formal modeling, there's usually an unavoidable level of complexity to it. This makes it harder to achieve the comprehension that leads to agreement.

Failure to reconcile the objectives, to bridge the gap in understanding between business and technology, is the main reason that process models have had limited success in the past. The really bad news is that BPMN alone also will not succeed!

Just as with spoken language, you can use BPMN and either succeed or fail. As with spoken language, successful use of BPMN depends on whom you want to communicate with and about what. You speak to your colleagues about the work you all know so well differently than you speak to your three-year-old about why the cat doesn't *like* to be pulled by its tail. Similarly, you will need other BPMN process models for coordinating with your co-workers than for presenting the future process to upper management. Decide for yourself if the latter scenario is akin to the toddler-and-cat situation.

On the one hand, different BPMN process models are required for specific audiences and topics so that they can be understood. On the other hand, each model must contain all the detail necessary for the topic. BPMN may be a *common language* for business and IT, but the phrasing will remain different nevertheless.

The following understanding is therefore imperative for your work with BPMN:

The precision and formal correctness of the process model must vary depending on the modeling objective and the expected consumers.

1.3.2 The customers of a process model

Whenever we model processes, we have to work in a customer-focused way. We must always keep the consumer of our model in mind. We must put ourselves in his or her place. This sounds simple, but few process models actually support this orientation.

As we have been saying, the knowledge, skills, and interests of the people who view our process models vary a great deal. In the following list, we have compiled the types we encounter in our BPM projects. These descriptions are for the roles played in relation to the project; they are not the titles of people in any organization. What we find is that the more experience an enterprise develops with BPM, the more consistently we see these roles fulfilled. We recommend that you become familiar with:

- **Process owner:** Process owners have strategic responsibilities for their processes. They are vitally interested in optimizing performance. They often have budget authority, but before they sign off, they need to be convinced that your improvement plan will work. In most companies, process owners inhabit the first or second tier of management. They may be members of management committees or heads of major divisions.
- **Process manager:** Process managers have operational responsibility for their processes. They report directly or indirectly to the process owners. They apply for improvement projects, acting as the ordering party for external services. Process managers are often low- or middle-level managers.
- **Process participant:** Process participants work with the processes and actually create value. Their relationship to the process manager varies greatly. In companies organized by functional divisions —sales, logistics, and so on —a process manager is a functional executive for the division in which the process is carried out. Process participants report directly to that functional executive. If the process is carried out across departments, which is common, especially in process matrix organizations (see figure 1.8 on the facing page) conflicts can arise between department executives. Process modeling alone cannot resolve such issues, which is why we do not examine them further in this book.
- **Process analyst:** The core competencies of process analysts are BPM in general and BPMN in particular. They support process managers as internal or external service providers through all stages of the BPM life cycle. A process analyst may be the contact for external service providers or may act as the process manager's representative. Within the company, process analysts usually have either their own sphere of competence in BPM, such as the business organization, or they are part of their IT divisions. It is rare, however, for a process analyst to be responsible for technical implementation.

The analyst may like technical work, may know BPMN from back to front, but his or her strengths are as an organizer and communicator. As the builder of bridges between business and IT, the process analyst is the center of every BPM project. About 70 percent of the people who claim or are assigned to this role, in our experience, are poorly qualified because they lack the proper analytic predisposition. The most important qualification of a process analyst is not a facility for sending out information, but a facility for receiving it. Good process analysts naturally want to understand everything thoroughly. At the

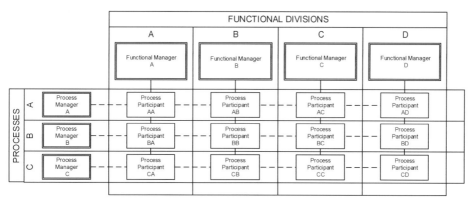

FIGURE 1.8 The process matrix organization.

same time, they have plenty of empathy in relating to the other people involved, and they can tailor their communication for every group. They remember every detail, but they also sensibly shield details from those for whom the details would just be a distraction.

Do project managers make good process analysts? No, nor should the project manager be the same person as the process analyst. Most project managers see themselves as "dynamic, action-oriented individuals" who constantly have to "get someone on board" or "pull chestnuts out of the fire." They may be extremely skilled at delegating responsibility although, to be honest, some are clueless windbags. It may seem ideal to have a good process analyst also manage a BPM project, but it rarely works.

- **Process engineer:** Process engineers use technology to implement the target state process modeled by process analysts. In the best cases, they do so in the workflow engine, which automates the process. You can call a programmer who programs the process logic in Java, C#, or another language a process engineer. The programmer's major work takes place during the implementation stage of the BPM life cycle, though the process analyst may get the process engineer involved at other stages as well.

Now that we've outlined the potential customers of a process model, we can talk about what the models should look like to keep these customers happy.

1.4 A method framework for BPMN

In our consulting projects and workshops, we have introduced a great many people from all kinds of enterprises to BPMN. From that collected experience, we have developed a practical framework for applying BPMN.

This framework helps us decide which BPMN symbols and constructs to use in which situations —and also when to hold back in the interest of simplicity. The framework focuses on projects with processes that need improved technological support and in which it is the target state that needs to be modeled. In principle, what we show as modeling patterns can also be applied to other scenarios such as the discovery, documentation, and analysis of current-state processes.

For this edition of the book, we revamped the way we visualize the framework. The following section introduces the new visualization, and then we explain why we changed it. Basically, we now find fault with a widespread approach to process-focused IT projects, and we want to present an alternative that our experience suggests is better.

1.4.1 The Camunda house

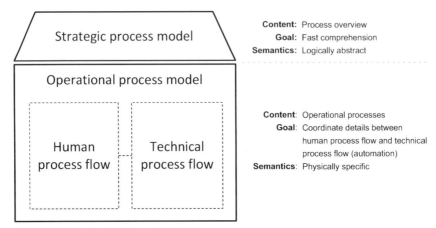

FIGURE 1.9 Camunda BPMN framework.

The *Camunda BPMN framework* in figure 1.9, or *Camunda house* for short, distinguishes between strategic and operational process models:

- **Strategic process model:** The primary target group for strategic process models are process owners and process managers. A secondary group early in the project may include process participants and process analysts. We provide the strategic model as a general, results-oriented representation of the process because we want to create the quickest possible understanding for an audience that has no special BPMN knowledge. We sketch the process in a few steps, but we don't show errors or variations. See chapter 3 for more detailed information on creating strategic process models.
- **Operational process model:** At this level, we investigate operational details of the actual process. It may contain human or technical process flows, and we model them accordingly. A human flow is handled by a participant while a technical flow is handled by software —preferably a workflow engine. Of course, the human and technical flows can interact. A human may trigger a technical flow in the course of doing his or her work, as in the case of calling a software function. Equally, a technical flow may require a participant to send an email, assign a task, and so on. The human flow thus is triggered by the technical flow. We handle developing human and technical process flows in chapter 4 and chapter 7.

The Camunda house is a purely methodological framework. In other words, it works independently of particular software tools, although certain tool functions may make it easier to apply. We deal with this in section 8.4.2 on page 224.

About half of this book is a detailed description of this framework. Because those chapters offer so much practical information, we encourage you to read them even if you are unconvinced of our framework's utility. If that's the case, just think of our framework as a classification system for our advice on applying BPMN practically.

Either way, we look forward to your comments and feedback, not just on this book, but also on the framework itself. By nature it's not a *perfect* approach, and it is subject to constant change and development. With your help, perhaps we can make it better for everyone!

Tooling

We developed the Camunda house specifically to represent projects involving a lone process or a manageable group of related processes. For now, we won't deal with modeling entire process landscapes. BPMN's portfolio does not encompass process landscapes. We *have* modeled process landscapes at a customer's request (we primarily used collapsed pools and message flows as described in section 2.9 on page 78), but we cannot recommend it. If you want a process landscape, you should use a more appropriate tool —perhaps a proprietary one that uses block arrows and rectangles and lots of colors. Of course, you can refine a process landscape with BPMN diagrams by linking the individual elements with flow charts.

1.4.2 The great misunderstanding

This is a confession. We declare ourselves guilty of spreading a deceptive image. The *Camunda BPMN framework* shown in figure 1.10 was used in a previous edition of this book. Released in German in 2009 and in English in 2012, it was a huge success. Hundreds of BPMN projects used the pyramid depiction of the framework for orientation. A large, international software vendor even included the pyramid in its marketing material. Unfortunately, it resulted in some misunderstandings.

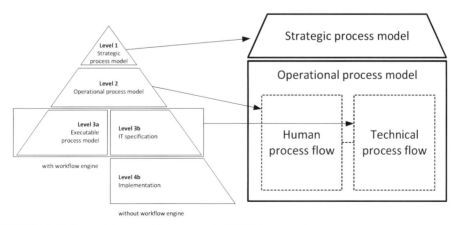

FIGURE 1.10 From old to new: The Camunda BPMN framework.

In the pyramid, we distinguished between strategic, operational, and technical levels. It seems similar at first to the Camunda house, but the Camunda house defines the technical level as a component called *technical process flows* within the *operational process model*, and not as a level of its own. The pyramid put the *operational level* in a position equivalent to what we now call *human process flows*.

This change was necessary because people too often assumed that the technical level was a refinement of the operational level, in other words, that the technical level merely added more detail. In reality, operational-level models (in the sense of the earlier framework) are often *more* detailed than their corresponding technical-level models. For example, think of a simple technical process flow —that triggers a complex manual task —which then requires a complex manual process.

Two related misunderstandings came up.

The first was a perception that the modeling on three levels had to take place in a fixed sequence, that the target-state process must be created first on the strategic level, and then on the operational level, and finally on the technical level. There's no need for that. It often makes more sense to create the operational or technical model first. Doing it this way allows you to develop a clearer understanding of the way process participants will have to do their work before you attempt to summarize or abstract it into a strategic process model. It is, in fact, common practice to conceive the technical and human flows of a process model *concurrently*, for example, in a workshop.

The second misunderstanding related to a strict separation of responsibilities. It was assumed that only the business side would define the strategic and operational levels while only the IT Department would define the technical level. We found this assumption most frequently in enterprises with difficult political situations, where cooperation between IT, operations, and business departments was less than ideal.

We should all understand that even a technical flow represents a *business model*. After all, it describes business requirements. It differs from a classic request document only in that the technical flow anticipates the executable source code —a major advantage of BPMN. The risk in such a strict segregation of responsibilities is that the technical model, while compliant with requirements, may become incomprehensible and unsatisfactory to the business.

It is a similarly serious matter not to involve IT sufficiently in the design of human processes. To believe that you can define a process purely from an operational perspective and only *then* align the technical implementation with it is … naive. Experience shows us repeatedly that operational decisions can and should be influenced by technological realities, either because what the business wants is technologically impossible (or perhaps infeasible for cost reasons), or because the technology can offer solutions that are not on the radar for the people defining operational requirements.

To summarize, you could say that the operational process model belongs both to the business and to IT. As a shared artifact, both parties should share in its development.

What does this thinking mean in terms of our approach to projects? Basically, it aligns with that of agile project organizations: The strict separation of concept from realization is as outmoded as the classic waterfall pattern of development. Most IT projects go better with iterative development, either in sprints within Scrum or otherwise, and it doesn't matter if the project is about process improvement or automation. The business and IT shouldn't work in isolation.

To be abundantly clear: Project participants may need to be shaken out of their comfort zones and motivated sufficiently to work honestly with "the other side." In our engagements during the last few years, the result of our strong encouragement for cooperation always has been the same: massive amazement at how productive a project can be. When IT and the business work side-by-side to define the target-state process at the strategic and operational levels, *including* technical flows, the technical flows can become executable within days or even hours.

As Thorsten Schramm of LVM Versicherung (a large insurance firm) put it during one of our workshops:

"It took only a few days to highly inspire the whole project team (consisting of people from both IT and business departments) for process modelling with BPMN, and right now the first improved processes are already emerging."

Thorsten distills our message nicely. Sometimes, the cooperation experienced within a workshop is just as meaningful as learning the BPMN methodology. BPMN thus can operate synergistically to produce positive change within the enterprise.

2 The notation in detail

■ 2.1 Understanding BPMN

What does a monkey know about the taste of ginger?

This Indian proverb expresses the truism that you can't fully appreciate what you don't understand. We see a corollary in the English expression, "Don't cast pearls before swine."

BPMN is a pearl not everyone can appreciate because not everyone understands it. If you are new to the standard, you won't regret spending some time to familiarize yourself with its underlying principles. For those who already know the BPMN specification, this chapter provides explanation and tips beyond the specification itself. It also describes the visual conventions we use when applying symbols. This is our modeling etiquette.

A full understanding makes BPMN an extremely powerful tool for any modern BPM project. In our experience, however, even those with high confidence in their BPMN knowledge still may fail to understand certain fundamental principles, and they often express surprise that sequence flows must not be drawn across pool boundaries.

2.1.1 Things BPMN does *not* do

BPMN was developed to model processes: logical, chronological sequences of events. That's all. Nonetheless, you often hear BPMN criticized for *not* representing:

- Process landscapes
- Organizational structures
- Data
- Strategies
- Business rules
- IT landscapes

We appreciate how important it is to incorporate these topics into process documentation. We also know that many process professionals come from the systematic world of Architecture of Integrated Information Systems (ARIS) (see section 2.12.1 on page 89). They have worked with event-driven process chains (EPCs), and they may regard BPMN as insufficient. But feasible (and even partly standardized) notations exist for the topics in the list above, and we are glad for it! It relieves BPMN of over-complication and keeps BPMN from being a monstrosity that nobody would want to compile, develop, or even understand. We remind those professionals that:

- BPMN process models are easy to combine with other types of diagrams. It is just a question of the tools used.
- BPMN provides extension options, including custom symbols. We explain this in section 2.11.2 on page 88.

Obviously it would be wonderful if BPMN could provide a complete, out-of-the-box alternative for the ARIS methodology. We admit that's not the case for the pure standard, but precisely because BPMN *is* a standard, software tools are now being created to use BPMN for the other necessary views.

2.1.2 A map: The basic elements of BPMN

When you draw a process diagram in BPMN, you use symbols that can be assigned to the categories shown in figure 2.1. We refer to these categories as the basic elements of BPMN.

In general, certain tasks have to be carried out during a process (*activities*), perhaps under certain conditions (*gateways*), and things may happen (*events*). What connects these three flow objects are *sequence flows*, but only within a *pool*. If connections cross pool boundaries, the process resorts to *message flows*.

Furthermore, *artifacts* provide additional information on the process, but these cannot influence the order of flow objects directly. Every artifact can connect to every flow object

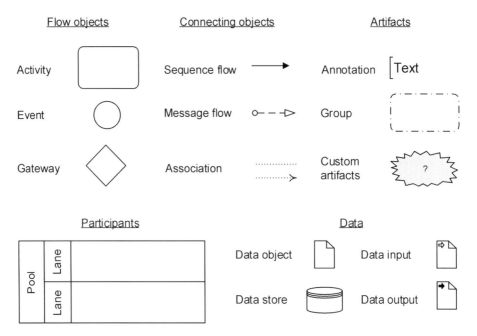

FIGURE 2.1 The basic elements of BPMN

through *associations*. (You can also incorporate your own symbols as additional artifacts into a BPMN palette all your own. We detail this option in section 2.11.2 on page 88.)

BPMN contains an additional *data* category. This refers to the creation, processing, and filing of information that may become relevant within the scope of process handling, thus the category's symbols usually connect to activities through associations.

There are three more aspects necessary to a full understanding of BPMN:
- The advanced ideas and rules behind this simple scheme
- The full range of symbols and
- The practical know-how to apply this stuff

The ideas and rules and the full range of symbols are explained later in this chapter. The practical know-how is acquired through experience, but we offer our knowledge in the subsequent chapters to help speed your progress. We've also devised a few recipes for applying BPMN. They may help you to avoid some traps that often snare beginners.

2.1.3 Perspectives in process analysis

Someone accustomed to modeling processes with other notation systems may have trouble adjusting to an extremely important aspect of BPMN: everything depends on perspective.

BPMN is based on the assumption that one or more *participants* can exist within one diagram. Do not, however, jump to the conclusion that a participant functions like a role, a department, or an employee! In BPMN, a participant is a *logical* element to which the following rules apply:
- There can be only one participant for each process. (This means logical participants; there may be many human participants.)
- The participant has complete control over the process flow.
- The participant is fully responsible for its process.
- Other participants cannot influence a participant's process; they may not even know how it works.
- If a participant wants to interact with other participants within the context of the process, the participant must communicate with the others, and they affect their own processes accordingly.

The same process may look completely different for each participant, and how it looks depends on its perspective. This results in different process models.

In BPMN, the symbol for a participant and for its process is the pool; each process gets its own pool. Logically, however, a participant can control more than one process.

If you learn to handle pools properly, you will have mastered the most significant principle of process modeling —assuming you're aiming for modern BPM aligned with necessary business IT. In section 2.9 on page 78, we detail this subject and also solve the riddle of why there can be only one logical participant for each process.

2.1.4 Models, instances, tokens, and correlations

In the specification for BPMN 2.0, Chapter 7 contains a section titled *Understanding the behavior of diagrams*. It introduces the idea that the behavior of the diagrams must be understood as well as the processes they describe. (Note: Because a diagram may contain several pools, a single diagram implies *n* processes). This is easier in theory than in practice because some process models are so complex that it becomes hard to know how to handle some circumstances. Remember the following:

- **Process model**: The basic description of a process. A diagram may describe one or more process models.
- **Process instance**: A process carried out in reality. One single customer complaint is an instance of the complaint process, for example. Some processes may be instantiated only a few times in a year, such as end-of-quarter reporting in the accounting department. Other instances occur more often. Think of the millions of credit-report requests in a year's time.
- **Token**: You can apply the token model, if you have a process model in mind and want to find out which process paths must or may be used during a process instance. A token is a concept we compare to a car: A car follows a road. At an intersection, its driver must decide to continue in a straight path or to turn left or right. Or perhaps the car turns *and* a clone of the car continues straight on. This is where the car metaphor breaks down, but we hope you get the gist: that the road system corresponds to a process model and that any particular route the car takes represents an instance. The token model can help you understand even the most complex BPMN process models, so tokens are also explained in the above-mentioned section of the BPMN specification. We apply this method frequently in examples throughout this book.
- **Correlation**: Do you ever get letters with a transaction key or a file number? When you reply, you are expected to reference the key or number to make it easier for your correspondent to allocate your communication properly. This allocation based on an unambiguous key is called correlation. Another example is when you pay a bill, and you are asked to write the invoice number on your check. If you don't comply, your payment may not be properly allocated, and the lack of correlation can lead to reminder notices, late-payment fees, and other unpleasantness. Correlation is often crucial to the success of processes, from both organizational and technical points of view. Some of the costliest mistakes come from carelessness with the issue of appropriate correlation.

2.1.5 Symbols and attributes

The BPMN specification describes the symbols provided for process modeling. It also describes the many attributes that you can assign to the symbols. Many of these attributes don't appear in diagrams, though they are stored in the modeling tool and used when a workflow engine executes the modeled process.

2.2 Simple tasks and none events

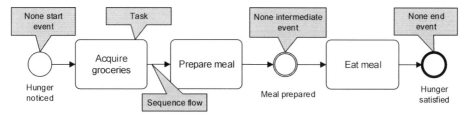

FIGURE 2.2 Our first process

Figure 2.2 shows a simple process triggered by someone being hungry. The result is that someone must shop for groceries and prepare a meal. After that, someone will eat the meal and have his or her hunger satisfied. You will easily recognize the following symbols and their meanings in the diagram:

Tasks

Tasks are the heart of the process. Ultimately, something has to happen to bring about a desired outcome. In BPMN, a task technically is part of the activities category, which also includes the subprocess explained in section 2.8 on page 66.

 Our modeling etiquette

When naming tasks, we try to adhere to the object-oriented design principle of using the [verb] + [object] pattern. We would say *acquire groceries*, for example, not *first take care of shopping for groceries*.

Events

Events describe significant things that happen before, during, or at the end of a process. The example in Figure 2.2 uses only *none events*. None events can be used in a process flow to indicate a status or a milestone. We explain about more event types later.

- **Start events** show which event causes the process to start.
- **Intermediate events** stand for a status that is reached in the process and that is modeled explicitly. They are used infrequently, but intermediate events can be useful, for example, if you regard reaching a certain status as a milestone and you want to measure the time until the milestone is reached.
- **End events** mark the status reached at the end of the process path.

Even for these simple events, we have to make further distinctions:

- Start events are catching events. That means something happened independent of the process, but the process has to wait for this event, or react to it.
- Intermediate events may occur, or they may be caused or triggered by the process itself (throwing events). The none intermediate event marks a status reached by the process and is therefore a throwing event. (Again, we will explain about more event types later, including more types of intermediate events to be classified as catching events.)

- End events take place when the process can no longer react to them. As a consequence, only the process can trigger them.

Our modeling etiquette

Events refer to something that has already happened regardless of the process (if they are catching events) and as a result of the process (if they are throwing events). For this reason, we use the [object] and make the [verb] passive in voice, so we write *hunger noticed*. BPMN does not require you to model start and end events for a process —you can leave them out —but *if* you model a start event, you must model an end event for each path. The same is true for end events that require start events. We always create our models with start and end events for two reasons: first, that way it's possible to determine the process trigger, and second, you can describe the final status of each path end. We only sometimes abandon this practice with subprocesses. More on this later.

Sequence flows

The sequence flow describes the time-logic sequence of the flow elements: tasks, events, and the gateways we describe later.

The process path taken by our token is also a sequence flow. It is born with the process instance because of the start event. Through the sequence flow and by means of the tasks and the intermediate events, it reaches the end event, where it is consumed and disappears. This also leads to the death of our process instance.

Our modeling etiquette

We always draw our process diagrams horizontally, from left to right, but there is nothing to keep you from orienting your flow differently. You may orient your diagrams vertically instead of horizontally, for example, although that is unusual.

2.3 Design process paths with gateways

2.3.1 Data-based exclusive gateway

Certain things can only be done under certain circumstances, so few processes always take the same course.

In our simple example (figure 2.3 on the next page), we want to go into the details of cookery. Driven by hunger, we think about what we are going to cook today. We only know three recipes, so we choose one. We can either cook pasta *or* cook a steak *or* prepare a salad. Let's say that these options are exclusive —we will never prepare more than one at a time. The point of decision on what to do next is called a *gateway*. We decide based on available data (the chosen recipe) and we follow only one of the paths, which is a data-based exclusive gateway. We abbreviate *exclusive gateway* as *XOR*.

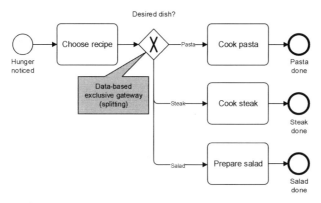

FIGURE 2.3 The XOR gateway.

Bear in mind that a gateway is not a task! You have to determine facts and needs before reaching a gateway. We will encounter this again in Business Decision Management (see section 4.5.4 on page 141).

$$\langle X \rangle = \langle \, \rangle$$

FIGURE 2.4 Both symbols mean the same.

BPMN uses two symbols for XOR gateways (see figure 2.4). They are identical in meaning. We always use the version with the X because it seems less ambiguous, but use what works for you.

 Our modeling etiquette

As in figure 2.3, we place the crucial question before the gateway. This is our convention, which has proved its value in our projects. Possible answers go on parallel paths after the gateway, which is how the BPMN specification shows them. We always work with XOR gateways as follows:

1. Model the task that requires a decision for the XOR gateway.
2. Model the XOR gateway after that. Create a question with mutually exclusive answers.
3. Model one outgoing path (or sequence flow) for each possible answer, and label the path with the answer.

An XOR gateway can have as many outgoing paths as you like. We start some paths in the upper left corner and the others in the bottom left corner, but these are just our style conventions.

By the way, it is not unusual to have three end events nor for the process to result in three end states. Recognizing this possibility can help you with more complex diagrams. Later, we will give more reasons for working with different end events. BPMN is not a block-oriented process notation, so you need not merge a split process path later —you can, but you don't have to.

Certainly, it may make semantic sense to merge the three paths. The meal is eaten after it's prepared, regardless of the recipe chosen. We can use the XOR gateway for merging also, and doing so leads the tokens from the three incoming paths into a single outgoing path. (See figure 2.5.)

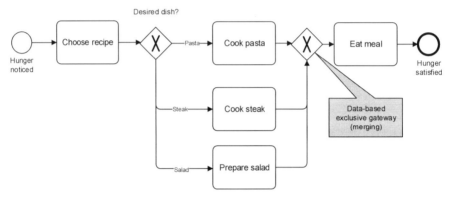

FIGURE 2.5 XOR gateways can also merge.

The double application of the XOR gateway —splitting and merging or *XOR split* and *XOR merge* —may confuse beginners. You can even model an XOR gateway that merges *and* splits at once! (See figure 2.6.) You have to decide if you prefer to compact your diagrams this way. For our part, we usually choose not to do that, and instead draw the two XOR gateways in succession. This method prevents misinterpretation.

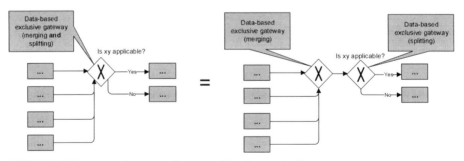

FIGURE 2.6 Two ways of representing a combined merge/split.

2.3.2 Parallel gateway

Suppose that now we want a salad on the side. If you want salad no matter what, you could model it as we have done in figure 2.7 on the next page.

Here, we've introduced another symbol, the (text) annotation. This is an artifact that you can associate with any flow object (in this case, tasks). You can enter any text; in our ex-

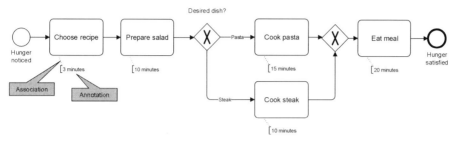

FIGURE 2.7 Preparing salad and main course.

ample, we entered the average time to carry out the associated task. The total of the task times equals the running time of the process, which was a total of 48 minutes for pasta and 43 minutes for steak. Congratulations: you've just analyzed your first process based on key data!

Still, this means waiting 23 or even 28 minutes until you can start to eat. Insufferable! You're really hungry, but what can you do? Maybe you don't prepare the salad first and then cook the pasta or the steak, but you work on both at the same time—in parallel. The appropriate symbol is the parallel gateway, or the *AND gateway* for short, as shown in figure 2.8.

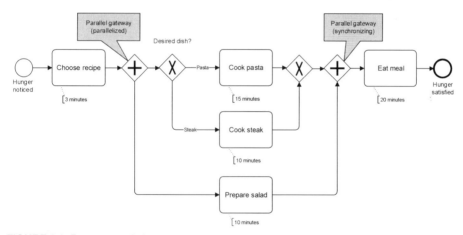

FIGURE 2.8 Preparing salad and main course at the same time.

Diagramming tasks as parallel does not make simultaneous processing compulsory. In contrast to the example shown in figure 2.7, it is also not imperative that you prepare the salad before starting other tasks. Parallel preparation does, however, reduce our total time by 10 minutes. It is classic process optimization to make tasks parallel as much as possible.

As the example shows, the process is not only parallel (it uses an *AND split*), but the paths also synchronize later (an *AND merge*). The reason is easy to understand: you can only start to eat after both main course and side dish are prepared.

How would the concept of tokens apply to an instance of this process? The token is born at the start event, it runs through the *choose recipe* task, and then it plunges into the AND split. One token emerges from the gateway for each path. That means two tokens in this example: The first token enters the XOR split, and its outgoing path depends on the recipe selected.

Let's assume we want to cook pasta. The token enters the task and stays there 15 minutes. At the same time, the second token enters the second, *prepare salad* task, where it stays only 10 minutes. After 10 minutes, it moves on to the AND merge. The number of incoming paths determines the number of related tokens the gateway is waiting for, so here, it waits for two tokens of the same process instance.

In our scenario, the second token arrives at the AND merge after 10 minutes, while the first token stays in *cook pasta* for a total of 15 minutes. This means the AND merge waits until the first token arrives —an additional 5 minutes. At that point, the tokens happily merge into a single token, which continues on the outgoing path.

Does that sound too abstract or technical? It is not. The AND merge behavior is identical to your own: The salad is ready, but the pasta is not, so you wait. When the pasta finally is ready, you eat.

Why the seemingly complicated token concept then? Think of 90 million process instances created by credit agencies, for instance, every year. Surely, these aren't executed in strict sequence. They overlap. To define and carry out such complex processes and their various parallel operations, branchings, mergings, and synchronizations correctly every day, the token approach is not only extremely helpful in conceptual design and implementation, but also necessary. We hope it is clear by now that process instances are not identical to tokens: Many tokens can run within the bounds of a single process instance.

Check your understanding with the following questions:

Question: Figure 2.9 shows the same process, but the AND merge was left out for lack of space, and the path from the *prepare salad* task leads directly to the XOR merge. What happens if we instantiate the process, and we decide in favor of pasta?

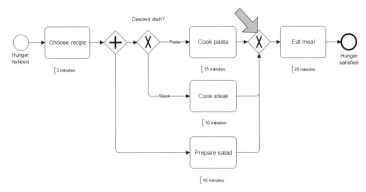

FIGURE 2.9 What happens in this process?

Answer: The token is generated and then cloned as always at the AND split. As soon as we finish preparing the salad, the token passes through the XOR merge and *eat meal* executes. Five minutes later, *cook pasta* also completes. Its token passes through the XOR merge and *eat meal* executes again! That's not the behavior we wanted.

Question: Figure 2.10 on the next page shows a process that consists of two tasks only. Once instantiated, how long does the process instance live?

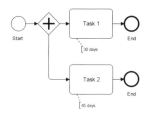

FIGURE 2.10 How long does the process instance live?

Answer: It lives 45 days, which corresponds to the run time of the process. Even though the token generated in the AND split passes through task 1 after 30 days and then is consumed by the upper end event, the second token stays in task 2 for an additional 15 days. The process instance continues to live until the second token is consumed by the lower end event.

Note: As long as just one token lives within the process, the process instance lives too! The instance cannot finish until all tokens generated are consumed.

2.3.3 Data-based inclusive gateway

We want to make our process even more flexible: When we are hungry, we want to eat
* Only a salad,
* A salad and "something real," like pasta or steak, or
* Only something real.

Using the symbols you have learned so far, you could model the situation as shown in figure 2.11.

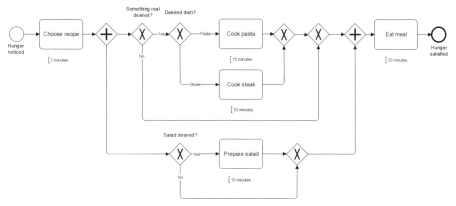

FIGURE 2.11 Various options in the combination of our meal.

If you want a more compact representation, you can use the data-based inclusive gateway —the OR gateway for short. (See figure 2.12 on the next page.) Use OR gateways to describe and/or types of situations, in which processing can flow along one, many, or all outgoing paths. OR gateways can keep diagrams from becoming overly complex.

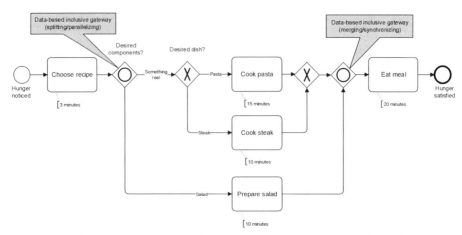

FIGURE 2.12 The OR gateway enables the compact representation of complex path variants.

We can use OR gateways to combine paths too: Depending on whether we want to eat just a salad *or* something real, or a salad *and* something real, we have to wait either for one token to arrive (merge) or for both tokens (synchronize) before we can eat. Note the difference between this and figure 2.11 on the preceding page, however. In the version without the OR gateway, we could have resolved not to prepare anything (neither salad nor something real), but we ate after this decision. The OR gateway excludes this absurdity. We have to decide at least in favor of a salad and/or something real, otherwise the token gets stuck in the gateway. Strictly speaking, the BPMN specification determines that a runtime error occurs in such a case, and that's important when it comes to technical process implementation.

In practice, handling OR gateways is not as simple as these examples imply. It's easy to understand that progress depends on waiting for another token to reach an OR merge. It can be harder to trace the synchronization rules with complex diagrams that sprawl across several pages. Just memorizing the conditions that apply at the OR split isn't a solution.

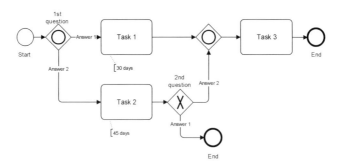

FIGURE 2.13 How long does the second gateway have to wait?

Consider figure 2.13: whether the OR merge needs to synchronize or not depends on whether the OR split runs through one or more paths. Here's the scenario: The first token reaches the OR merge after 30 days. Because answer 2 applied to the previous OR split too, another token is on its way, and it will stay in task 2 for another 15 days. This task is completed, so it becomes possible that a decision made at the XOR split results in the second token being routed through the answer 1 path, and being consumed by the end event. What happens to the first token at the synchronizing OR merge? *The OR gateway must register that the second token has vanished, and it must forward the first token.*

This could cause problems in three circumstances:

- You come across an OR merge in your process manual on page 10, and you have to rummage through the previous 9 pages to understand what conditions require which waiting times.
- You implement such a process in an organization that makes a person responsible for task 3 but permits that person no control over the process.
- A workflow engine runs the process and controls the synchronizing behavior. It is expensive to implement such a check, and it is bound to fail. In some cases it may be impossible.

There are a couple of reasons for using the OR gateway —with caution.

Question: Can we model the process as shown in figure 2.14?

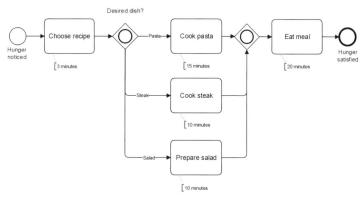

FIGURE 2.14 An incredibly (?) compact version.

Answer: Sure, this makes the model more compact, but it changes the meaning. This process model produces the following outcomes:

- We eat only pasta.
- We eat only steak.
- We eat only salad.
- We eat pasta and salad.
- We eat steak and salad.
- We eat pasta and steak.
- We eat pasta, steak, and salad.

And the last two outcomes aren't what we intend!

2.3.4 Default flow and getting stuck

There's another aspect to working with XOR and OR gateways. (To simplify matters, let's set the salad aside for now and focus on real meals.) What happens if we want neither pasta nor steak? In the previous models, this situation meant that our token could never get beyond the XOR split for *desired dish*. According to the BPMN specification, that throws an exception. In other words, a runtime error occurs.

Don't get angry because we are talking about throwing exceptions! We'll come back to this issue and show why it doesn't concern only IT.

The so-called default flow protects us from runtime errors. We indicate the default flow with the small slash shown in figure 2.15. The principle behind default flows is simply that all outgoing paths are examined; when none of the other paths apply, the process uses the default. Don't mistake the default flow for the usual flow, however. The symbol does not mean that the default applies most of the time. That's a different question.

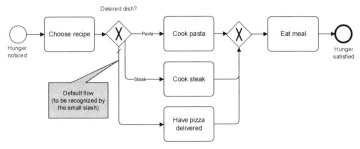

FIGURE 2.15 The default flow.

 Our modeling etiquette

You don't have to use a default flow, of course. You can draw a normal sequence flow instead and label it *other* or whatever you like. We use the default flow any time there's a risk of getting stuck, and we want to avoid disruption to the organization. If a diagrammed decision has Yes or No outflows only, risk is zero; more complex decisions present greater risk.

In our models, default flows help us to determine if we have limited the risk of getting stuck. In terms of aligning business and IT goals, this is certainly good business practice. ∎

2.3.5 Complex gateway

The complex gateway is a category apart. While it isn't used often, there are situations that justify its use. An example: we want to order pizza. We peruse the menu of our favorite supplier, but just for a change, we also look on the Internet. Once we find something we want to try after researching *both* sources, we order the pizza.

How can we model that? The attempt shown in figure 2.16 on the facing page results in ordering the pizza only after the research in *both* sources completes.

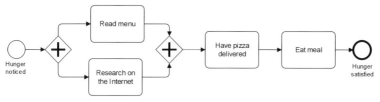

FIGURE 2.16 Pizza research with AND merge.

In figure 2.17, neither is an option: Based on the token concept, we would execute the *order pizza* task twice. (Remember the test question in section 2.3.2 on page 30?)

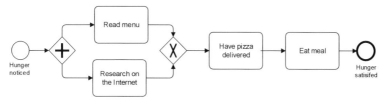

FIGURE 2.17 Pizza research with XOR merge.

Nor does the OR merge in figure 2.18 solve the problem: When a token arrives at the OR merge, the process waits for corresponding tokens that may never get there. The OR merge behavior is thus the same as an AND gateway.

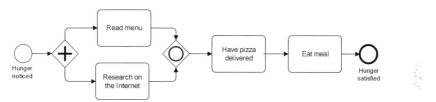

FIGURE 2.18 Pizza research with OR merge.

The solution is the complex gateway combined with an annotation, as shown in figure 2.19. As soon as one of the two tasks completes, the complex merge sends the token to the *order pizza* task. When the next token reaches the complex merge, it is consumed. It vanishes.

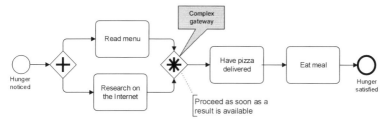

FIGURE 2.19 Pizza research with complex merge.

Here's a similar situation: Assume we execute four tasks at once. There's a fifth task to execute once three of the first four tasks complete. For example, we ask four friends what pizza place they want to order from. Once three friends have offered opinions, we decide. We can model our synchronizing behavior with a complex gateway. (See figure 2.20.)

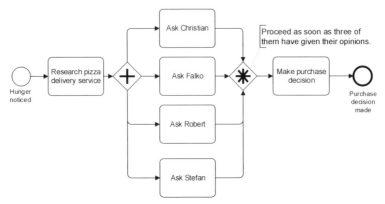

FIGURE 2.20 Using complex gateways to realize *m* out of *n* merges.

In principle, a complex gateway also can be applied as a split —to summarize several different gateways in one symbol to save some space, for instance. The OR split from the process in figure 2.14 on page 35 could be replaced with a complex gateway by writing the split semantics in an annotation. That doesn't really make sense, though, and we have never used the complex gateway as a split nor seen it used in any practical model.

2.4 Design process paths without gateways

Some people don't like gateways. They think gateways make process diagrams too comprehensive or even inflated, and they would rather do without all those diamonds. While gateways *are* optional —you can instead model the logic of the XOR, AND, and OR gateways directly with the tasks —you have to be careful. It's rare that you can eliminate gateways entirely.

Figure 2.21 on the next page illustrates an alternative to the OR split as well as to the XOR merge. The upper and the lower process models are equivalent, but the upper model shows two flows routing directly to task 4. It also represents the OR split with conditional flow symbols: the small diamonds connected to task 1. Conditional flow symbols may connect only to tasks or subprocesses, and only as outlets. They may not be used with gateways or events.

If you read section 2.3 on page 28 carefully, you likely see the problem with this: If only one of the two conditions applies, everything is okay, but if both apply, they generate two tokens in the OR split and so trigger task 4 twice thanks to the XOR merge. This isn't necessarily wrong, but it probably isn't intended. And that brings us to the first problem associated with gateway abstinence:

We cannot model synchronizations (that is, AND merges) without gateways.

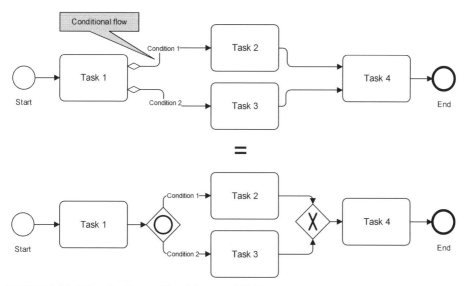

FIGURE 2.21 OR split with conditional flows and XOR merge.

The second problem is that we can't combine conditional checks. We can't represent the process logic shown in figure 2.22 without gateways because of the intermediate event.

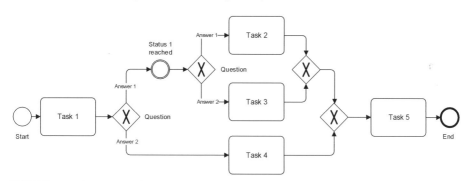

FIGURE 2.22 Combined XOR gateways.

The third problem is that conditional flows follow the same semantics as the OR split. In other words, the defined conditions must not exclude each other. Because the OR split is compatible with the subsequent XOR split, this isn't crucial, but modelers and those who use their diagrams need to be aware of this. Otherwise, in our experience, misunderstandings quickly result.

Would it be better to use gateways all the time? No, there's no need for that either. A simple loop, for example, can be better off without XOR merges because it's less confusing for the inexperienced. And because BPMN permits multiple flows from start events to end events, the diagrams can be nicely compact. We modeled the process in figure 2.23 on the following page with and without gateways to illustrate this. (Yes, technically speaking, the models are not identical: The upper one includes the XOR gateway syntactically, so several paths must be used. It requires that conditions 1 and 2 never occur at the same time. This is not the case in the lower model, where both conditions can apply.)

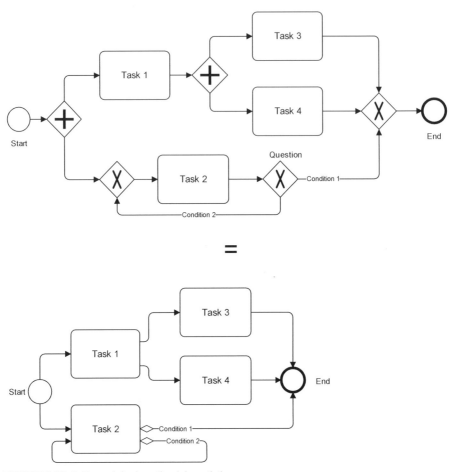

FIGURE 2.23 Both models describe (almost) the same process.

2.5 Lanes

We have talked about *what* to do in our processes, but we have not yet explained *who* is responsible for executing which tasks. In BPMN, you can answer this question with lanes.

Figure 2.24 on the next page shows that the tasks in our sample process were assigned to particular people. We can derive the following process description from the assignments: If Christian is hungry, he chooses a certain recipe. Depending on what Christian chooses, he can either take care of it himself (cook pasta), or he can get his roommates on board. If the latter, Falko cooks steak and Robert prepares salad. In the end, Christian eats. The three

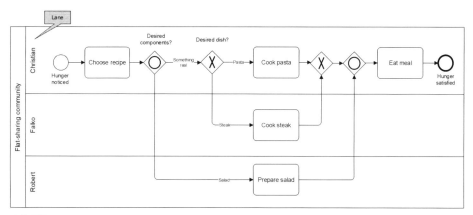

FIGURE 2.24 Responsibilities represented using lanes.

lanes (Christian, Falko, Robert) are united in one pool designated *flat-sharing community*. We discuss pools in detail in section 2.9 on page 78.

In the example, lanes equate to people, but this meaning is not specified by BPMN. You can designate the lanes as you like. In practice, lanes are often used to assign:

- Positions in the primary organization, for example, accounting clerk.
- Roles in the secondary organization, for example, data protection officer.
- General roles, for example, customer.
- Departments, for example, sales.
- IT applications, for example, CRM system.

 Tooling

Some tools enable you to assign the elements in your diagram to different categories or views, such as executing positions, responsible positions, supporting IT applications, and so on. You can also show the process from the respective view. This changes the lanes, and arranges the elements accordingly. ∎

Incidentally, lanes have a long history in the world of process modeling. They're analogous to a swimming pool in which swimmers swim only in the lanes to which they are assigned. Swimlane representations are common to different process notations.

 Our modeling etiquette

BPMN does not specify that you have to order tasks either vertically or horizontally. In figure 2.25 on the next page, the process starts in the top left corner and ends in the bottom right, and that is our convention, but you can model it from the bottom left to the top right as well. The essential thing is that you decide on a style for structuring your diagrams, and then apply it consistently. Keeping to your standard makes your diagrams easier to read from one to the next. ∎

In BPMN, lanes can also interlace to illustrate refined responsibilities. (See figure 2.25.)

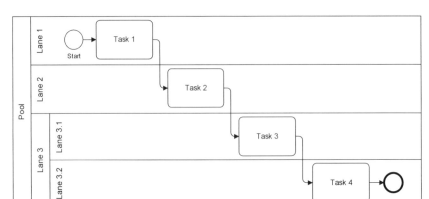

FIGURE 2.25 Interlacing lanes.

Handling lanes often is trickier than you may expect. In our little process, for example, we assume that the tasks are clearly distributed. But what if Falko and Robert want to eat too? A representation like that in figure 2.26 would be syntactically wrong. It is not permissible to have a flow object (activity, event, gateway) positioned outside a single lane.

The solution for keeping Falko and Robert happy is to duplicate the *eat meal* task and to assign this task to each person (figure 2.27 on the facing page). This also makes sense content-wise, because the task actually is completed three times. There is still the possibility of misconception, however, since it is not evident that the three men eat together. It may not matter if Falko and Robert dine with Christian, but in cases where cooperation is intended —perhaps the task is *furnish expert opinion* and you want a joint opinion, not a collection of individual ones —you could apply a group frame as shown in section 2.11.1 on page 87.

Note: In our process diagrams, we don't separate lane captions from the lanes themselves. This complies with BPMN version 2.0, which explicitly forbids such a separation. This is a

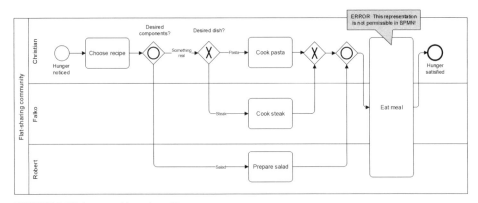

FIGURE 2.26 Incorrect lane handling.

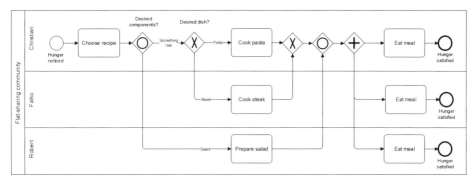

FIGURE 2.27 Correct lane handling.

change from version 1.2, where it was permitted. You may encounter BPMN diagrams like figure 2.28, and the tool you work with may only allow lanes with separate lane headers.

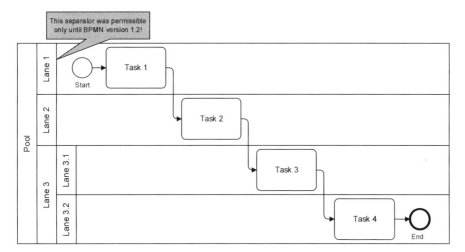

FIGURE 2.28 The lane separators between lane header and lane body were allowed only until BPMN 1.2.

2.6 Events

2.6.1 Relevance in BPMN

Tasks and gateways are two of three flow elements we've come to know so far: Things (tasks) have to be done under certain circumstances (gateways). What flow element is still missing? The things (events) that are supposed to happen. Events are no less important for BPMN process models than tasks or gateways. We should start with some basic principles for applying them. In section 2.2 on page 27, we saw:

- Catching events and throwing events
- Start events, intermediate events, and end events

Catching events are events with a defined trigger. We consider that they take place once the trigger has activated or fired. As an intellectual construct, that is relatively intricate, so we simplify by calling them catching events. The point is that these events influence the course of the process and therefore must be modeled. Catching events may result in:

- The process starting
- The process or a process path continuing
- The task currently processed or the subprocess being canceled
- Another process path being used while a task or a subprocess executes

Throwing events are assumed by BPMN to trigger themselves instead of reacting to a trigger. You could say that they are active compared to passive catching events. We call them throwing events for short, because the process triggers them. Throwing events can be:

- Triggered during the process
- Triggered at the end of the process

Start events are therefore events that always occur. The process cannot trigger an event before it has even started. The simplest application of a start event is shown in figure 2.29. When the event occurs, the process starts.

FIGURE 2.29 Once event 1 occurs, the process is started.

Note: The question mark in the circle indicates that this event can be allocated to a certain type. So far, we have only covered none events. The possible event types are explained in the following sections.

Different events may trigger the process, which could be modeled as shown in figure 2.30. It is important that each event triggers its own process instance.

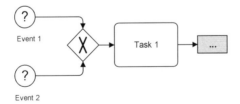

FIGURE 2.30 Once events 1 *or* event 2 occurs, the process is started.

On the other hand, suppose you want to model several events that have to take place before the process starts. A lot of people would model this situation as shown in figure 2.31 on the facing page.

This is intuitive, but unfortunately it is not correct, and few BPMN beginners understand why it is not correct. The reason is that the AND merge does not support the correlation

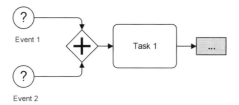

FIGURE 2.31 Bad: Technically speaking, this model would lead to a deadlock.

already mentioned in section 2.1.4 on page 26, so the process will not recognize the two events as being associated. We will explain this problem in greater detail in section 2.6.14 on page 58, and we will describe how BPMN provides the solution.

The process may require that a specific *intermediate event* occurs, as shown in figure 2.32. After task 1 completes, event 1 has to occur before task 2 can complete. With the token approach, the token waits at event 1 until it occurs. Only then does the token continue, and it starts task 2.

FIGURE 2.32 After task 1, the process waits until event 1 has occurred. Only then does it proceed to task 2.

Note: The none event (as explained in section 2.2 on page 27) is *not* a catching event. It belongs to the throwing events.

How can we represent that a process has to wait for two events? What we show in figure 2.33 is flawed. After task 1 completes, the token continues and waits for event 1 to occur. If event 2 occurs while the token is waiting on event 1, the token will not notice it. Even worse, if event 1 occurs after event 2, the token continues and then waits for event 2 to occur. Since event 2 already occurred, the token will wait forever.

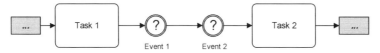

FIGURE 2.33 Sequential intermediate events can only be recognized one after the other.

The semantics of catching events is therefore *not* to check for a condition that already may have been fulfilled, but to treat the catching event as a transitory signal that vanishes immediately after the occurrence. The process therefore can handle the event only if it is in a *ready-to-receive* state at exactly the moment it occurs. This details can usually be ignored in purely functional process modeling, however, it must be adhered to in technical process modeling (section 7.4.4).

If we need to wait for two events that may occur independently, but both events must occur before the process can continue, we represent the situation as in figure 2.34 on the following page.

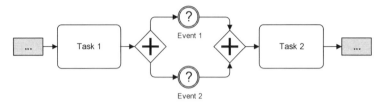

FIGURE 2.34 Using the AND gateway to wait for several events at the same time.

We can model attached intermediate events with BPMN. These do not explicitly require waiting, but they do interrupt our activities, both tasks and subprocesses (which will be discussed later). Such intermediate events are attached because we position them at the boundary of the activity we want to interrupt. A token running through the process shown in figure 2.35 would behave this way:

- The token moves to task 1, which starts accordingly.
- If event 1 occurs while task 1 is being processed, task 1 is immediately canceled, and the token moves through the exception flow to task 3.
- On the other hand, if event 1 does not occur, task 1 will be processed, and the token moves through the regular sequence flow to task 2.
- If event 1 occurs only after task 1 completes, it ceases to matter.

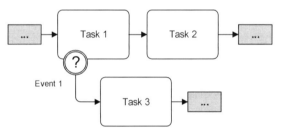

FIGURE 2.35 Event 1 cancels task 1 and starts task 3.

Attached intermediate events do not have to result in canceled activities because of the non-interrupting intermediate event. It sounds awkward, but it is useful. The token moves through the process section shown in figure 2.36 on the facing page as follows:

- The token moves to task 1, which starts accordingly.
- If event 1 occurs while task 1 is being processed, the token is cloned. Task 1 continues to be processed while the second token moves to task 3, which is now also processed. This procedure may even take place repeatedly, that is, the event can occur many times. Each occurrence results in another cloned token.
- If event 1 does *not* occur, task 1 will be completed, and the token moves through the regular sequence flow to task 2.
- If event 1 occurs only after task 1 completes, it ceases to matter.

Throwing intermediate events are triggered by the process. That means a token occurring at such an event triggers it, then immediately moves on. Throwing events do not lead to

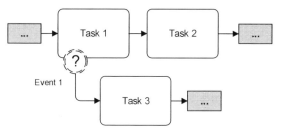

FIGURE 2.36 The occurrence of event 1 results in starting task 3, while task 1 is being further processed.

canceled activities, which is why they can never be attached. They occur only in the sequence flow. We already know the none intermediate event, which can be used to model the entry into a defined status. This is a throwing event too.

In the following sections, we introduce the event types to be used when working with BPMN. We also explain how you can react to different events using the event-based gateway. The event types are:

- Message
- Timer
- Error
- Conditional
- Signal
- Terminate
- Link
- Compensation
- Multiple
- Parallel
- Escalation
- Cancel

2.6.2 Message events

Sooner or later, most processes require communication, which can be represented in BPMN by means of the message event. You'll recognize it as the small envelope. The general application of the message event is shown in figure 2.37 on the next page.

The meaning of *message* in BPMN is not restricted to letters, e-mails, or calls. Any action that refers to a specific addressee and represents or contains information for the addressee is a message. In figure 2.38 on the following page for example, the pizza ordering issue has been fully modeled: We choose a pizza, and we order it. We then wait for the pizza to be delivered. After delivery, we eat. Notice that there is no *order pizza* task.

What's shown in figure 2.39 on the next page would in fact be wrong: The throwing intermediate event *pizza ordered* implies that we have ordered a pizza. If a corresponding task were added, it would result in a double definition and therefore be meaningless.

2 The notation in detail

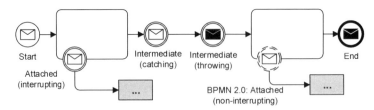

FIGURE 2.37 Applying the message event.

FIGURE 2.38 Ordering and getting pizza as a message event.

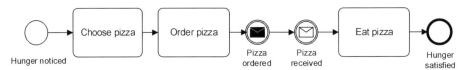

FIGURE 2.39 Wrong content: According to this process model, we would order the pizza twice.

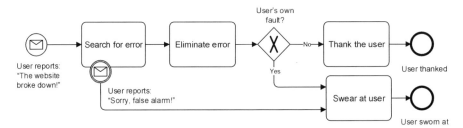

FIGURE 2.40 The attached message event results in the cancellation of the task *Search for error*.

In figure 2.40, we show a message leading to cancellation. In this scenario, we administer a web application. When a user notifies us that the website does not work, we immediately search for the error. But maybe the user is mistaken, and the website is fine. Maybe the user's Internet connection is defective. If the user tells us about the false alarm, we cancel the search and swear at the user for wasting our time. If the error is actually found, however, we eliminate it and simultaneously figure out who caused the error. If the user caused the error, we can swear at the user for a different reason. If the user is not at fault, however, we thank him or her graciously for letting us know about the problem.

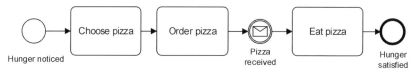

FIGURE 2.41 Our convention: tasks for sending, events for receiving messages.

 Our modeling etiquette

We are not always happy with the throwing intermediate event. Implying a *send message* task without modeling it explicitly can easily confuse inexperienced consumers of our models. We choose not to use throwing intermediate events for messages and instead use a task. (See figure 2.41.) In section 2.7 on page 61, we explain that there are special BPMN task types for sending and receiving messages.

2.6.3 Timer events

The timer event is often used when working with BPMN because it is so flexible to apply. A clock icon represents the timer event. You can see it applied in figure 2.42. You can use timer events to start processes:

- Once, at a scheduled time
- Repeatedly at scheduled times
- At timed intervals
- Relative to other events

As an intermediate event, a timer event can stop a process until:

- A scheduled time arrives.
- A defined span of time has elapsed.
- A time relative to another event expires.

Figure 2.43 on the following page shows a few examples of applications. Time moves on no matter what we or our processes do, so timer events can exist only as catching starts or intermediate events.

You can model countdown times with an attached timer event. They are used this way frequently. You can specify upper time limits —the maximum time allowed for a processing

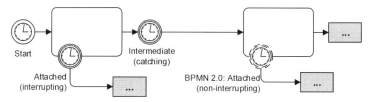

FIGURE 2.42 Applying a timer event.

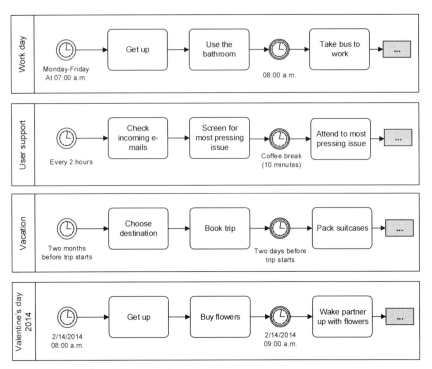

FIGURE 2.43 Examples of timer events.

task—for instance. Figure 2.44 shows a process in which a task may take a maximum of 30 minutes. If the time expires before the task completes, the *choose pizza* task is canceled, and we cook pasta instead. In either case, we eat the meal at the end.

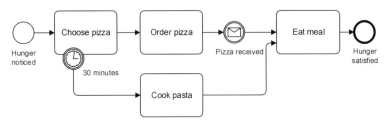

FIGURE 2.44 The timeout for the *choose pizza* task is 30 minutes.

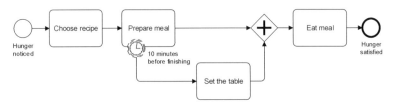

FIGURE 2.45 You can attach timer events that do not lead to cancellation, but instead generate another token.

Timer events can be non-interrupting. Figure 2.45 on the facing page shows another example of this. Before we can eat, we have to prepare the meal and set the table, but we only start setting the table 10 minutes before the meal is ready.

2.6.4 Error events

Do your processes run completely error-free? If not, you can identify potential errors in your models as a step toward eliminating them, or as part of modeling escalation processes. In BPMN, error events are represented by a flash symbol. Apply them as shown in figure 2.46.

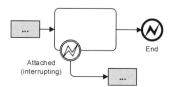

FIGURE 2.46 Applying an error event.

The BPMN specification does not specify what an error may be. As the modeler, you have to decide that. Section 4.5.1 on page 134 has some hands-on tips.

An error is a serious event in BPMN, so it can be modeled only as an attached intermediate event. This means that an error during task execution must be handled in a specific way: As a throwing event, it can be modeled only at the end of a process path so that the participant knows the process has failed. The parent process should likewise recognize the failure. (We explain the interaction between parent and subprocesses in section 2.8 on page 66. You'll also find an example of applying an error event there.)

2.6.5 Conditional

Sometimes we only want a process to start or to continue if a certain condition is true. Anything can be a condition, and conditions are independent of processes, which is why the condition (like the timer event) can only exist as a catching event (figure 2.47).

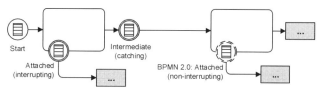

FIGURE 2.47 Applying a conditional event.

We can enhance our pizza process with conditions. If we want to have frozen pizza, the process starts as shown in figure 2.48 on the following page. We take the pizza from the freezer and turn on the oven. But we only put the pizza in after the temperature in the oven reaches 180 ° C, and we only take it out to eat after it is done.

FIGURE 2.48 Baking pizza under fully modeled conditions.

If we know how long the pizza needs to cook, we can specify this in the process model by substituting a timer event for the last conditional event. The whole thing would then look as shown in figure 2.49.

FIGURE 2.49 Baking pizza with indicated baking time.

2.6.6 Signal events

Signals are similar to messages, which is why you can model them in BPMN as events just as you can with messages (figure 2.50). The symbol for a signal is a triangle. The essential difference between a signal and a message is that that latter is always addressed to a specific recipient. (An e-mail contains the e-mail address of the recipient, a call starts with dialing the telephone number, and so on.) In contrast, a signal is more like a newspaper advertisement or a television commercial. It is relatively undirected. Anyone who receives the signal and wants to react may do so.

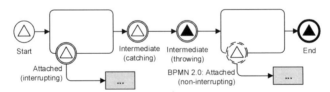

FIGURE 2.50 Applying the signal event.

We saw a new frozen pizza on TV, and we are keen to try it. Figure 2.51 illustrates this new situation.

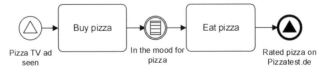

FIGURE 2.51 Pizza signals.

We buy the pizza, but we keep it in the freezer until we're really hungry for pizza. That's a conditional event. After trying the new pizza, we go to Pizzatest.de to rate the new product.

That's a signal. It is a signal for the general public too. (Pizzatest.de actually exists, by the way, which proves again that you can find simply *everything* on the Internet!)

2.6.7 Terminate events

Let's look at the abstract example in figure 2.52. We already discussed (simple) Key Performance Indicator (KPI) analysis in section 2.3.2 on page 30, and we therefore know that this process always takes 55 minutes. After task 1, tasks 2 and 3 can be processed simultaneously. Processing task 2 takes more time than does processing task 3, which is why it determines the runtime of the process. A token that runs through the process is cloned in the AND split. The first token stays in task 2 for 45 minutes; the second token stays in task 3 for 30 minutes. The second token arrives at the none event first, where it is consumed. After 15 more minutes, the first token arrives at the upper none event, where it is consumed too. Since no more tokens are available, the process instance finishes after 55 minutes.

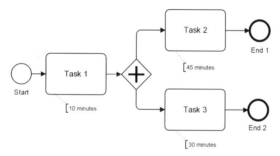

FIGURE 2.52 The process always takes 55 minutes.

So far, so good, but what happens if we already know that, after having completed task 3, task 2 has become redundant? This is a frequent situation with parallel task executions related to content. In such cases, we can apply the pattern shown in figure 2.53.

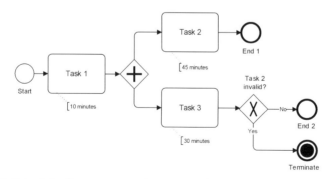

FIGURE 2.53 Potentially, the process terminates immediately after task 3 completes.

We use the terminate event to make sure that *all* available tokens are consumed immediately. That leads to the termination of the process instance, consequently, you can use the terminate event as an end event only. (See figure 2.54 on the next page.)

FIGURE 2.54 Applying a terminate event.

2.6.8 Link events

The link event is a special case. It has no significance related to content, but it facilitates the diagram-creation process. As shown in figure 2.55, you can draw two associated links as an alternative to a sequence flow. Here, *associated* means there is a throwing link event as the *exit point*, and a catching link event as the *entrance point*, and the two events are marked as a pair —in our example by the designation A. Sometimes we use color coding to mark the association.

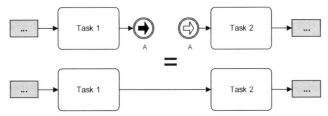

FIGURE 2.55 Associated link events can replace a sequence flow.

Link events can be very useful if:

- You have to distribute a process diagram across several pages. Links orient the reader from one page to the next.
- You draw comprehensive process diagrams with many sequence flows. Links help avoid what otherwise might look like a spaghetti diagram.

Link events can be used as intermediate events only (figure 2.56).

FIGURE 2.56 Applying a link event.

2.6.9 Compensation events

In practice, we apply compensation icons (see figure 2.57 on the facing page) only to transactions even though BPMN permits other uses. (See section 2.8.5 on page 74.) We execute tasks in our processes that sometimes have to be canceled later under certain circumstances.

Typical examples are:

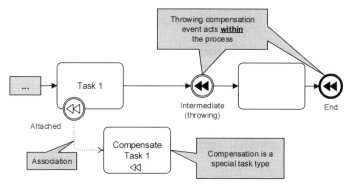

FIGURE 2.57 Applying a compensation event.

- Booking a train or airline ticket
- Reserving a rental car
- Charging a credit card
- Commissioning a service provider

In figure 2.58, we see this process: On Friday at 1 p.m. we agree with our partner either to go to the theater or to spend the evening with friends. In both cases, we have to do something binding, either to reserve the theater tickets or make the arrangements with our friends. When evening arrives, perhaps we no longer feel like going out at all. We then have to cancel the arrangements we made with the theater or our friends before we can collapse in front of the TV in peace.

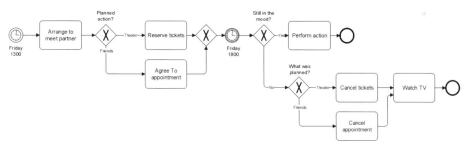

FIGURE 2.58 A possible process for the weekend.

We can represent the latter part of the model more compactly with a compensation event, as shown in figure 2.59 on the next page. If we don't feel like going out, we have to cancel all our arrangements; we don't have to check which ones to cancel.

There are special rules for handling compensations:

- Throwing compensations refer to their own processes, so the event is effective within the pool. This shows how this event type differs from a throwing message event.
- Other attached events can take effect only while the activities to which they are attached remain active. In contrast, an attached compensation takes effect only if the process triggers a compensation *and* the activity to which the compensation is attached successfully completes.

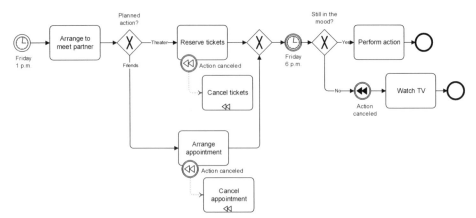

FIGURE 2.59 The same process as shown in figure 2.58 on the preceding page, applied to the compensation event.

- Attached compensation events connect to compensation tasks through associations, and *not* through sequence flows, which would otherwise be common usage. BPMN thus emphasizes that compensations are beyond the regular process sequence; executing one is an exception.
- The obligatory compensation task is a special task type that we explain with other task types in section 2.7 on page 61.

 Our modeling etiquette

This example may be too simple to illustrate how much work this construct can save you. If you think of the complex business processes that frequently require compensations, however, you'll see how much leaner your models can be. You'll also be quick to spot the circumstances that demand compensations. We use compensation events only occasionally to describe complex processes. ∎

2.6.10 Multiple events

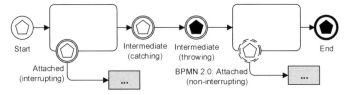

FIGURE 2.60 Application of the multiple event.

We can use the multiple event (figure 2.60) to summarize several events with a single symbol. The semantics are simple:

- If we model the multiple event as a catching event, *only one* of the summarized events has to occur to start or continue the process or to cancel the task.
- If we model a multiple event as a throwing event, it means that *all* of the summarized events are triggered.

Figure 2.61 applies the multiple event to our pizza scenario. In the example, we try a new pizza after having seen it on TV or after a friend recommended it. After eating it, we will rate the pizza on Pizzatest.de and in turn inform our friend if we also recommend this pizza.

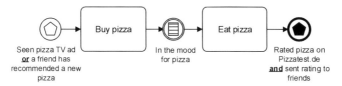

FIGURE 2.61 The multiple event summarizes events.

The model in figure 2.62 describes the same process, but the events are fully modeled.

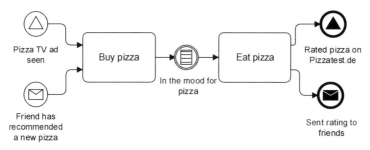

FIGURE 2.62 An alternative for figure 2.61

 Our modeling etiquette

You have to decide if multiple events serve your purposes. We concede their benefit in rough functional process descriptions, but they cease to be as useful in the more advanced technical-implementation phase. You can't afford to leave relevant details hiding in the descriptive text. We don't find the multiple event to be intuitive, nor is it helpful on a functional level. It may make your diagrams larger to model all events separately, but the resulting diagrams will be both more comprehensive and more comprehensible. The bottom line is that we have never used this symbol in practice, nor have we seen anybody else doing so. ∎

2.6.11 Parallel events

The parallel event (see figure 2.63 on the following page) supplements the multiple event. While a catching multiple event has XOR semantics —it occurs as soon as *one* of its contained events occurs —the parallel event uses AND semantics. It doesn't occur until *all* of its contained events occur. Because the throwing multiple event already implies AND semantics, the specification defines parallel events as catching events only.

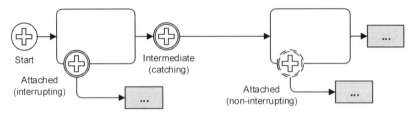

FIGURE 2.63 Application of the parallel event.

2.6.12 Escalation events

The escalation event (see figure 2.64) shows communication between parent and subprocesses. We discuss it in section 2.8 on page 66 with the help of an example.

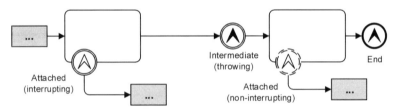

FIGURE 2.64 Applying an escalation event.

2.6.13 Cancel events

You can use the cancel event only in the context of the transactions we discuss in section 2.8.5 on page 74. That section also has examples of applying this event type.

2.6.14 Event-based gateway

We learned about the exclusive data-based (XOR) gateway option in section 2.3.1 on page 28 as a way to use different paths without regard to the data being processed. In figure 2.65 on the next page, we had to choose a recipe (pasta, steak, or salad) first, and depending on result of the *choose recipe* task, the XOR gateway routed us to the *cook pasta*, or *cook steak*, or *prepare salad* task accordingly.

Users of other process notations recognize this type of branching, but BPMN gives us another way to design process paths: the event-based gateway —event gateway, for short. This gateway does not route based on data, but rather by which event takes place next. To understand the benefit, consider the process shown in figure 2.66 on the facing page: We order pizza and wait for it to be delivered. We can eat only after we receive the pizza, but

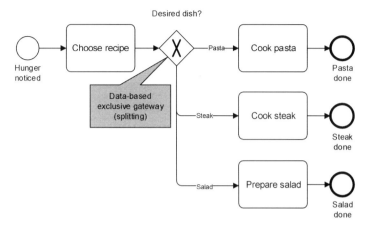

FIGURE 2.65 An XOR gateway decides routing based on available data.

what if the pizza doesn't arrive after 60 minutes? We'll make an anxious phone call, that's what! We can model this with the event gateway (figure 2.67). Now, in contrast to the data-based XOR split, the token waits at the event gateway for one of the subsequent events to occur. Once any one event occurs, the token takes the respective path. If other events then take place, they are ignored. This is XOR semantics.

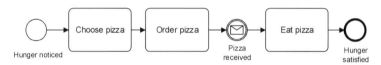

FIGURE 2.66 According to this model, we may wait forever for pizza to be delivered.

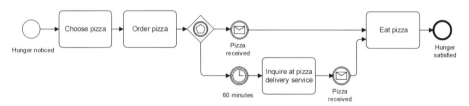

FIGURE 2.67 After the gateway, the path that receives the event first is used.

As you can see in figure 2.68 on the following page, not all intermediate events combine with the event gateway. You can, however, combine it with the receive task, which we discuss in section 2.7 on page 61.

As an instantiating gateway, the event gateway can be used to start a process. You can combine them with other events to trigger a process and, as shown in figure 2.69 on the following page, they can be merged through XOR merges.

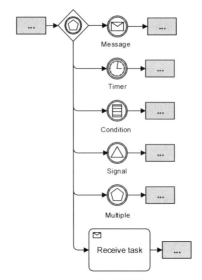

FIGURE 2.68 Applying an event-based exclusive (XOR) gateway.

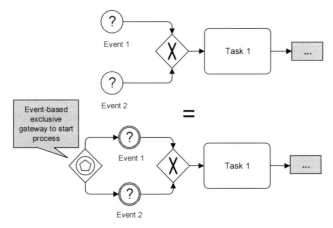

FIGURE 2.69 The event gateway can be a starting point, but it must be of the instantiating type.

 Our modeling etiquette

We find it cumbersome and non-intuitive to modeling start events with event gateways. Instead, we use XOR merges without event gateways.

2.6.15 Event-based parallel gateway

There is a variation on the event gateway: the event-based parallel gateway. Use of this symbol expresses that all subsequent events have to occur before a process can be started completely. It therefore provides correlation not provided by the simple AND merge.

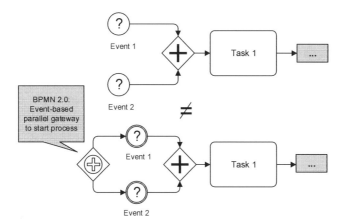

FIGURE 2.70 The lower model works, the upper one (strictly speaking) does not.

The lower model shown in figure 2.70 causes the following behavior:
- If event 1 occurs, the process instance is started and a token is born.
- The new token waits at the AND merge.
- If event 2 occurs, the related process instance already started is identified. (This is correlation.) At event 2, another token is born.
- The second token also moves to the AND merge, where it merges with the first token. Only a single token leaves by the outgoing path.

The *upper* model shows that the allocation to the running process instance would not be carried out. Instead, two isolated instances start in which a token waits forever at each AND merge. This *strict correlation semantics* of BPMN doesn't always further the goal of making process models easy to understand!

2.7 Special tasks

2.7.1 Typification

So far, we have used only tasks of undefined types, though BPMN provides the opportunity to work with task types just as it does for event types. Primarily, task types are intended to model processes that are technically executable. Task types are applied infrequently in practice. We know from experience, however, that task types can be particularly useful when modeling engineering requirements.

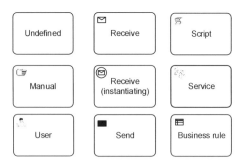

FIGURE 2.71 Task type symbols in BPMN.

Types of tasks include:

- Manual
- User
- Service
- Receive and send
- Business rule
- Custom

Manual tasks: Tasks executed by a human being that do not affect the completion of a task assigned by the workflow engine. All the tasks from our various pizza processes are manual types.

Other examples:

- File a document in a folder
- Clarify an incorrect invoice by phone
- Talk with customers at the counter

User tasks: User tasks are executed by people too, but they are assigned by a workflow engine, which may, for example, place these tasks in each user's task list. After the human finishes a task, the engine expects confirmation, usually including data input or a button click. User tasks are part of the Human Workflow Management.

Typical task examples from the world of Human Workflow Management are:

- Check an invoice
- Approve an application for vacation
- Process a support request

Service tasks: Service tasks are those done by software. These are program functions applied automatically as a process executes. BPMN normally assumes that this function is provided as web service, though it can be another implementation. The service task is a component of process-oriented implementation integration, which explains why it is so similar in concept to Service-Oriented Architecture (SOA).

Typical examples from the world of implementation integration are:

- The credit rating provided by a rating agency, obtained as XML through HTTP during a credit check

- Booking an invoice received as EDIFACT through X.400 in SAP R/3
- The offer of substandard goods by an online auction house, as a web service

Receive and send tasks: Receiving a message can be modeled as a separate task. This task type is an alternative to the catching message event, which is why the symbol for the event defined in BPMN is an empty envelope. If a receive task is to instantiate a process, that is, the receive task replaces the message start event, this is shown by a small event symbol in the top left corner. The same principle applies to send tasks. These tasks are technical, and the workflow engine executes them. Therefore, they mainly are used for calling web services asynchronously through message queues and accepting service requests for asynchronous processing.

Script tasks: Scripts execute directly in the workflow engine, so they must be written in a language that the workflow engine can interpret.

Business rule tasks: This task type is used solely to apply business rules. We discuss this further in section 4.5.4 on page 141 and section 7.2.5 on page 195.

Custom task types: You can define your own task types with individual symbols to customize your diagrams and to make them express conditions in your organization better. Your BPMN tool must provide this option, of course. We have yet to encounter anyone who has done this —most people don't even know it's possible. Even so, we can imagine task types for:

- Phone calls
- Signatures
- Approvals or rejections
- Archiving

2.7.2 Markers

In addition to those various types of tasks, we can mark tasks as loops, multiple instances, or compensations. Markers can be combined with the assigned types.

Loops

A loop task repeats until a defined condition either applies or ceases to apply. Perhaps we suggest various dishes to our dinner guests until everyone agrees. Then, we can prepare the meal (figure 2.72).

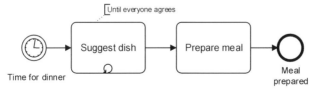

FIGURE 2.72 We keep suggesting dishes until everyone agrees with a suggestion.

Do we absolutely need the loop symbol for this process model? No, we could just model a return with gateways, without gateways, or both. We discussed these methods in section 2.3 on page 28 and section 2.4 on page 38. It becomes a question of which alternative in figure 2.73 you prefer, because they all are equally correct syntactically, and they are semantically identical to the process shown in figure 2.72 on the preceding page. Depending on what you choose (the loop symbol, gateways, or conditional flows), apply it in your models in a standardized way.

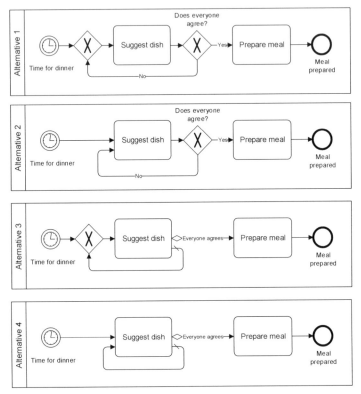

FIGURE 2.73 All four variations represent the same process as in figure 2.72 on the previous page.

In the example, we executed the task first and checked afterwords to see if we needed it to execute again. Programmers know the principle as do-while loop. However, we can also check for a condition before the task instead of afterward. This occurs rarely, but it makes sense if the task may not execute at all.

You can attach the condition on which a loop task executes for the first time or, as shown in the example, apply the condition on repeated executions as an annotation to the task. You can store this condition as an attribute in a formal language of your BPMN tool as well. That makes sense if the process is to be executed by a workflow engine.

Multiple task

The individual cycles of a loop task must follow each other. If for example we live in a flat-sharing community and the roommates feel like eating pizza, the *choose pizza* task must be repeated for each roommate before we can order. You'd sit together and pass a menu around until finally everyone has made a decision. There are student apartments where they *do* handle it like that —more evidence that students have too much time on their hands! It is much more efficient for all roommates to look at the menu at once, and they choose a pizza together. You can model this process using the *multiple task* (figure 2.74). A multiple task instantiates repeatedly and can be executed in sequence or in parallel, with the latter being the more interesting case.

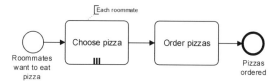

FIGURE 2.74 Using the multiple task to make tasks dynamically parallel.

Do you think the example is absurd? How does your company check invoices for group orders, such as for office supplies? Do you forward the invoice from one employee to the next, so that each person can sign off on the items he or she ordered, before you pay the invoice? If so, you live in a flat-sharing community, and you urgently should consider optimizing your process. Automating invoices is still one of the top BPM projects, and the top goal of such projects often is one of parallelization.

Compensation

We explained the benefit of the compensation event in section 2.6.9 on page 54 by means of an example. The compensation task type is applied exclusively in the context of a compensation event. Accordingly, it is integrated in the process diagram only by associations, never by sequence flows.

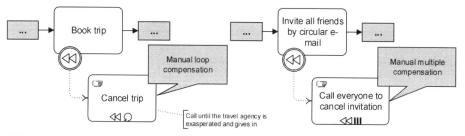

FIGURE 2.75 The compensation and loop/multiple markers can be combined both with each other and with task types.

The possible combination of the compensation with a loop or multiple instance as shown in figure 2.75 is worth mentioning. In this case, both markers are placed in parallel. As with the other markers, the compensation can be combined with the task types already introduced. A manual compensation task that repeats until it succeeds or that executes repeatedly and in parallel as far as possible (figure 2.75 on the previous page), is therefore eminently practical.

2.7.3 Global tasks and call activity

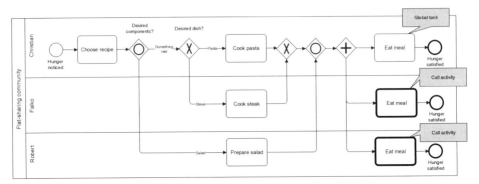

FIGURE 2.76 The process from figure 2.27 on page 43 as it had to be represented in BPMN correctly.

Global tasks differ from the regular tasks in that you can reference them by means of a *call activity*. Call activities have a thicker frame than other activities, as the diagram in figure 2.76 shows.

2.8 Subprocesses

2.8.1 Encapsulate complexity

The examples in this book either deal with simple processes, or they diagram complex processes superficially so that the models fit on one page. When modeling your process landscape, you don't have this luxury. You have to rough out your processes so that you can get the general ideas in place and recognize correlations. Then you have to develop a detailed description, so that you can analyze exactly where the weak points are or how you'll have to execute the process in practice. The possible top-down refinements or bottom-up aggregations mark the difference between true process models and banal flow charts, between sophisticated BPM software products and mere drawing programs.

BPMN provides us with the subprocess to help with the expanding/collapsing view. A subprocess describes a detailed sequence, but it takes no more space in the diagram of the parent process than does a task. Both tasks and subprocesses are part of the activities class and are therefore represented as rectangles with rounded corners. The only difference is the plus sign, indicating a stored detailed sequence for the subprocess. (See figure 2.77 on the facing page.)

What good is that to us? That depends most on how your BPMN tool supports the following options for connecting subprocesses with their parent processes:

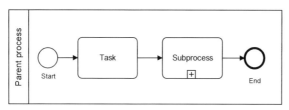

FIGURE 2.77 A task and a subprocess.

- **Representation in a separate process diagram**: The subprocess symbol links to a separate diagram. If your BPMN tool displays the process model in a web browser, for instance, clicking on the symbol would open a new page to display the detail diagram. (See figure 2.78.)

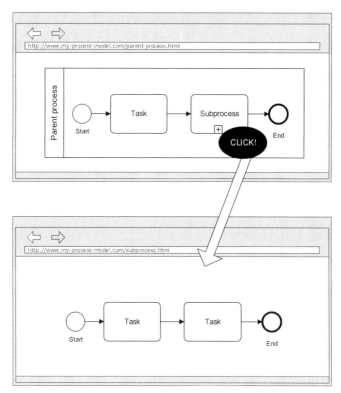

FIGURE 2.78 The details of the subprocess are shown in a separate diagram.

- **Expanding in the process diagram of the parent process**: The activity with the plus sign is called a collapsed subprocess. The plus sign suggests that you could click on it and make the subprocess expand. The BPMN specification provides for this option, though not all tool suppliers implement it. Figure 2.79 on the following page shows how the subprocess was directly expanded in the diagram of the parent process. A tool supporting this function enables you to expand and collapse the subprocess directly in the diagram, respectively, to show or hide details.

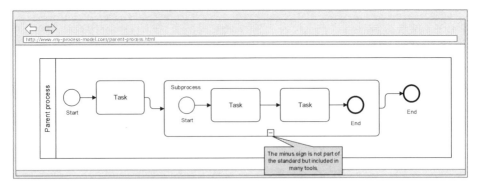

FIGURE 2.79 The subprocess expands directly in the diagram of the parent process.

Direct expansion may seem appealing, but often it is not useful in practice. Expanding the subprocess requires that all the adjacent symbols in the diagram shift to make room. This can result in sluggish performance with a complex diagram, and it can be visually... nasty. The most important thing is that your tool provides for linking and that you can usefully navigate through the diagrams. In other words, it supports the first option above. Yes, it can be helpful to have your subprocess modeled and expandable directly from the parent process. That means process segments remain localized, and you can attach events too (see section 2.8.3 on page 71). This is, however, the less important option.

The sequence flow of the parent process ends in both cases at the left edge of the subprocess. The next sequence flow starts at the right edge. This means that sequence flows are not allowed to exceed the boundaries of the subprocess, which not every beginner knows, and which becomes a problem when a subprocess expands.

Visualize a token that behaves as follows:

- The parent process starts, and a token is born.
- The token runs through the task and arrives at the subprocess, which causes the parent process to create an instance of the subprocess.
- Within the subprocess, a separate token is born which runs through the subprocess from the start to the end event, but the token of the parent process waits until the subprocess completes.
- When the subprocess token arrives at the end event, it is consumed, which completes the subprocess. Now the token of the parent process moves to its own end event.

The encapsulation in subprocesses that we're describing isn't restricted to two levels. You could just as easily have a parent process as a subprocess, or you could model further subprocesses on the level of a defined subprocess. How many levels you use and the level of detail you apply to model them is up to you. BPMN doesn't specify this, and there can be no cross-company or cross-scenario cookbook to define levels. Participants in our BPMN workshops don't like this, but there's no point in hiding the fact nor attempting to explain it away. In the following chapters, we work often with subprocesses in explaining our best practices, but the truth is the number of refinement levels and their respective levels of detail is always situational. It depends on the organization, the roles of the project participants, and the goals for the process you're modeling.

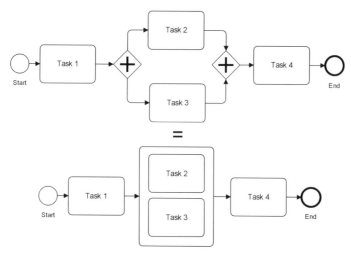

FIGURE 2.80 A subprocess can be used to replace the AND gateways.

You may remember that we explained in section 2.2 on page 27 that you can work without start and end events. Without them, you can make the parallelization shown in the top part of figure 2.80 somewhat more compact. In this example, start and end events were used in the parent process, but not in the expanded subprocess. That's completely legitimate, but we don't do this ourselves for two reasons:

1. It increases the risk of confusing inexperienced consumers of the model.
2. It is easy to confuse the representation with the ad hoc subprocess to be introduced later in the book. We use that a lot.

The example shows that subprocesses in BPMN practice are used not only to refine processes in terms of content; they are also a "technical stylistic device" for creating diagrams. The following sections illustrate this.

2.8.2 Modularization and reuse

In version 1.2, BPMN differentiated between embedded and reusable subprocesses by assigning an attribute to a subprocess. In version 2.0, BPMN maintains this differentiation in principle, but it is defined differently. A subprocess now is embedded intrinsically, and it can be reused only by defining it as a global subprocess, and then referencing it by means of a call activity. We therefore refer to embedded subprocesses and global subprocesses in the following.

An embedded subprocess can occur only within a parent process to which it belongs. An embedded subprocess cannot contain pools and lanes, but it can be placed within the pool or the lane of the parent process. Furthermore, an embedded subprocess may have only a none start event; start events such as messages or timers are not permitted. An embedded subprocess has essentially nothing more than a kind of delimited scope within the parent process, which may serve two goals:

1. To encapsulate complexity (as already described)

2. To formulate a "collective statement" on a part of the parent process by attaching events or placing markers. We deal with this option later.

On the other hand, global subprocesses may occur in completely different parent processes. There are a great many subprocesses that, in practice, are used over and over. A good example is the procurement of an item because a customer ordered it or you need to re-stock supply. Another example is invoicing because you've delivered or repaired an item as shown in figure 2.81. In the example, notice that call activities differ from regular activities by their considerably thicker borders.

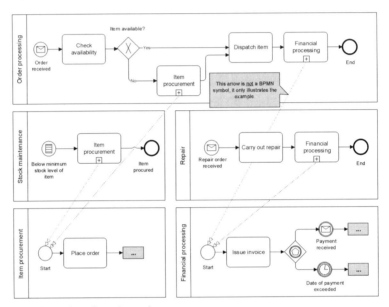

FIGURE 2.81 Examples of reusing subprocesses.

The connection a global subprocesses has to its parent is considerably less close, and they can have their own pools and lanes. You can think of the participant responsible for a subprocess as a service provider for various parent processes. It is a like a shared service center.

The loose connection also affects data transfer between the parent and the subprocess. BPMN assumes that embedded subprocesses can read all the data of the parent process directly, but an explicit assignment is required for global subprocesses to be able to read it. That may seem like merely a technical aspect at first, one that modelers and the consumers of their models care to know about but won't wish to bother with. After some consideration, however, you may see the impact this difference makes on the organization. Consider this: When your accounting department wants to issue an invoice for a repair, it always needs:

- A billing address
- The date of performance delivery
- A description of performance
- An amount to invoice
- An expected date of payment

The owners of order processing, not just the repair department, must provide this data. Accounting will want the data in a standard format, won't it? This corresponds well to what BPMN calls required data mapping between parent processes and global subprocesses. (Do you notice how often these weird techie issues correspond to the organizational needs and expectations of a process?) BPMN simply forces us to formalize many matters that seem self-evident, or that remained unconscious or forgotten in the process design. Formalization is our best chance of keeping up in a fast-changing environment with ever more complex processes.

2.8.3 Attached events

We already learned about intermediate events that can be attached to tasks. The same events can be attached to subprocesses as well, which opens up a wide range of opportunity in process modeling. As shown in figure 2.82, we can represent how a spontaneous dinner invitation leads to canceling our cooking process. In the process shown, however, we could ignore the invitation if our meal had already been prepared and we already ate it.

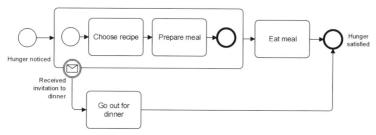

FIGURE 2.82 The catching event cancels the entire subprocess.

Where message, timer, and conditional events are involved, the parent process always aborts the subprocess when reacting to external circumstances. With error, cancellation, and escalation events, however, the subprocess reports these events to the parent process. This isn't as abstract as it may sound.

In the bottom right of figure 2.83 on the following page, the item procurement task can fail because the item is no longer available. Because item procurement is a global subprocess, it triggers an error event to tell the parent process that something went wrong. In business terms, this may mean that the customer who wanted to buy the item tells a salesperson that his or her order failed because the item is out of stock. A clerk then orders more of the item to replenish inventory.

It is interesting that parent processes can handle the error message differently. While the disappointed customer must be informed within the scope of the order process, it is sufficient for the stock maintenance process to delete the item from the catalog. The respective parent processes decide what circumstances require canceling the subprocess and what happens next. That's a principle that you can use to build flexible and modular process landscapes.

The signal event serves two functions. A parent process can react to a signal received from the outside while it executes a subprocess —this is much like a message event. But we

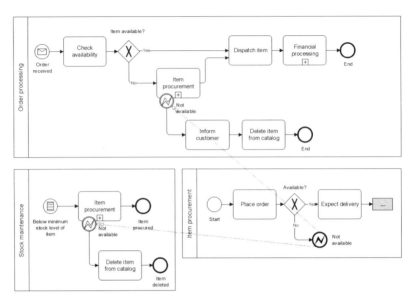

FIGURE 2.83 The subprocess reports an error to its parent.

also use the signal event to let the subprocess communicate things other than errors to the parent process. Primarily, this is because we can't model this type of communication with message events. BPMN assumes that we always send messages to other participants who are outside of our pool boundaries; the communication between parent and subprocess doesn't fit that mold. We don't use signal events for directed communication, but rather to broadcast information akin to advertisements on the radio.

A better alternative is the escalation event (see figure 2.84 on the next page).

The subprocess can use an escalation event to report directly to the parent process, and the message won't be regarded as an error message. Also, the parent process can receive and process messages from escalation events without canceling the subprocess because non-interrupting intermediate events can be attached.

2.8.4 Markers

You can apply the loop, multiple instance, and compensation task markers that we described in section 2.7.2 on page 63 in a fashion similar to the way you apply subprocesses. You can use them to model even complex loops as shown in figure 2.85 on the next page. The top and bottom parts of this diagram are equivalent.

One marker available only for subprocesses is called ad hoc. Recognize it by the tilde character as shown in (figure 2.86 on page 74). Use the ad hoc subprocess to mark a segment in which the contained activities (tasks or subprocesses) can be:

- Executed in any order,
- Executed several times, or
- Skipped.

2.8 Subprocesses

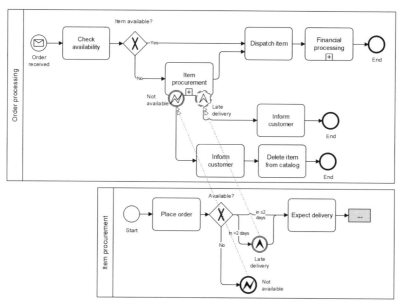

FIGURE 2.84 The escalation event informs the parent process that something needs to be done.

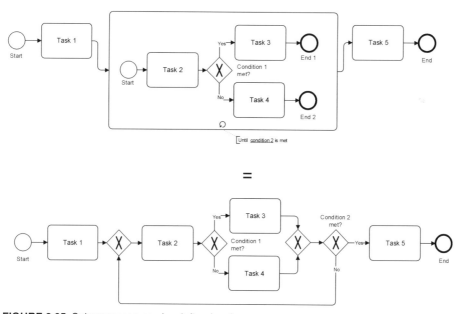

FIGURE 2.85 Subprocesses can be defined as loops.

Any party who executes this subprocess decides what to do and when to do it. You could say that the barely structured nature of what happens inside this subprocess reduces the whole idea of process modeling to an absurdity because what happens and when are the things we most want to control. On the other hand, this is the reality of many processes, and you can't model them without representing their free-form character. Frequent exam-

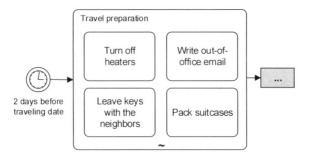

FIGURE 2.86 Travel preparation may include, but does not have to include, these tasks.

ples are when a process relies largely on implicit knowledge or creativity, or when different employees carry out a process differently. You can use the ad hoc subprocess to flag what may be an undesirable actual state. Doing so could be a step on the path to a more standardized procedure.

BPMN specifies which symbols must, which may, and which are forbidden to occur within an ad hoc subprocess. They are:

- **Must**: Activities
- **May**: Data objects, sequence flows, associations, groups, message flows, gateways, and intermediate events
- **Forbidden**: Start and end events, symbols for conversations and choreographies (discussed later)

By means of the specification, mixed forms —so-called weakly structured processes —can be modeled as shown in figure 2.87.

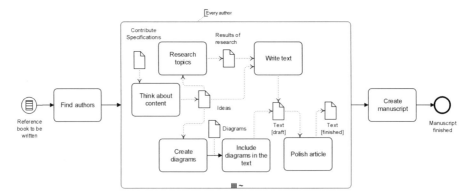

FIGURE 2.87 The processes of the individual authors are not subject to a predefined structure.

2.8.5 Transactions

Many processes work in an all-or-nothing fashion: either all steps must be carried out successfully or nothing must be done at all. The compensation event, which we discussed in section 2.6.9 on page 54, can undo tasks already completed without having to model the undoing in detail. The transaction is a special subprocess, which also helps us in such cases. We explain this in figure 2.88 using the following example:

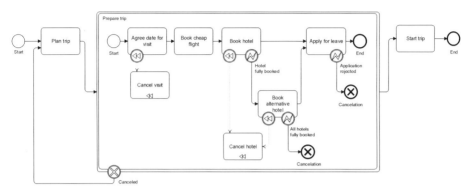

FIGURE 2.88 The double border marks a transaction, in this case the expanded subprocess *travel preparation*.

Suppose you want to visit relatives overseas. After deciding to make the trip, you start preparing for it. First, you make a firm plan with your relatives regarding the date and length of your visit. Second, you book a discount flight, and you reserve a hotel room (to avoid being an excessive burden on your hosts, despite their protests to the contrary). Third, you schedule vacation time with your boss. If all goes well, you can start the trip.

What happens, however, if the hotel you wanted is booked and you can't find another? What if the boss denies your vacation request? You have to cancel the travel preparation transaction. The cancel event exists for this purpose. You can only use it within transactions. If you cancel a transaction, it triggers a compensation of all tasks to which corresponding compensation tasks were assigned. You therefore sadly inform your hosts that you won't be able to come at the agreed date, and you cancel the hotel reservation, if any. Because you booked a discount flight, the airline will not refund the ticket price. (You curse them silently.) After compensating for all the tasks already executed, you leave the transaction through the attached cancel event, and you start over with preparations for a different travel plan.

This process is flawed. Because of the cursed airline's poor refund policy, it would make more sense to book the flight only after the other details are confirmed. Book it at the end of, or outside of, the transaction to minimize risk. That's the point: transactions are for critical processes in which even the smallest risk has to be taken into account. If you arrange your vacation time with the boss in advance, the risk of having your request rejected seems small, but it hasn't been reduced to zero, has it? An important bit of work may come in, and your non-binding agreement with the boss may evaporate. Transactions provide security for scenarios like this.

2.8.6 Event subprocesses

We locate an event subprocess within another process or subprocess. Recognize them by their dotted-line frames.

A single start event triggers an event subprocess, and this can only happen while the enclosing process or subprocess remains active. For event subprocesses, there can be interrupting (continuous line) and non-interrupting (dashed line) events. This is the same differentiation made as for attached intermediate events. Depending on the type of start event, the event subprocess will cancel the enclosing subprocess, or it will execute simultaneously. You can trigger non-interrupting event subprocesses as often as you wish, as long as the enclosing subprocess remains active.

Okay, that's pretty abstract, but we can demonstrate how an event subprocess works with an example. (See figure 2.89.)

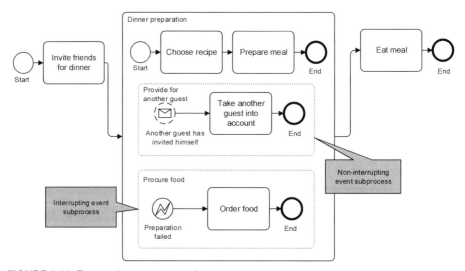

FIGURE 2.89 Event subprocess examples.

We invited a couple of friends for dinner. This starts the *dinner preparation* subprocess of choosing a recipe and then preparing the meal. While we are doing that, the telephone rings. Another guest invites himself to dinner. Spontaneous as we are, we just increase the amount of food or set another place at the table without interrupting the meal preparation. If an accident happens during preparation, however, the error immediately triggers the interrupting event subprocess for remedial action. We order food for delivery. When this event subprocess completes, we exit the enclosing subprocess through the regular exit and attend to eating the meal.

You can see in figure 2.90 on the next page how event subprocesses are represented in collapsed state: The frame is a dotted line, and we have again used the plus sign to represent collapsed subprocesses. In the top left corner, we also have the start event triggering the subprocess.

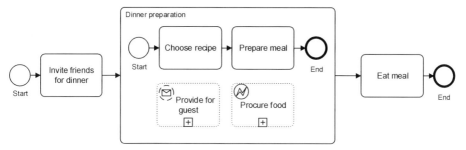

FIGURE 2.90 Collapsed event subprocesses.

The event types that can trigger non-interrupting event subprocesses are:
* Message
* Timer
* Escalation
* Conditional
* Signal
* Multiple
* Multiple parallel

There are two more types for the interrupting event subprocesses:
* Error
* Compensation

Are you wondering if you could model the example without event subprocesses and instead just attach events? Yes, you could. We did it that way in figure 2.91. In terms of sequence, the process works identically to the one shown in figure 2.89 on the facing page. There is, however, a small but important difference: In the second model, adding an additional guest and ordering the alternative meal do not take place within the *dinner preparation* subprocess, but within the parent process instead. This has the following consequences (which apply particularly to global subprocesses):

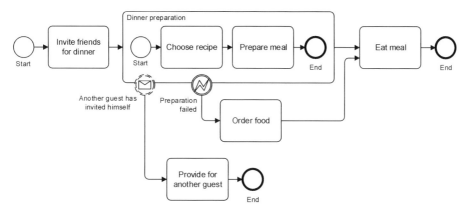

FIGURE 2.91 Compare this process to the one shown in figure 2.89 on the facing page.

- If responsibility for the subprocess lies with another parent process, two different roles take care of executing the subprocess and handling the related events. If the handling takes place within the subprocess, the same role has to take care of it.
- If the subprocess is global and thus reusable, each parent process must specify how it reacts to both events. On the other hand, if handling takes places within the subprocess, it is reused as well —for good or ill.
- Global subprocesses cannot access directly the data of the top-level process (or their parent processes); some data mapping is required. Data mapping is not required with an event subprocess.

2.9 Pools and message flows

2.9.1 The conductor and the orchestra

In section 2.5 on page 40, we described using lanes to assign responsibility for tasks or subprocesses to different task workers. Lanes always exist in a pool, and the pool boundaries represent process boundaries from start to end. To BPMN, the pool represents a higher-ranking instance compared to its lanes. The pool assumes process control —in other words, it assigns the tasks. It behaves like the conductor of an orchestra, and so this type of process is called *orchestration*.

In figure 2.92, the conductor arranges for Falko to process task 2 as soon as Robert completes task 1. The conductor has the highest-level control of the process, and each instrument in the orchestra plays the tune the conductor decides upon.

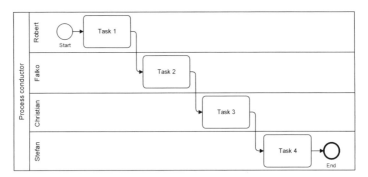

FIGURE 2.92 Tasks and task workers.

Do you think this is unrealistic? Many experienced process modelers have problems with this way of thinking. They would prefer to model a process sequence like that shown in figure 2.93 on the next page on the assumption that no almighty conductor exists in their company, and that individual task workers have to coordinate and cooperate on their own.

To coordinate cooperation with BPMN requires explicit modeling. You assign each task worker a separate pool, and the process passes from one to the next as a message flow (as

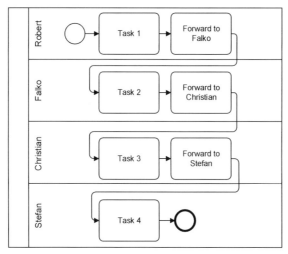

FIGURE 2.93 The task workers provide for the respective successor to start the processing.

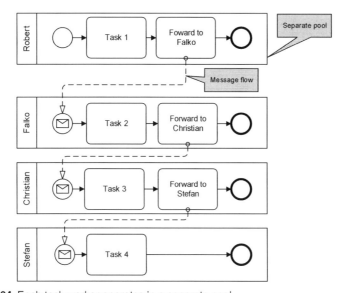

FIGURE 2.94 Each task worker operates in a separate pool.

shown in figure 2.94 on the facing page). In principle, this creates four independent conductors. These have control over their respective mini-processes, but they can't do anything other than to send messages that trigger their successor processes.

That seems complicated —and you don't have to choose the coordinated cooperation method for practical modeling. It reveals a basic principle, however, that you must understand. Even though BPMN lanes look very much like those of other process notations, they represent an entirely different way of thinking, which we attribute to BPMN's origin in the world of process automation. In that world, the workflow engine controls all tasks in the process, even though different task workers may execute them. So the workflow engine equates to the mysterious, almighty process conductor.

Have you heard of service orchestration in connection with Service Oriented Architecture (SOA)? That's almost exactly the task of a workflow engine, except that these services are not only fully automated web services; they also can be tasks executed by human process participants as directed by the workflow engine. What does that signify, however, for purely functional process modeling, in which you also describe processes *not* controlled by such a workflow engine? There's no general answer to that question.

You can eliminate pools and work just with lanes, modeling the message exchange as normal tasks as shown in figure 2.93 on the previous page. That's traditional, and it's a pragmatic solution during, say, a transitional period that allows your co-workers to adapt. In the medium and long terms, however, avoiding pools denies you a powerful device for increasing the significance of process models.

The next chapter explains the most important rules to be observed when working with pools and message flows. Meanwhile, we show the usefulness of this new thinking by example. One thing to remember is that if you strive to harmonize your functional and executable process models to achieve a better alignment of business and IT, you inevitably face this type of process modeling whether you use BPMN or not.

2.9.2 Rules for application

When working with pools and message flows, you may model the following things (see figure 2.95):

- Catching message events, which message flows enter
- Throwing message flows, which message flows exit
- Tasks, which message flows enter *or* exit
- (Expanded) subprocesses, which message flows enter or exit

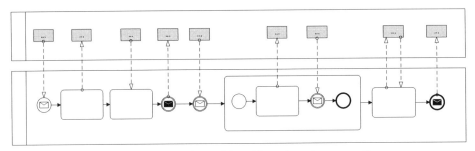

FIGURE 2.95 **Acceptable** constructs for working with pools and message flows.

The following constructs violate the BPMN specification and therefore must *not* be applied (see figure 2.96 on the next page):

- Sequence flows exceeding pool boundaries
- Message flows *not* exceeding pool boundaries
- Events with message flows that are not of the message type

2.9 Pools and message flows

* Events, which message flows enter *and* exit
* Message flows with arrows at the beginnings and the ends
* Gateways with message flows

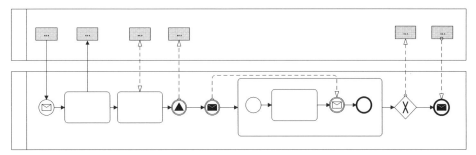

FIGURE 2.96 Forbidden constructs for working with pools and message flows.

2.9.3 The art of collaboration

We examined the process represented in figure 2.97 in connection with the event-based gateway.

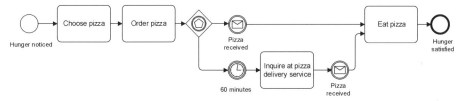

FIGURE 2.97 After the event-based gateway, the path at which the event arrives first is used.

Now consider the broader picture, and think about how this process happens from the point of view of the pizza delivery service. Presumably, it looks like figure 2.98: As soon as we receive an order, we bake the pizza. Our delivery person takes it to the customer and collects the money, whereby the process completes successfully.

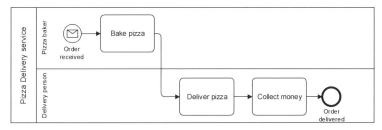

FIGURE 2.98 The sales process of the pizza delivery service.

We want to link the two processes, that is, to examine the interaction of customer and delivery service from a neutral perspective. We can try to model this interaction by means

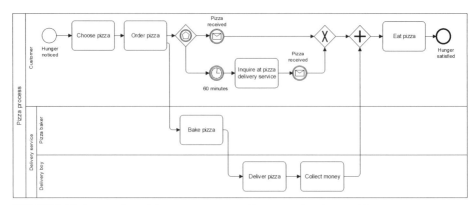

FIGURE 2.99 An overview of the pizza process with one pool and several lanes —a poor solution.

of a pool and lanes as in figure 2.99, but it doesn't work well: There are tasks and events that reference interaction within the pool —waiting for the delivery, for instance, or collecting the money. Other tasks are carried out by roles oblivious to their partners, such as baking the pizza and eating the pizza. It is impossible to differentiate the two visually. Strictly speaking, the diagram is not semantically correct because message events always refer to messages received by the process from outside, and that's not the case here.

If we go with pools, the whole process looks like figure 2.100. Both processes in the combined representation would look just as they did before, but now they connect through message flows. BPMN calls this form of visualization a collaboration diagram. It shows two independent processes collaborating.

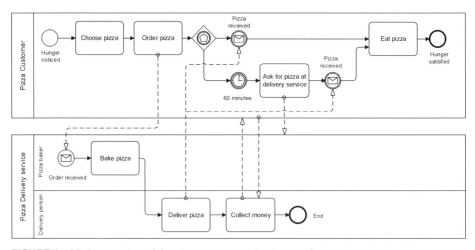

FIGURE 2.100 An overview of the pizza process using two pools.

In two cases, the message flows do not end in an activity or event, but at the participants' respective pool boundaries. The first one comes from the *inquire at delivery service* task; the second one connects to the *collect money* task. The rationale behind the first one is that our inquiry does not influence the sequence flow of the deliverer. The pizza service may provide information or speed up its order processing in anticipation of a new order, but the baking, delivering, and collecting of money doesn't change just because an inquiry came in. As for the *collect money* messages, there's a flaw in the model of the customer process: we have to pay for the pizza *before* we eat it, and that task is still missing. We added it to figure 2.101, and now we can connect the message flows directly to the *pay for pizza* task.

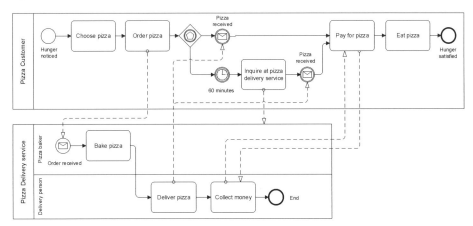

FIGURE 2.101 In the customer's process, the *pay for pizza* task has been added.

2.9.4 Collapse pools

It often happens that we don't know the processes of all parties in detail. We may know the processes of our own company, for example, but not those of a partner company. As long as our partner and we adhere to agreed-upon interfaces, such as receiving or sending certain messages, things can still operate smoothly. As customers of the pizza delivery service, we expect the deliverer to:

* Accept pizza orders,
* Deliver ordered pizzas and collect the money, and
* Be available for inquiries.

As customers, we have little interest in the deliverer's internal process. Maybe he bakes and then delivers the pizza; maybe when he's out of supplies, he gets another pizza service to bake the pizza and deliver it. That's his problem —we simply expect to receive our pizza. In modeling such cases, we can hide the deliverer's process and collapse the pool (see figure 2.102 on the next page).

We could go a step further and collapse the customer's pool too (see figure 2.103 on the following page). Now we see only the messages to be exchanged, assuming that we label the arrows to give us the general idea. The downside is that we can't recognize interdependencies any more. We can't see if the inquiry always goes out, or only takes place under certain conditions —the actual case. BPMN fixed this problem in version 2.0 by introducing a new type of diagram, the so-called choreography diagram that we describe in section 2.13 on page 94.

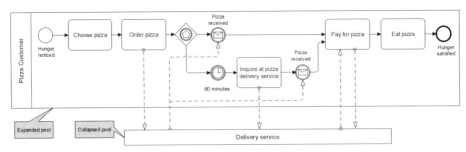

FIGURE 2.102 The deliverer's pool is collapsed, which hides the process details.

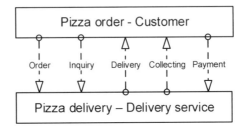

FIGURE 2.103 Both pools are collapsed, and only the message flows are marked.

2.9.5 Multiple instance pools

We showed in section 2.7.2 on page 63 and section 2.8.4 on page 72 that tasks or subprocesses can be marked as multiple, which means that these elements instantiate several times during execution. BPMN applies this principle to pools too.

Because a pool always represents a participant, we name the construct *multiple participants*. Figure 2.104 shows how to apply it. We defined three participants: customer, agent, and supplier. If the agent's process is instantiated, it does so because a customer places an order. This causes the agent to execute the *invite offer* task repeatedly. The supplier pool now has the same marker as the task that executed repeatedly. At a glance, this shows that

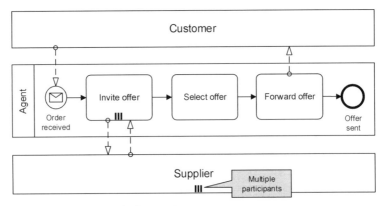

FIGURE 2.104 BPMN allows multiple participants.

it is not always the same supplier, but that several suppliers are involved. After obtaining all the offers, one is selected and forwarded to the customer.

The multiple instance participant always helps us when we want to show the interaction of processes in collaboration diagrams. Some processes may instantiate only once while others instantiate several times within the scope of cooperation.

2.10 Data

In the description of a process, BPMN focuses on the sequence flow: the sequence of tasks, gateways, and events. All other potentially relevant aspects to the process execution are treated as less important. The same applies to information or documents used in, or generated by, the process. You can account for these aspects in your diagrams by modeling so-called data objects, which represent all kinds of information regardless of their physical nature. They can include paper documents, abstract information, or electronic data records.

Data objects are coupled to flow objects and sequence flows by means of (data) associations. In addition to their designation, they can be assigned a specific status, which is marked by square brackets in BPMN. Typical statuses for data objects are:

- Generated
- To be checked
- Checked
- To be revised
- Revised
- Rejected
- Approved

The abstract example in figure 2.105 on the next page shows the following interaction of pools 1 and 2: In task 2.1, pool 2 generates the data object 2.1 with the initial status A, which we visualize by means of the directed association from task toward data object. Task 2.3 needs this data object as input, which is why we have drawn another directed association there. Furthermore, task 2.3 consumes the output of task 2.2.

Because these tasks directly follow one another, we can omit the directed associations, and we can connect data object 2.2 directly to the sequence flow. This is just a visual shortcut of the input/output relationship. Task 2.3, in turn, transforms data object 2.1 from status A to status B, and it sends it through a message flow directly to pool 1. Pool 1 waits for this message and then forwards the received data 2.1 to task 1.3, where it is transformed from status B to status C.

You have to pay attention when using message flows and directed associations in the same diagram, because they look similar. The most important distinctive features are:

- Message flows are dashed, the beginning of the line is a small circle, and the arrow is a closed triangle.

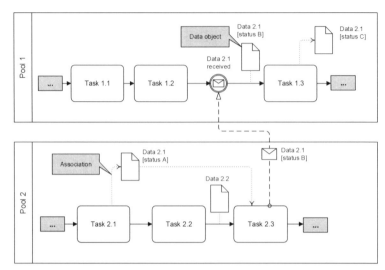

FIGURE 2.105 Examples of working with data objects.

- Directed associations are dotted, the beginning of the line is unmarked, and the arrow has an open base.

BPMN defines data as an additional category aside from flow objects and artifacts. This relevance is based primarily on the desire to execute BPMN process models directly, and this requires explicit observance of data. For collaboration diagrams, there are a couple of other interesting symbols besides the message object. We have applied them to the deliverer's pizza process in figure 2.106.

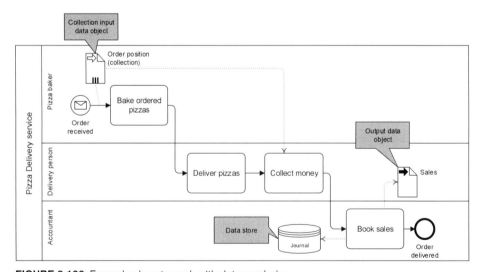

FIGURE 2.106 Examples how to work with data symbols.

Any new pizza order that the deliverer receives serves as input for the process. Recognize this as the arrow in the top left of the diagram. The order may include one or more pizzas (as expressed by the usual symbol for multiple instances), and the *bake pizza* task must execute a corresponding number of times. The number of instances also corresponds to the number of items in the *collection input data object*. The *collect money* task requires the object for the delivery person to ask for the correct amount. The accountant enters the sale in a journal. This sale is the output of the process, recognizable by the black arrow. The journal is a *data store* that exists, unlike the data objects, regardless of the specific process instance. The journal remains available long after the process instance has ended. If the pizza company was more up to date, its accountant could use software or a database.

2.11 Artifacts

2.11.1 Annotations and groups

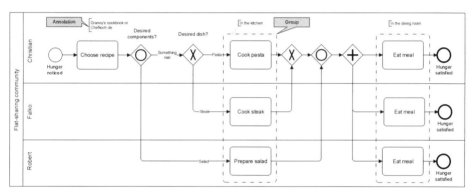

FIGURE 2.107 Annotations and groups.

We use annotations to supplement our diagrams. Annotations can contain almost anything you find useful, and you can connect them to other elements with associations. Usually, we use annotations to provide insight on the execution of tasks (see figure 2.107). (In figure 2.7 on page 31, we used annotations to record the average processing times; in figure 2.72 on page 63, we used them to explain what condition cancels a looping task.)

In figure 2.107, we noted that the food is to be prepared in the kitchen but eaten in the dining room. Because this information refers to several elements in the diagram at the same time, we can group them. Like all artifacts, groups do not influence execution semantics, so don't confuse them with things like subprocesses. You can apply groups any way you like —even across pool boundaries. Groups can be extremely useful for marking off parts of your models to which only certain conventions apply. We will return to this possibility in subsequent chapters.

2.11.2 Custom artifacts

BPMN allows you to introduce symbols that suit your own modeling conventions and particular information needs. In figure 2.108, we expanded the process of delivering pizzas with a bicycle and a computer. These appliances help us execute tasks. Apply the same rules to custom symbols as to all artifacts: connect them with associations to any flow object; place them in any position in the diagram.

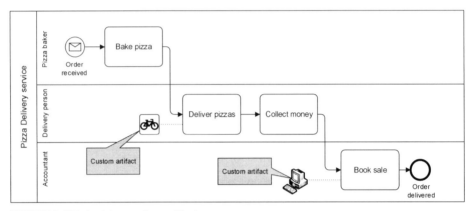

FIGURE 2.108 Applying custom artifacts.

 Tooling

You can use custom artifacts only if your BPMN tool supports them. Relatively few products do, unfortunately.

2.12 Comparison with other notations

Many people interested in BPMN already know other process modeling notations. They wonder if switching is worthwhile and what they have to watch out for. In this section, we compare four other notation systems —the ones we encounter most often in our practice —with BPMN. The primary weakness in all of them, which leads us to prefer BPMN, is that they lack the ability to model the interactions of participants acting autonomously. As we saw earlier, simple swimlane representations are insufficient for modeling collaboration. A secondary reason to prefer BPMN is the greater precision it provides, compared to the other notation systems, for handling events.

2.12.1 Extended event-driven process chain (eEPC)

The event-driven process chain (EPC) is a component of the ARIS methodology developed at Saarland University in cooperation with SAP AG. The resulting BPM software, ARIS Toolset, integrated tightly with the ERP (enterprise resource planning) solutions by SAP. Processes implemented in SAP products consequently were documented as EPCs, and that's a major reason they've been implemented so widely. It also made EPC dominant as a notation until 2008. Now, however, it has become apparent that EPC will be superseded by BPMN. Many EPC process modelers are preparing to switch, although that's not always easy because of differences in the approach. Meanwhile, ARIS offers process modeling with BPMN as well.

The EPC consists of the three basic symbols: function, event, and connector. Similar to gateways in BPMN, connectors can function as exclusive branches (XOR), and/or branches (OR), or in parallel (AND). The difference between data- and event-based branches does not exist in EPC. The extended version added symbols to describe organizational units, data, and application systems. You can reference subprocesses through so-called process paths or process signposts.

Converting EPC process models into BPMN is comparatively simple, as shown in figure 2.109 on the following page, though you need to be careful when converting events. EPC interprets possible data states the same way as it interprets events —incoming messages that trigger a process, for example. You mustn't model data-based decisions as event-based gateways, but rather as data-based gateways. Given EPC's name, it is ironic that BPMN is superior for modeling events. EPC neither differentiates between start, end, or intermediate events nor does it recognize different types such as message or timer. EPC doesn't let you attach events, so it is difficult or impossible to model monitoring functions, troubleshooting, or escalations. Another advantage of BPMN is in how it lets you treat an application as a data object: we could have attached our application as an input to the *check application* task (as in EPC), but instead, we attached it to the sequence flow between the start event and the task. You can thus see at a glance that the document was not already available in the company, but that it was sent there.

EPC still has lots of users. They have a history with EPC, they are used to working with it, and they may find it hard to internalize the new paradigm that BPMN represents. Given the shortcomings of EPC for modeling process automation, however, you should not consider it for modern BPM projects.

2.12.2 UML activity diagram

The activity diagram is one of 13 diagram types defined in UML (Unified Modeling Language) version 2. Like BPMN, UML is managed by the OMG (Object Management Group), though only since 1997. No one should mistake BPMN as a successor to UML, because UML is a general language for modeling software systems. Though it was not developed for modeling business processes, UML activity diagrams have been used often for process modeling —especially for IT projects. One frequent use has been to diagram target state processes as part of developing engineering requirements for new software.

90 2 The notation in detail

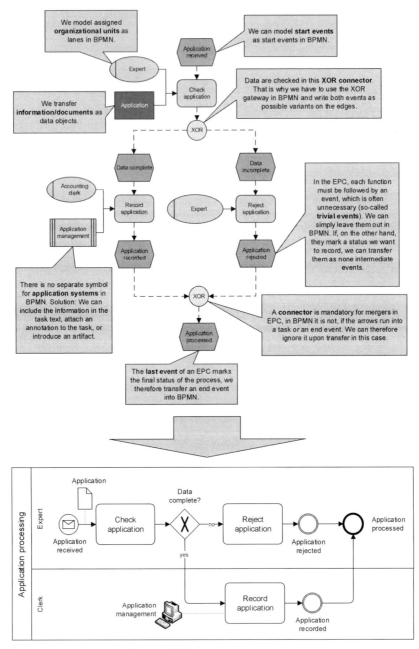

FIGURE 2.109 Converting EPC into BPMN.

UML's notation for activity diagrams is more comprehensive than EPC's. It contains a couple of symbols specific to software that have no direct equivalent in BPMN, including processing objects and object parameters in individual actions. Most of the current UML symbols for modeling business processes can be converted with no problem. What does become difficult is if you work with interruptible activity regions that cross several lanes. It would be a tidy solution to transfer these into BPMN as embedded subprocesses, but we can't do that because subprocesses in BPMN must not cross lane boundaries. The only solution is to define the subprocesses as global (and thus reusable), and to model the pool and lanes. That may be ugly, but it is the only way to make it work. (See figure 2.110 on the next page.)

Activity diagrams remain important for specifying software-related detailed sequences. Their integration in the UML framework supports this, as does the standardization by the OMG. But we think BPMN is still better for requirements engineering of process-driven applications, particularly if you also need to document process functions. Defining processes that the workflow engine executes directly is BPMN's specialty. No other notation can match it.

2.12.3 ibo sequence plan

The ibo sequence plan is implemented in Prometheus, which is BPM software from ibo Software. Like EPC, Prometheus is a proprietary notation system. We include it here because it is based on the conventional and widespread flow diagram. (ibo is a management consulting agency with more than 25 years of experience. Most of its customers are from the German-speaking financial world.) Though the ibo sequence plan is well established among process managers, ibo has discovered the advantages of BPMN. It has integrated BPMN into Prometheus.

Most of the symbols of the sequence plan transfer easily into BPMN, as we illustrate in figure 2.111 on page 93. The only problem is when you have a temporal interruption in your sequence plan. This can only be modeled as a timer event if it is caused by a process owner who deliberately does nothing for a certain period, and who then continues the process. We already examined sequences in which an interruption served as an indicator. We *could* continue the process after a countdown expired and because something else needed to happen. That does not work in BPMN. The only solution is to model the event that we're waiting on as a type (a message or a condition, perhaps), and to append an annotation to show how long it usually takes for the event to occur. That gives us a clean control flow without losing the indicator for the average wait time.

2.12.4 Key figures and probabilities

Can BPMN analyze and simulate processes? People who have worked with other notation systems ask this regularly, but the answer may not be a matter of methods but one of tools. What BPM software do you use? Does it let you store key figures and probabilities as well as the corresponding analysis?

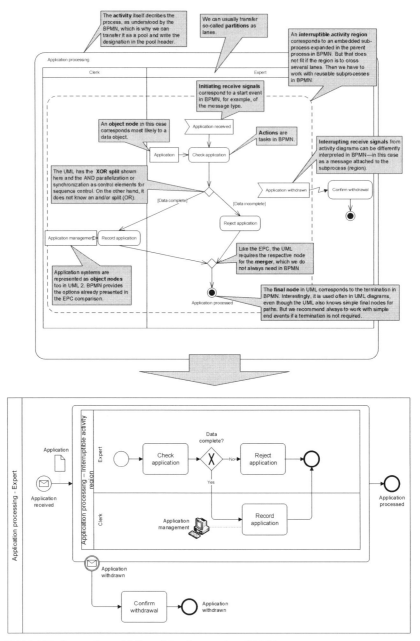

FIGURE 2.110 Converting a UML activity diagram into BPMN.

To be honest, the BPMN specification —even at version 2.0 —does not provide attributes to integrate key figures in process analysis. You could regard that as a regrettable deficit in the standard. On the other hand, simulation is particularly complex, and few people or organizations are willing to spend the time and money to implement it consistently. If the

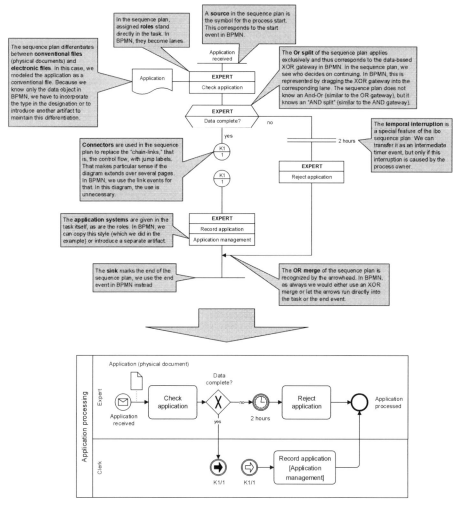

FIGURE 2.111 Converting an ibo sequence plan into BPMN.

BPMN specification represented all aspects of process simulation, the document would probably be 50 to 100 pages longer than it is. The shift in focus might even undermine BPMN in terms of the things it does well.

Figure 2.112 on the next page shows how the key figures lead time (LT), idle time (IT), and cycle time (CT) can be visualized in a process diagram along with probable outcomes. After an application arrives, it sits for about two hours before it is checked. The check takes 15 minutes, then the expert decides whether to reject or record it. Nine times out of ten, the application is recorded. We have modeled possible intermediate states, and we can offer the first analysis: The processing time from receipt to recording is 160 minutes. Rejects take only 140 minutes because the process bypasses the holding time on the clerk's desk. Taking all probabilities into consideration, we know that the average running time for the process is 158 minutes. Appropriately, we note this at the end event.

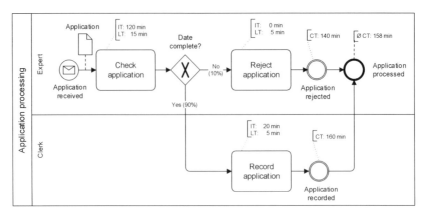

FIGURE 2.112 Possible representation of key figures in BPMN highlighting how the key figures, lead time (LT), idle time (IT), and cycle time (CT), can be visualized.

This is merely one example. Different BPMN tools offer different ways to define key figures, and they provide a variety of ways to depict and to use them. The extent to which process simulation is carried out makes further demands on the process model. Further dependencies may include the occurrence probability of multiple, the capacity of resources, and so on.

2.13 Choreographies and conversations

We showed in section 2.9 on page 78 that BPMN attaches particular importance to the interaction of different participants. BPMN even describes two additional modeling methods for this. We have so far seen little value in these methods for real-life projects, but we'll explain their potential. At the bottom right of figure 2.113 on the next page is our pizza collaboration from section 2.9 on page 78. It was merely decorated with the message objects (the envelopes), and we have positioned them on the message flows.

In the middle of the picture, notice the corresponding *choreography diagram*. This diagram reduces our view of the process to the exchange of messages between participants. In section 2.9.4 on page 83, the pools of both participants were collapsed. Choreography diagrams are considerably more accurate because we can still recognize the fundamental sequence. In the earlier diagram, it appeared that the customer only asked for delivery if 60 minutes elapsed since his or her order. That would be strange. In contrast, a choreography diagram models only the tasks that are relevant to the message exchange, and they do it only once for both participants. This makes the diagram much clearer. The sending participant has a white background; the receiving or reacting participant has a gray background. It does not matter if you place the participants above or below the task. Choreography diagrams can also define subprocesses to be modeled as choreographies.

The top part of the figure models the content of a matching *conversation*. This is the most compact way to represent the participants and their collaboration. A conversation in this regard stands for messages that are exchanged and logically connected to each other. In

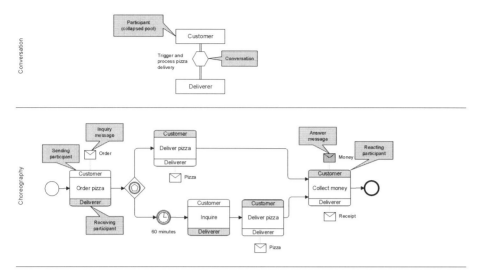

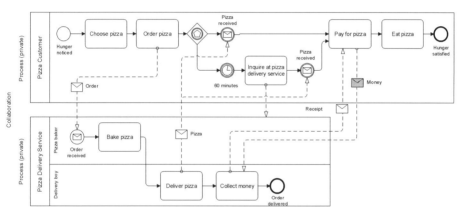

FIGURE 2.113 The pizza story as conversation, choreography, and collaboration.

other words, they correlate. In most cases, a conversation should stand for one collaborative process only. To be precise, we note that conversations in BPMN are not a separate type of diagram, but a variant of a collaboration diagram.

When do such diagrams make sense? Some BPMN experts regard them as superfluous, but we disagree. A one-person business may have little need for process modeling, but the systematic examination of processes —from an organizational *or* a technological perspective —only becomes more important as an organization grows larger and more heterogeneous.

As the number of people collaborating in a process increases, the less you can depend on implicit understandings and coordination among them, and the more important process modeling becomes. The same applies even more clearly to process implementation beyond the limits of IT systems. Both choreography diagrams and conversations can represent useful maps for situations where you have to recognize quickly the critical points in a collaboration. If required, you can then model them in more detailed collaboration diagrams.

3 Strategic process models

3.1 About this chapter

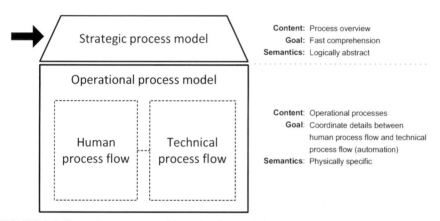

FIGURE 3.1 Strategic process models in the Camunda house

3.1.1 Purpose and benefit

You must be able to depict a process from start to end at the strategic level. Such strategic process models are necessarily rough. They are necessarily compact. The audience to bear in mind is likely to be the executive in charge of a company division. He or she may be a process manager or a process owner. The strategic process model also serves process participants, analysts, engineers, and external partners. Yes, these other audiences will need —and they are likely to *insist* upon —more detail, but they also need to have the strategic view if they are to work together toward a goal that makes sense for the organization.

To be readily comprehensible, your strategic diagrams may need to include information on computer systems or human tasks, but the diagrams must remain compact. The point at this stage is to create something that everyone can grasp, and, at a glance, know what the process does, for whom it is done, and the basic sequence of how it gets done.

Consider a strategic model when needs like these exist:

- To clarify what is and is not part of a process.
- To identify resources for a process and assign responsibilities.
- To identify key performance indicators and specify their characteristics. An example KPI may be that a process has a maximum run time of 24 hours.
- To review a process initially in the course of an improvement action.

3.1.2 Model requirements

The chief requirement of a strategic process model is that it is easy to understand —even for people with no experience in BPMN. The model must be comprehensible so that it will be accepted as a means for helping the situation. The title of Steve Krug's book on web usability is wonderfully suggestive when it comes to strategic process models:

Don't Make Me Think!

It also must be abundantly clear who the customer of the process is. Process management philosophy is that a process exists only for carrying out a defined task for a defined customer. Ensuring customer satisfaction is the purpose that defines many performance characteristics, and these characteristics are often the focus for improvement projects.

No one can grasp a process at a glance if the model extends across several pages. Our standard for a strategic model is to fit it onto a single sheet of standard-sized office paper. Orient the paper horizontally, and you automatically have something compatible with PowerPoint. It doesn't help to squeeze in as many lines and boxes as possible. For our strategic models, we limit ourselves to 10 or fewer flow objects and not more than eight artifacts.

In the purposefully plain model we're describing, you can't use the whole array of BPMN symbols. (This isn't the time for compensation events or multiple-instance tasks in any case.) Does the model lose some of its expressiveness? Sure. Does it become less precise? Not necessarily, though it does make for a less granular representation than you might otherwise prefer. Limiting yourself to ten flow objects and eight artifacts is very restrictive too, although you can choose which symbols to use and which to set aside for the sake of simplicity. You can even use custom symbols as artifacts. We'll discuss custom symbols later in this chapter; meanwhile, section 3.3 on page 102 presents a set of symbols that we find useful for strategic diagrams.

The second compromise is a semantic one. In section 3.2 on page 101, we give an example that shows how the semantics of strategic process models cannot be fully consistent. We struggled with this at first, but what we finally came to accept was that insisting on consistent semantics in strategic process models just made the models too complicated. The complexity interfered with the understanding and acceptance we needed from our target audiences, and so the models failed. Now, we knowingly accept inconsistencies, but *only* at the strategic level, mind you!

We remain strict with syntax, however, and we make certain our strategic models are syntactically correct. (The available BPMN tools check syntax and so help to enforce correct syntax anyway.) As a rare exception, we admittedly diverge from the BPMN syntax, but only if the divergence is minor in nature, permitted by the tool, and offers a clear advantage in creating understanding.

Our modeling etiquette

The principle for strategic process models is: Make the syntax as correct as possible, but allow inconsistent semantics if necessary.

3.1.3 Procedure

When do we model strategic processes? We do it either after the initial process discovery, when we have a general idea of an existing process, or at the beginning of process design, when we are configuring the new or improved process (see figure 3.2).

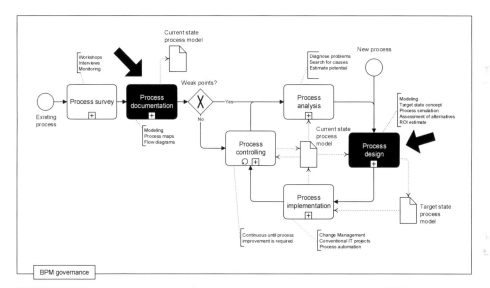

FIGURE 3.2 Strategic process models can be generated in two stages of the BPM life cycle.

It is significantly harder to do an initial discovery of a process than most people think. Sometimes you have documents such as standard operating procedures available, but most of the time you have to interview the process participants or the process managers. These may be one-on-one interviews or group interviews carried out as part of a workshop.

The advantages of a workshop are that you can gain several perspectives at once, and that the participants start feeling invested in the BPM project early on. That can increase acceptance. Workshops can be exhausting, however, because everyone perceives the process differently, because they all want to have their pet variations and contingencies considered, and because they already know what goes wrong. When different departments or teams participate —usually the case because of the comprehensive nature of the processes —discussion can quickly devolve into political squabbling. By then, you stand little chance of creating a differentiated process model. Imagine you've drawn only two rectangles when you hear the first interjections:

- "Before we can confirm the delivery date, we have to check the order details for completeness."
- "But we don't always do that after the order was received! Sometimes we have to check the customer's credit first."
- "But only if the contract volume exceeds 300,000!"
- "And if it is not a class A customer!"
- "Yes, right, that would have to be checked too then. Who takes care of that?"
- "The account executive."
- "In our department, his assistant does. At least, if the account executive is busy."
- "Seriously? Do they even permit that? In our department, he always gives the account executive the order so she can check it!"

And so on. Every BPM expert knows that his or her attempt to get a bird's eye view of the process gets lost in the croaking of the frogs who, naturally, have only a frog perspective. Unless you chair the workshop with an iron fist, the disaster takes its course: Everybody either gives up in exasperation or, even worse, agrees on a process model that looks complete but isn't, one that may even be wrong. You may as well give up too, since your process model will only gather dust in some little-used cabinet!

When you chair an initial survey workshop, use the following as a mantra:

> All process models are incomplete —but some of them are useful!

We credit statistician George E. P. Box for inspiring this thought. What it means is that you should *never* attempt to model a process in a greenfield approach, to try to account for every contingency and any possible variation. It simply will not work out. Instead, you should communicate at the beginning of the workshop that you want to start with just a general idea of the process. Set the following goals for this first iteration:

- We want to record the process from start to end.
- We want to record the process in a maximum of eight steps.
- We want to record the standard procedure only.
- We want to record the regular responsibilities.
- We want to record neither the weak points nor to devise improvements.

If you set these goals at the beginning of the workshop, you and your frogs can achieve the first-iteration bird's eye view you need, and you can do it in a span of 30 to 45 minutes! You must be careful to stay on target, however. Whenever a frog tries to escape back to the swamp, you have to stop him!

This first iteration is important psychologically. When it's done, the group will feel a flush of success, and they will see that the process can be managed after all. From this basis, you can launch into the gritty details of the process in subsequent iterations.

Can we start using BPMN in the first iteration? It isn't necessary, but yes, we can, and doing so has a benefit: It gives the group a good initial feel for the symbols and practices. You can also use index cards. For some time now, we have been experimenting with BPMN symbols attached to a white board with magnets. You can move them around easily during the discussion.

3.2 Case example: Recruiting process

Robert, a Human Resources manager, wants to improve the recruiting process. He believes that his staff members do too many tasks by hand that could be handled more efficiently by software. Moreover, he's tired of hearing complaints from other departments about how long it takes to fill vacancies.

Robert is convinced that most of the delays are because the managers of those other departments spend too much time vetting candidates. Also, they don't provide enough information with their requisitions, and they are slow to respond to questions. He can't prove his suspicions though.

Talking with us, Robert describes the recruiting process:

"When a department wants to fill a vacancy, the manager notifies me by e-mail. They fill out a form —it's just an Excel spreadsheet —where they enter the job title, and a job description, and their requirements, and..."

We interrupt Robert. The point, we explain, is not to discuss the cells in his Excel spreadsheet. We are interested in the basic sequence. The other stuff comes later.

"Oh, okay. So they notify me of the vacancy by e-mail. I have to check to whom I forward the e-mail, and that depends on who's available at that moment. Usually I just ask around, since we are all in one office anyway."

Again, we have to dampen Robert's talkativeness. Patiently, we explain that the point is merely to record the most important process steps and to set aside any operational details. He seems taken aback, but he continues:

"Well, then it's simple: We post the job and wait for appropriate applications. We check the applications, select a candidate, and fill the position. Essentially, our job is done if the selected candidate signs an employment contract, even though we have to yet record his or her information in the personnel files. Is this still too much detail?"

It is. For us, however, we can now extract the following key data about Robert's process:

- The process is triggered by a department's requirement to fill a vacancy.
- A job is posted, applicants apply, applications are checked, and the vacancy is filled.
- The process has reached its target when the vacancy is filled, in other words, when an employment contract is signed.

Based on the key data, we build the process model in figure 3.3 on the next page, which Robert understands right away, although we did have to explain a little about the conditional event that triggers the process. We deliberately put the end event in the department's lane to follow the BPM principle of starting and ending processes with the customer.

As a BPMN adept, did the semantic inconsistency of the model catch your eye? If we imagine a token running through the process, we have a huge problem with the *submit application* task and also the *check applications* task. If a single application was submitted, it is impossible to check several applications. That is a contradiction in content, a semantic inconsistency.

The problem doesn't get better by changing the task description to the plural form *submit applications*. That makes it look as though one applicant applied for the job repeatedly, and that's probably nonsense too. The truth is that there is no formal, clear, syntactically

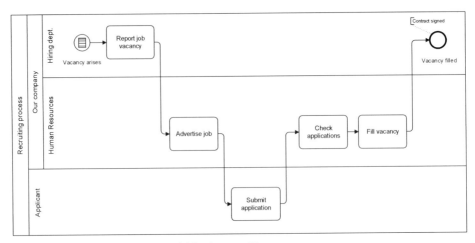

FIGURE 3.3 Strategic process model for the recruiting process.

correct solution for this, assuming that we want the model to remain as easy to understand as it is now.

What does Robert say about our problem? Probably nothing. For him, the connection between these tasks is obvious, and he grasps the basic sequence of the process at a glance. We have achieved what we needed from the strategic process model, so we smile and nod and keep quiet about the semantic inconsistency.

The representation has another shortcoming: You can't tell from the diagram that examining the job applications involves the requesting department as well as Human Resources. We accept this inaccuracy at the strategic level as well, since we haven't started the detailed analysis phase yet. If we model a task or a subprocess involving more than one process participant, we assign the activity to the lane of the party responsible for successful completion.

■ 3.3 Restricting the symbol set

As we showed in Chapter 2, BPMN has more than 50 symbols. That's far too many for strategic process models, and it is why we use only a subset of symbols. Use any subset you choose for strategic process models, but our suggestions follow.

3.3.1 Pools and lanes

After reading section 2.9 on page 78, you should assess figure 3.3 critically. After all, BPMN requires a conductor for each process, one who orchestrates (assigns tasks to) all the people and systems in the process. But this process isn't controlled by a workflow engine, so there is no conductor here. When the requesting department sends its request to Human

Resources, there is no forwarding of the instance, so you should model it as a message flow. Also, you should assign the requesting department to another pool.

In figure 3.4, we did assign the requesting department to another pool. It now reports its vacancy explicitly in the form of a message to HR and, if the vacancy can be filled, the requesting department is informed likewise.

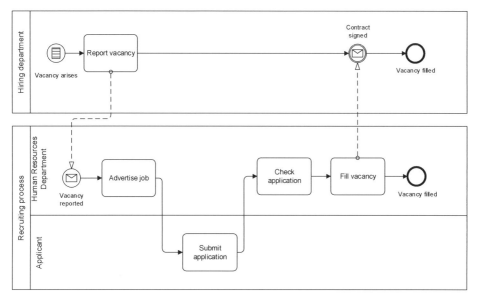

FIGURE 3.4 Reassigning the requesting department to a separate pool.

While this representation has its charm, a problem still exists: The applicants are not orchestrated by a conductor either. (A conductor for this pool would have equal control over both applicants and HR.) Figure 3.5 on the next page shows the collaboration when each party has its own pool.

The more we detail our model of the collaboration, the more questions arise, and the more we can detect inaccuracies and inconsistencies. How does an applicant learn about the vacancy? If he or she responds to a published notice, we should model this with a signal event, not a message. And the diagram still shows that we are waiting for one application instead of several, nor is it clear that we check applications immediately upon receipt or collect them all before checking. Finally, it appears that the applicant only has to submit an application to achieve employment. No interview required!

We could clarify all these issues with Robert and revise the model accordingly, but that's not the purpose of the strategic process model. Robert grasped the meaning of figure 3.4 with little explanation. It is doubtful that he would react well to our later diagrams if he encountered them when we weren't there to explain the symbols for the signal event or the different cardinalities of instances (one job posting, many applications). Robert wouldn't understand the model at first glance, and he wouldn't accept it any more. Consequently, we put figure 3.5 on the next page aside for further development at the operational level.

For strategic process models, we usually abstain from using multiple pools unless the customer is external to the organization. In such cases, a separate pool lets us model an

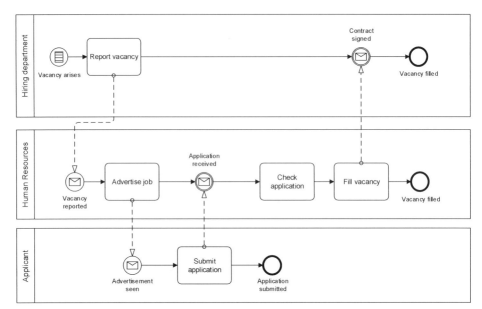

FIGURE 3.5 Each party is assigned its own pool.

overview of order processing, for instance, or complaint handling in the second pool. In figure 3.6, we show the customer as a collapsed pool so that we can focus on the process sequence at the time an order is received. Wouldn't it be nice if we could model all processes this way?

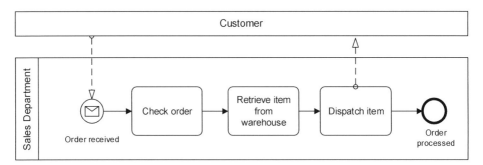

FIGURE 3.6 The customer as a collapsed pool.

We can't. The recruiting process example shows why we can't. In reality, we often have external partners that cannot be assigned to their own pools without making our strategic diagram so complex that it no longer serves our needs. On the other hand, we often deal with processes involving internal customers such as the hiring department in the recruiting process.

3.3.2 Tasks and subprocesses

Tasks often appear in our strategic models, but subprocesses appear only rarely. Task typing (see section 2.7.1 on page 61) is something we don't do for strategic process models though, and we also abstain from applying markers (see section 2.7.2 on page 63) with one exception: the loop marker. That is intuitive for most people, so we use it for strategic process models.

Our modeling etiquette

When we explained tasks in section 2.2 on page 27, we said our convention is to use the *verb + object* pattern —*report vacancy*, for example. When designating subprocesses at the strategic level, we do things a little differently. We nominalize them —turning *post job* into *job posting* and *check application* into *application checking*. In some cases, nominalization produces something that sounds a little unfortunate, but there are two advantages: First, this practice differentiates tasks from subprocesses. Second, compared to tasks, subprocesses are discussed more often and in more depth. The nominalized forms help participants express themselves more constructively: "The application checking is still too complex. We have to...." Does this seem like splitting hairs? Is it pedantic? Our experience has shown that the devil is always in the details of project communication and software development. Careless language quickly leads to costly misconceptions; it is worth paying attention to such details. ∎

Subprocesses should refine processes and process models. In the recruiting process model, we could define the steps *advertise job, submit application, check application,* and *fill vacancy* as subprocesses. It's likely that they stand for complex operations and not simple tasks. From what Robert told us, the *report vacancy* task, however, seems to be limited to completing and sending an Excel spreadsheet. That doesn't sound like a complex operation, so we leave it as a task. To represent this thinking, we come up with figure 3.7.

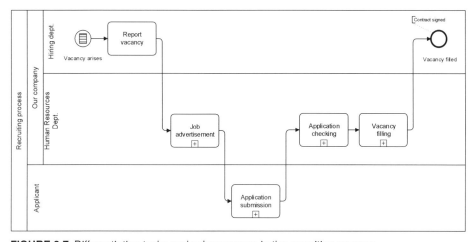

FIGURE 3.7 Differentiating tasks and subprocesses in the recruiting process.

The question now is if we want to model collapsed subprocesses fully on the strategic level. Usually, we don't do that because the point of the strategic level is *not* to show detailed operational sequences. We can't make it correspond smoothly to the subprocesses level of detail anyway because of the semantic inconsistencies already described.

3.3.3 Gateways

The recruiting process shown in figure 3.7 on the previous page is based on the assumption that we can fill vacancies when and as we like. That's not the reality, because sometimes we can't find a qualified candidate. We could model this and other special cases with gateways, but not at the strategic level.

At the strategic level, we only deal with the so-called *happy path*, meaning that we show the process path and results that we'd *like* to see. Most of the time, the happy path is sufficient. But if a process has different triggers, as in a customer-driven process, for example, we do sometimes have to model multiple paths at the strategic level. This is the time for a gateway.

We recommend using gateways as follows (refer to figure 3.8 on the facing page):

- Use XOR gateways for splits, that is, when *no* conditional flows exit directly from tasks. XOR gateways are easier to intuit than conditional flows. Target audiences understand a split when they see it.
- Merge tasks *without* XOR merge. In other words, let arrows flow directly into tasks. Such gateways (especially loops) only confuse inexperienced users; besides, omitting them results in more compact diagrams. Although we must use the gateways for merges in front of intermediate events and AND gateways, those should not appear at the strategic level.
- Use the AND gateway with *no* direct exit from the tasks to synchronize and make parallel. Parallel parts of a process need to be synchronized again later, so the AND gateway should be used in both cases to make the representation uniform and to avoid confusion.
- Do *not* use the OR gateway. It quickly results in meaningless constructs if you're not careful. Theoretically, you can represent any OR gateway by combining XOR and AND gateways. Again, however, this kind of complexity should not be part of a strategic diagram.
- Do *not* use the complex gateway. This representation of complex splitting and merging logics does not belong at the strategic level.

3.3.4 Events and event-based gateway

We recommend using start and end events at the strategic level to mark the start and the end of the process. You could do without these symbols, and the recruiting process would look like figure 3.9 on page 108. The diagram is more compact, but you can't see the process trigger or its desired end condition. That's a particular problem for the start-to-end presentation we're trying to create at the strategic level.

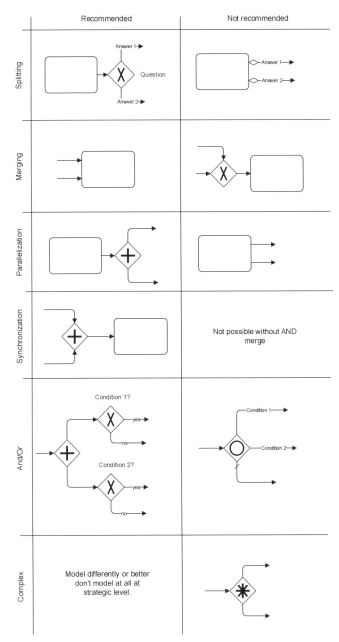

FIGURE 3.8 Recommended uses for gateways at the strategic level.

Compared to start and end events, intermediate events often require a little explanation. It is difficult for many people to understand at the outset that a catching event means that the process waits for that event to occur. We have to label them descriptively to make the

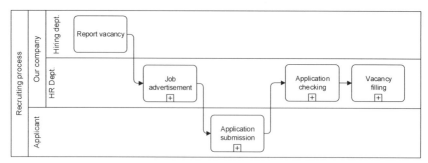

FIGURE 3.9 The recruiting process without start and end events.

meaning clear. With the exception of none events, catching intermediate events are too complicated for the strategic level.

We only permit some of the possible event types at the strategic level:

None events may be used as start, intermediate, and end events. The intermediate event can indicate process status during the execution. Process owners readily accept this kind of status as milestones they can use to monitor progress. In figure 3.10, we show two milestones defined for the recruiting process. At the strategic level, process models are sometimes so clearly laid out that you could define a milestone for every step. In such lovely cases, it is probably better to leave explicit milestone indicators out of the diagram just for simplicity's sake.

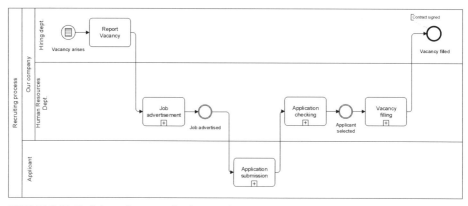

FIGURE 3.10 Defining milestones for the recruiting process.

We permit *message* and *timer* events as start events and intermediate events at the strategic level. The symbols are virtually self-explanatory.

The *conditional event* is problematic because people don't recognize it right away. It can be useful at the strategic level, however, because process owners want to see at a glance which conditions trigger a process or when a process has to execute. A common example is the tendering process, which, for compliance reasons, has to start as soon as an order exceeds a certain amount. This is why we include the conditional event in our strategic level *toolkit*. We use it often.

We try to apply a type to every process start event. In other words, we model it as a message or a timer or a conditional event. We succeed almost every time. If none of these events apply, we consider first if we have chosen the correct process start —if our pattern matches the process, or if the process actually starts earlier or later than we thought. Once in a while, we model a none type start event at the strategic level. If we fully model a subprocess, that none start event is important for correct syntax because a subprocess can only be started by its parent process.

Intermediate events can be also attached to tasks and subprocesses, but we avoid using them in this context at the strategic level because they indicate an exception. We want to record only the standard sequence for now. We also exclude the event-based gateway from strategic diagrams; reacting to events is an inappropriate level of detail for the strategic level.

3.3.5 Data and artifacts

Text annotations are permitted at the strategic level. We use them often. In the recruiting process example, annotations helped us to add information to the *vacancy filled* end event, namely that the employment contract was signed at that point.

People easily understand the group frame, so it is permissible at the strategic level, but we find that it gets used infrequently because strategic models are clear enough without it. Inexperienced modelers often mistake the group frame for an expanded subprocess, so you may want to hide the group frame at first. You can reveal it after the modelers' understanding has grown.

Data objects quickly result in visual overload. On the other hand, they can make two things readily apparent:

1. The essential input and output parameters of a process or a subprocess.
2. The type of communications between process participants.

The second item technically is a message-flow domain. Because we deliberately avoid using multiple pools —and hence their message flows —at the strategic level, we resort to data objects.

When we ask the Human Resources manager, Robert, how information is transmitted in his recruiting process, he says, "We receive requirement notifications by email. We then post the job notices to our website and also on the major Internet job sites. We receive applications by postal mail and email, though the email responses have been growing as a proportion of the total."

We can model Robert's communication by using data objects attached to the sequence flows by means of associations (see figure 3.11 on the next page). We usually attach the essential input and output data to the sequence flow between the start event and the first task or between the last task and the end event. That may not be correct in a formal sense because the output is not passed to the end event, but it is intuitive and therefore workable at the strategic level.

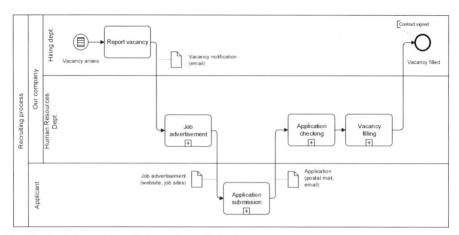

FIGURE 3.11 Data objects indicate forwarded information.

3.3.6 Custom artifacts

As described in Chapter 2, you can add your own symbols to BPMN as long as you only use them as artifacts. You can connect artifacts only by associations to flow objects (tasks, gateways, or events) to prevent them from influencing the sequence flow. They represent references to things beyond the main sequence.

In our experience, artifacts are well suited to the strategic level for meeting the particular requirements of your process owners. One classic is to represent the software systems used for individual tasks of subprocesses. We usually use a cuboid for this. The cuboid is used for the same purpose in Unified Modeling Language (UML) use case diagrams, which is why it makes sense to us.

When we ask what IT systems the recruiting process uses, Robert says, "So far almost none. The job description is created in Excel; all the other things are done without any special software." Find the corresponding representation in figure 3.12.

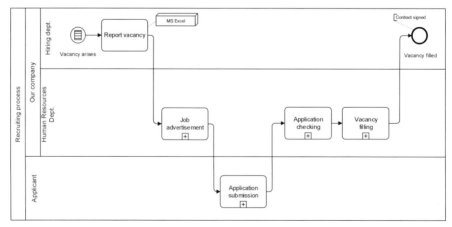

FIGURE 3.12 Software use is restricted to Microsoft Excel.

Depending on the industry and the particular needs, you can introduce custom artifacts for completely different purposes. Suppose the insurance sector faces regulatory pressure regarding minimum requirements for risk management. This makes identifying risks in the process documentation necessary; you can use a custom artifact to flag the risks associated with execution of tasks and subprocesses.

3.3.7 Hide and reveal symbols

You can see the extensions added to the recruiting example for milestones, data forwarding, and IT systems in figure 3.13. This information is particularly helpful for discussing a process, but because they tend to overload a diagram and add to the potential confusion, not all users of the diagram will want to see them. It is useful to be able to hide and reveal the extra symbols as needed. This is a question we often get in our BPMN workshops; here are our notes:

- Hiding and revealing is not a feature of the notation. This feature must be provided by the BPMN tool you work with.
- Several of the BPMN tools make it easy to hide and reveal artifacts such as data, annotations, or custom symbols.
- Hiding and revealing is more complicated for none intermediate events because they attach to the sequence flow. When you hide them, you get unexplained and unsightly gaps unless your tool is intelligent enough to rearrange the diagram accordingly. (Suppose an XOR merge was applied before an event that suddenly became redundant because the arrows could enter the task after the event directly.) So in general, hiding and revealing flow objects like activities, events, and gateways is problematic, which is why most BPMN tools do not provide a hide-reveal feature, or they limit its function.

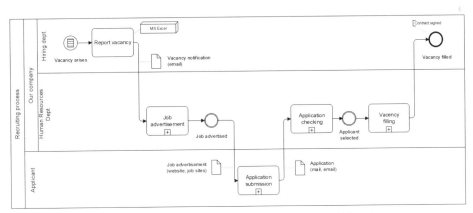

FIGURE 3.13 The recruiting process, including milestones, data, and IT systems.

3.4 Process analysis on the strategic level

After making our first, rough survey of the recruiting process and documenting it, we can do two things:

1. We can start a detailed survey to model the actual state of the process at the operational level.
2. We can content ourselves with the documentation at the strategic level.

The choice depends on the purpose of the model. If we aim for ISO certification, or if we want to provide the model to process participants as a guide for their daily work, it needs to be more detailed.

Recall that our Human Resources manager is unhappy with his process, and he wants to embark on a project to improve it. He has described the symptomatic weaknesses. Remembering the BPM life cycle, we can now start with analysis to get to the bottom of the weaknesses and devise ideas for improvement (figure 3.14). A detailed survey and documentation of the current state can be helpful for this analysis, but to be honest, the cost-benefit ratio is high enough to discourage it in practice. More often than not, we use the strategic process model to guide our search for causes during analysis.

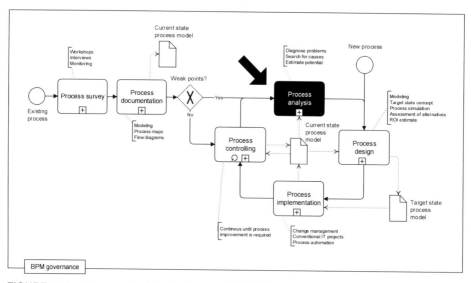

FIGURE 3.14 Process analysis in the Camunda BPM life cycle.

How does searching for causes work? The main thing is that we listen. We listen not only to the process manager, but also to the customer of the process and, of course, to the process participants. How we proceed and what tools we use always depends on the complexity of the process, but a workshop or two involving these three parties is usually enough to identify the weak points of the process and their causes. We don't want to discuss the interpersonal and political aspects —these quickly become a problem in such workshops. Perhaps they are a topic for a different kind of book.

Here we draw a brief picture of a workshop called *Analysis of potentials in the recruiting process*. The participants are:

- Process manager: Robert.
- Customer: Falko, Sales Manager and representative of the hiring departments.
- Process participants: Marina, Christine, and Stefan, clerks in the Human Resources Department.
- Process analyst: you!

After the usual introductions and explanations of purpose, you display the process model from figure 3.13 on page 111. You let it sink in. You apply your well-honed skills as a moderator to engage the participants in analyzing weak points. You list an obvious symptom, for instance, and ask the participants to confirm, correct, or amend your observation. You write the results on red index cards and attach them to a white board. They are:

- The process takes too long.
- The process is too intricate.
- The process is not transparent enough.

The complaint about the long processing time comes from Falko. Robert complains about the intricacy of the processing. Both of them agree that more transparency is needed to support comprehension of the process in whole and in its parts.

Working with the participants, you then extract the causes that account for the symptoms. Step by step, you identify and list on your red cards the causes of the causes. Some of the symptoms or causes may be attributable to a certain subprocess or task, and this will be well marked by the card affixed next to it. Other symptoms and causes will apply to the process as a whole.

All the workshop participants quickly agree that too many activities in the process are executed manually. "There must be a technical solution," is a unanimous verdict.

Robert's criticism that the vacancy notifications from the hiring departments are often incomplete, unclear, or incorrect, is of course not received enthusiastically by Falko, but Falko cannot deny that mere notification is usually insufficient. More clarifying details have to change hands between the hiring departments and HR.

For his part, Falko faults the Excel template provided by HR for the notifications. "These things are a catastrophe! Confusing and without any assistance or explanation. You can't even see which details are mandatory and which are optional!"

One ticklish issue involves holding times: the periods between task assignments and when they actually occur. Robert and Falko blame each other. They accuse and defend their respective staffs without useful facts to back up their statements. At this juncture, you, as diplomatic moderator, get the squabblers to agree that excess holding times harm the process, but that the causes cannot yet be clearly established nor responsibility apportioned.

The result of the workshop is the causal chain as shown in figure 3.15 on the following page. You deduce four solutions to be pursued within the scope of an improvement project:

- Reduce manual activities.
- Minimize correction loops.
- Make the current status of each operation visible at all times.
- Record and assign responsibility for idle times.

You may suppose that the solutions will be IT-enabled, though that's not always the case in practice. We do not mean to suggest that software is the solution to every problem. BPMN

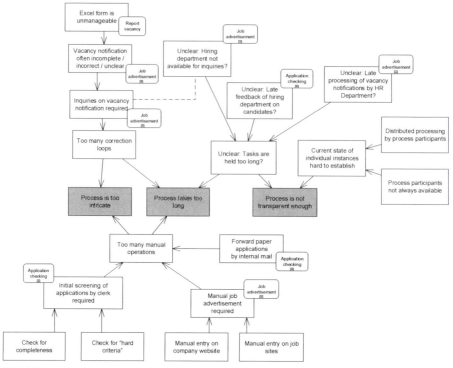

FIGURE 3.15 Causal chain, showing weaknesses and their causes.

development started with the need to improve processes by means of IT, however, and that is why our example reflects that kind of scenario.

In the BPM life cycle, you now enter the *process design* phase to devise an improved target-state process. This is the time for the operational level.

3.5 Conversations and choreographies

The possibilities provided by BPMN for modeling conversations and choreographies haven't yet established themselves in real-world situations. We don't find them in our customers' projects, and we only use them on rare occasions. If you're interested, the next section provides some thoughts about using them in the described use case.

Looking at the recruiting process as a conversation (figure 3.16 on the next page), two possibilities present themselves: In the simplest case, just represent that there are three participants in the process and that they are conversing with each other. The other possibility is to add a multiple symbol to the applicant to show that, while only one hiring department and the Human Resources Department participate in the conversation, more than one applicant may participate. Certainly it helps to indicate the different cardinalities, but the success of doing so depends on users who understand the symbols. Apart from that, the conversation diagram is good for representing all the parties in a single view.

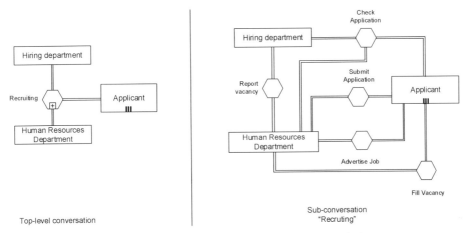

Top-level conversation   Sub-conversation "Recruting"

FIGURE 3.16 The recruiting process conversation at two levels of granularity.

We can refine this conversation and fully model its sub-conversations. The plus sign in the hexagon of the top-level representation indicates a refinement similar to the symbol for a subprocess in our process diagrams. We can see in the refined representation that not all the participants participate in all sub-conversations. The applicants, for example, do not participate in the vacancy notifications; the hiring department doesn't participate in posting the job.

There's a semantic problem with this representation: The job posting is not a message received directly by the applicant; it is modeled by means of the conversational relationship. We tend to allow the semantic flaw in the interests of clearness and comprehensibility, just as in our process diagrams. One advantage a conversation diagram has over the sequential representation in a process diagram is that we can take the different communications relationships between participants into account without having to accept a complicated representation with multiple pools and their related message flows.

The representation as a choreography in figure 3.17 on the following page is even more precise because it also considers the order of communication. We can see the different messages. It is a mixture of conversation and process diagrams because we still see the various participants in the choreography of tasks and subprocesses. One advantage in this is the more differentiated examination of cardinalities: The job advertisement takes place once, and it is a message from the Human Resources Department to a number of applicants. (No, the semantics are not really correct, but we accept this for simplicity's sake.)

In the next, *application submission* step, multiple applicants send their applications to the Human Resources Department. It is correct to represent *application submission* without a multiple instance, because this subprocess is executed only once by each applicant. The application check, conversely, is executed as often as applications are received, in other words, multiple times. It is completed separately for each applicant, however, which has its effect on the *applicant* communication partner. Each applicant gets a separate invitation and a separate interview, so the applicant gets no multiple instance symbol in this

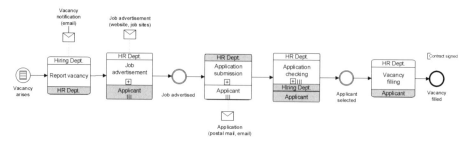

FIGURE 3.17 The recruiting process as a choreography.

subprocess. The last subprocess, *vacancy filling*, takes place only once, and the chosen applicant signs a contract.

The advantage of the choreography diagram is that it compactly represents the communications relationship between process participants. It is ideal for providing overviews of communication-intensive processes. The question is if choreography diagrams can be understood and accepted by target groups at the strategic level. In our experience, it is hard enough to introduce the regular symbols of BPMN to such groups.

4 Operational process models

4.1 About this chapter

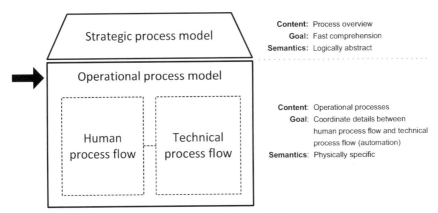

FIGURE 4.1 Operational process models in the Camunda house.

4.1.1 Purpose and benefit

It is at the operational level that process models begin to reveal operational details in the form of human and technical flows. Process participants reference operational process models (the human flows, that is) every day. Process analysts examine them to identify improvements. Also, operational process diagrams can be the starting point for technical process implementation in the form of technical flows —ideally by a workflow engine. The operational process model obviously describes more detail than does the strategic model, but this leads to a problem:

A whole process is a complex interaction between people and IT systems as they carry out tasks. The *process analyst* is concerned with getting to the heart of these interactions so that he or she can devise organizational or technical improvements. The analyst's question is:

> How is the work done, and how can we do it better?

The *process participant* only cares about the aspects of the process that concern him directly. He wants to know:

> How should I do my work?

When a process requires technology to be implemented, the *process engineer* gets involved. He or she has to understand what the technical implementation is meant to achieve from a functional point of view. The process engineer asks him- or herself:

> What does the engine have to achieve?

It isn't easy to reconcile the three roles, and answering their questions is the challenge of the operational level. If you meet the challenge successfully, the benefits are:

- The logic of the operational process model is consistent between operations and the technical implementation. In other words, the process actually works as documented.
- The understanding gap between business and IT shrinks. The parties can discuss the same process model, and they can recognize both the technical effects of business requirements and the impact technical implementations may have on operations.
- If the process is implemented by a workflow engine, monitoring and reporting on the process can become much more substantial and immediate.

In short, if you master the operational level, you will have found the common language of business and IT —at least as far as process modeling is concerned.

4.1.2 Model requirements

Just as with the strategic level, operational process diagrams must be syntactically correct. Although some semantic irregularities can be tolerated at the strategic level, we can't allow them in operational models. The operational level describes how work is actually done, so there can be neither contradictions in content nor formal mistakes.

As you develop the operational model for any project that includes technical implementation by means of a workflow engine, another requirement arises: All the questions that the process engineer must ask to understand the desired outcomes need to be answered. After all, the technical model itself becomes executable.

Precision serves the process participants too, because they should be able to refer to the model for how to accomplish the work. At the same time, it is best not to burden participants with complexity that doesn't serve them. After all, the participants' core competence is the work itself, not BPM. For participants, the process model is just a means to an end, something they may reference only once in a while.

4.1.3 Procedure

An operational process model has to be sufficiently precise but not overly complicated. To achieve that apparently contradictory goal, we provide a view of the process model specific to each role. Figure 4.2 on the next page depicts what we mean. If the process participants see a view that represents only their perspective, they are satisfied. The participants know what to do and when to wait for others to complete their portions of the process without being distracted by the details of what the others do.

Viewer	Process participant	Process analyst	Process engineer
Central problem	How should I do my work?	How is the work done?	What does the engine do?
View	Own orchestration	Entire collaboration	Orchestration of the workflow engine

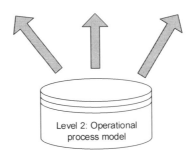

FIGURE 4.2 The roles and their views at the operational level.

The core idea of the operational level is to differentiate consistently between orchestration and collaboration. As explained in section 2.9 on page 78, each participant gets his or her own pool. This presents the participant's experience as its own, closed process. Reserve the diagram that shows the collaboration among these processes for the process analyst, who presumably can handle the complexity.

Treat the workflow engine as a participant with its own pool, and the process engineer can focus on it. Note that in this approach we are following the BPMN idea of a conductor for each pool who controls its processes. BPMN presumes a workflow engine even when a human serves in place of an actual workflow engine.

Aside from the improved views, this differentiation is important because in practice, the entire process is almost never controlled completely by a workflow engine. There are always decisions to be made and tasks to be carried out by humans. To represent the process completely in a model, we have to account for the human activities. We accomplish this when we assign a separate pool to each participant, whether human or not.

The process analyst plays a major role in achieving a differentiated model. He or she must comprehend BPMN fully and be able to model the process from different participants' points of view. If the target state process is to be implemented in a workflow engine, he or she must develop and maintain the model in all its representations, from the strategic to the technical.

This is an example of the process analyst's steps:

1. Review the target state process at the strategic level. (See chapter 3.)
2. Resolve the lanes into separate pools. (See section 4.2 on the next page.)
3. Model the human flows, that is, the target-state process from each participant's point of view. (The participants and the process manager must settle upon these details. See section 4.3 on page 122.)

4. Model what the participants do that will be supported by the workflow engine and how it will do so. This also must be settled between the manager and participants. (See section 4.4 on page 125.)

5. Model the technical flows, at least to the extent that these can be derived from the participants' processes. The process analyst or the process engineer can do this. The operational model won't be directly executable, but the process engineer can enhance the model for that purpose. (See section 4.4.2 on page 127.)

6. Finalize and document other requirements such as templates, data, and business rules. Group these around the process model by referencing them from their relevant symbols in the diagram (See section 4.4.3 on page 129.)

This is only one approach. If it makes sense to you, you can start from the technical flow and work bottom up, or you can work outward from an operational process model. Frequently, it is the operational process model that comes into existence first because the business and IT got together during a workshop, and they developed the human and technical flows concurrently.

After developing the model, show the views to the people affected. This takes a tool with good presentation functions. The ability to expand and collapse pools is especially valuable, since the expand/collapse function means you can avoid having a lot of different diagrams with redundantly modeled pools. For more on tool support for BPMN in general and our framework in particular, see section 8.4.2 on page 224.

■ 4.2 From the strategic level to the operational level

We often create a strategic model of the process before we model it at the operational level. For our recruiting process example, we created the strategic process model in section 3.2 on page 101. We depicted it in figure 4.3 on the facing page, and in section 3.4 on page 112, we discussed the process' weak points. We learned that the process sequence itself is not that bad; most of the friction comes from insufficient technological support. Now the process modeling needs to extend to the operational level. First, we'll examine the sequence solely from an organizational standpoint. Second, we'll think through what a workflow engine can contribute to improving the process.

Chapter 3 described how strategic process models often contain semantic contradictions. These make it impossible to refine the model directly, but strategic views often differ significantly from operational views. You can assume that a strategic process model rarely changes. At the operational level, you can expect changes more often. That's another reason for the principal structure of models at this level to be technically compatible with the even more detailed implementation models to follow.

As a consequence, while we will reference the strategic process model often, we have to develop the operational model afresh. That may sound like a problem, but in practice it usually is not: The strategic model doesn't take that much time to create, and it achieves clarity about strategic purposes and outcomes that you shouldn't need to revisit while de-

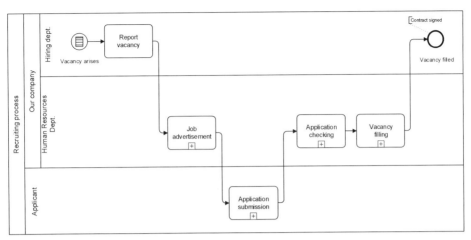

FIGURE 4.3 The recruiting process at the strategic level.

veloping at the operational model. Also, because the strategic level changes so infrequently, you need not worry about duplicating effort to maintain it through updates.

The recruiting process example has a semantic difficulty at the strategic level: the different cardinality of instances. It looks as though every applicant for a job gets that job, even though everyone understands that's not the real-world expectation. Everyone assumes that the normal course of events is that several applicants submit applications, that Human Resources checks a corresponding number of applications, and that a single applicant ultimately fills the vacancy. Another difficulty is that we don't know our applicants nor their number. These are two reasons that, when it comes to creating an operational model, we cannot represent the applicant as a lane in the same pool as the other participants.

A valid operational model also has to specify the interaction between the hiring department and Human Resources more realistically. It's not as if HR carries out the *job advertisement* and *application checking* tasks without consulting the hiring department. The process analysis (section 3.4 on page 112) showed that the two departments communicate actively; it is the ineffectiveness of their communication that causes most of the friction and ambiguity. What makes the most sense therefore is to model the processes of these participants in separate pools. That allows an explicit examination of the organizational interfaces. It also allows us to provide each participant with information relevant to his or her role, and we can exclude irrelevant information. Irrelevant information is a huge over-complication!

Figure 4.4 on the next page shows the recruiting process after moving the lanes into separate pools and accounting for the activities that require exchanges between participants. The applicant still reacts to the signal of a job being advertised, but the three short lines at the bottom center of the applicant pool indicate that there potentially are multiple applicants. (Refer to section 2.9.5 on page 84.) The possibility of multiple applicants is why we modeled an AND split after the message *application received* event; it shows that HR is not waiting for a single application but will instead process any applications received. The terminate event at the end of the HR pool means that this activity will continue only until an applicant is selected and successfully employed.

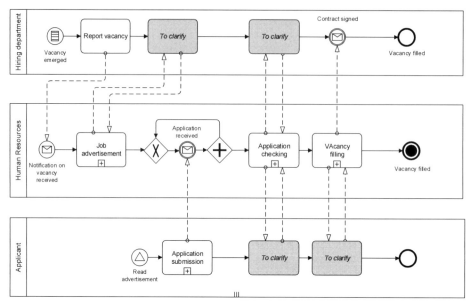

FIGURE 4.4 Start of transfer to the operational level.

Open issues remain to be settled and modeled. Not only do we have to define the *to be clarified* activities, but we have possible special cases to account for. What if:

- an applicant is rejected as unqualified?
- not even one applicant is qualified?
- not even one application is received?

Examining this entire process at the operational level easily could exceed this book's goal of illustrating principles and methods. In the following sections, therefore, we elaborate only on the part starting with identifying the personnel requirement through advertising the job. (To explore the complete example, visit BPM-Guide.de/BPMN.)

4.3 Processes of the participants

As already described, the process analyst models processes at the operational level. Where does he or she get the operational details needed? Usually from the process participants themselves, that is, the people working in the process. For the *post a job* process, we'll interview Falko first, because he's the manager of the hiring department. Falko describes his contribution this way:

"When I see that we need a new staff member, I report the vacancy to Human Resources. I then wait for them to send me the job description so that I can check it before they publish the advertisement. I may have to request a correction to the job description, but otherwise I release it. And sometimes HR has additional questions about tasks or qualifications, so I make myself available for clarifications."

When we model Falko's process, we may include the Human Resources clerk in the diagram to complete the picture. When we collapse the clerk's pool, however, figure 4.5 results.

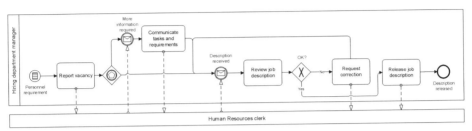

FIGURE 4.5 The *post a job* process from the hiring department manager's point of view.

Note: BPMN 2.0 does not allow sequence flows to flow directly into an intermediate event following an event gateway. This prohibition seems unnecessary to us, and we advocate that it be removed in future versions of the specification. For the time being, try representing this type of scenario as shown in figure 4.6.

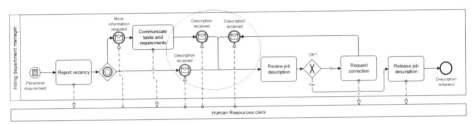

FIGURE 4.6 The current version of BPMN 2.0 requires this representation, which seems inefficient and unnecessary.

Christine, the Human Resources clerk, has a different point of view about the *post a job* process: "When a job vacancy is reported to me, I write a job description based on the details I'm given," she says. "If there are ambiguities in those details, I have to ask the hiring department about them. After I finish the description, I submit it to the hiring department for it to be checked, then I wait for it to be released. Sometimes they do that right away, but sometimes they reject it and ask for corrections. In that case, I correct the description and submit it again to be checked. Once the description is finally released, I publish the advertisement for the job."

When we collapse Falko's pool and show Christine's, the result looks like figure 4.7.

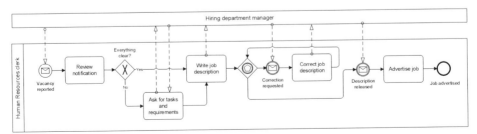

FIGURE 4.7 The *post a job* process from the Human Resources clerk's point of view.

What have we achieved so far? We have explicitly modeled the operational details of the *post a job* process. At the same time, we created two process models that are not overly complicated on their own.

The consumers of our models must have some basic knowledge of BPMN. They must:

- understand events —intermediate events in particular.
- understand the difference between a data-based and an event-based gateway.
- understand the difference between the sequence and the message flow.

The burden on the users of our models is greater at the operational level than it is at the strategic level. The first target audience for the operational level is the process analyst, who can use the model as the basis for a detailed analysis as well as for an IT implementation. We show this later. In all likelihood, the process analyst developed the model in BPMN, so his or her understanding of the model can be presumed.

The second target audience is the participants whose work the model represents —Falko and Christine. They should be partners with the process analyst in a dialog about improvements, and they should at least understand the models. You may find them both later using the diagrams as a guideline for their work, helping to answer the questions "How should I do my work?" and "What do I have to do next?"

So, will participants like Christine and Falko accept the models? Our experience shows that they will, provided that:

- Each participant sees only his or her own pool and not the full complexity of the process. This requires that the process model be developed accordingly and an adequate tool used to present it.
- The participants were provided with a basic briefing on BPMN, and a simple key or legend to explain the symbols. As the process analyst, you probably will have to do the instruction yourself. Tools often provide a key or legend.

Of course we can view *post a job* as a whole by expanding both pools, and we can show it to Christine and Falko as a detailed collaboration diagram (figure 4.8 on the facing page). But isn't it obvious how much more complicated this diagram is, compared to separate views of the pools? Would the process participants be more likely or less likely to accept and use the more complex diagram? In any event, the entire collaboration only matters to the process analyst. In the following two sections, we will deal with collaboration diagrams as we consider process automation.

BPMN provides the option to hide the complexities of the collaboration in a choreography diagram (figure 4.9 on the next page). The advantage is that this represents the interaction between participants more compactly. It is therefore good for orienting the process analyst. On the other hand, a choreography diagram omits internal steps that do not help communication between participants. You can't see, for example, that the Human Resources clerk executes the *advertise job* task. We regard choreography diagrams as sometimes useful additions to operational level collaboration diagrams, but usually they can't take the place of collaborations.

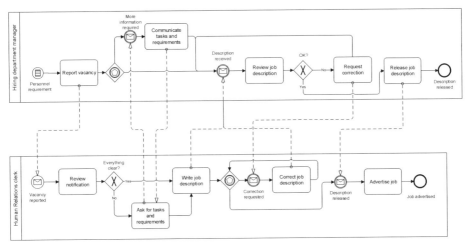

FIGURE 4.8 *Post a job* as a collaboration diagram.

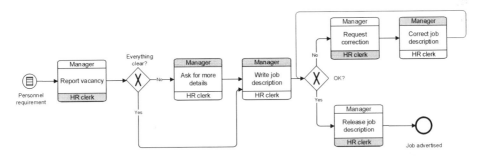

FIGURE 4.9 *Post a job* as a choreography diagram.

4.4 Preparing for process automation

Describing a process from an organizational perspective is only one task of modeling a process at the operational level. It's not even the most interesting task! The holy grail actually is the smooth transfer from human to technical flows, in other words, from the functional to the executable process model.

In section 1.1.4 on page 4, we show how an executable process model can be interpreted directly by a workflow engine to combine human workflow with service orchestration. Since this is also central to the IT perspective on BPM, we focus on this approach in the following sections and in Chapter 5 (see figure 4.10 on the next page). An alternative would be to implement the process logic without a workflow engine, but in a general programming language such as Java or C#. That's a scenario we'll address in section 4.4.5 on page 132.

4.4.1 Designing for support by a workflow engine

The desired technical implementation for a process can be discussed and documented with the models we did for the individual participants. Let's now consider the participants

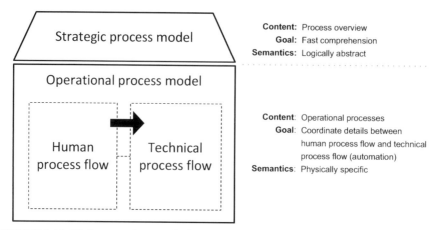

FIGURE 4.10 We focus on the transfer from human to technical flows.

as users of software, and let's see what performance they expect from an automated process. In this thought experiment, the workflow engine itself becomes a participant with which the user exchanges messages.

Falko, as hiring department manager, describes the desired support in the *post a job* process:

"I record a vacancy in a form on our portal and then send it. If the job description is ready to be checked, I want to see it in my to-do list on the portal. I process the task by reading the description, and I either request corrections or I release it. After the job advertisement runs, I want a short email notice that everything worked out."

If you remember Falko's process model from figure 4.5 on page 123, you will recognize his description, but there are two major differences:

- The Human Resources Department's reaction to requests is not to be shown as a task on the portal. It is still processed by email or phone.
- The confirmation message about successful postings is new.

Now we expand on the process model:

- We subdivide it into lanes called *HR portal* and *Other*.
- We assign all the tasks to be executed on the portal to its lane. For our purposes, a message event represents a human task that displays in the task list. A task with an outgoing message flow means that the user has completed a human task. The XOR gateway shows that the task may have different results, such as *request correction* or *release job description*.
- The first task in the HR portal lane is *"report vacancy*. This is not a task that was assigned to the user by the workflow engine because it does not follow the corresponding message event. It is possible, however, for the user to trigger the process, that is, to effect an instantiation. If so, the workflow engine must provide the corresponding option, usually by means of a form available on the portal, which can be filled in at any time.
- The request made by the Human Resources Department, as well as the reaction to it, are assigned to the Other lane because neither are realized on the portal, but rather through

the usual channels: phone or email. The message conveying that the advertisement was published also belongs in the Other lane. Although the workflow engine sends that message, it reaches the user by email, and not as a notification in the portal.

The result is in figure 4.11, which shows the workflow engine as another participant, but still with the pool collapsed.

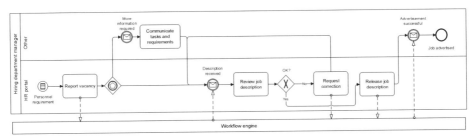

FIGURE 4.11 IT support of the hiring department's manager regarding the job posting.

Now we learn something new from Christine, the Human Resources clerk: "A vacancy report appears as a new entry in the task list of the HR portal. This is where I write the job description and then forward it to the hiring department for verification. Forwarding it completes the task. If I have to correct the description, that comes up on my task list too. If the hiring department releases the job description, however, I essentially receive notice by the appearance of an *initiate advertisement* task. In that case, I specify the advertising channels on the portal and then initiate the advertisement. If the advertisement runs successfully, I want a short notice that everything worked out."

Applying the principles discussed in this chapter results in figure 4.12, but with one difference: The user doesn't trigger the process any more. Falko already took care of this. Christine only has to react to the new entry in her task list on the portal. You will recognize this by the start event of the message type.

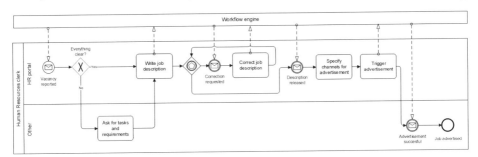

FIGURE 4.12 IT support of the Human Resources clerk.

4.4.2 Required processes of the workflow engine

We will now define the first version of the technical flow. As process analysts, we don't need as much input from the process participants now. We can turn our attention to the process engineer. We consult with the process engineer to determine how to implement the process with the workflow engine. We show the pools of the human participants in a collaboration diagram, and we expand the pool of the workflow engine as another participant, dividing the workflow engine pool into three lanes:

- The hiring department manager gets a lane, as does the Human Resources clerk. All the tasks placed in these lanes are user tasks, which is to say, tasks for humans to complete.
- The third lane is for fully automated tasks. These are things like interface calls (service tasks) or internal program fragments (script tasks). You can also store whole subprocesses in this lane.

The process steps to be implemented in the engine result directly from the behavior of users Falko and Christine. The process starts because Falko reports a vacancy by filling in a form on the portal. He sends it, which is represented by the start event of the message type. The workflow engine then assigns the *write job description* task to Christine. Once Christine completes her task, the engine assigns the *check job description* task to Falko. Falko can either release the description or ask for a correction. Depending on Falko's choice, the engine will assign either *trigger advertisement* or *correct job description* to Christine. If she has to correct it, the job description returns to Falko as another *check job description* task. This loop repeats until Falko releases the job description.

The engine assigns *trigger advertisement* to Christine after Falko releases the description. First, she has to specify the channels through which the job is to be advertised, and then she has to initiate the action. This tells the engine that Christine has completed *trigger advertisement*. The engine then executes the *publish advertisement* subprocess, which consists mainly of interface calls. (It is encapsulated as a subprocess at this point in order to avoid overloading the diagram.) At the end, the workflow engine sends confirmation emails to both Falko and Christine to inform them that the advertisement was successfully published.

The collaboration diagram in figure 4.13 on the facing page shows the technical process flow, which is executable in the workflow engine. There is some redundancy within the diagram because the users are represented in their own pools, but they also have lanes in the pool for the workflow engine. This is important for separating responsibilities: The participants always decide on the routing within a pool, that is, they determine which path exits an XOR gateway.

Christine, for example, decides if she can write the job description without further input or if she has to get Falko to clear up discrepancies. The workflow engine can't do that; it doesn't even notice this decision. On the other hand, the workflow engine does decide if Christine needs to execute *correct job description* or *trigger advertisement* next because the corresponding XOR gateway is in its pool. The workflow engine makes this decision based on Falko's decision following his review.

Our collaboration diagram solves a problem that arises frequently when attempting to evolve a functional (operational) process model into an executable one: mixing control instances in a single pool. As we keep saying, people and workflow engines almost always have their respective decisions to make within a process. Until you segregate control instances into appropriate pools, it will be difficult to achieve a model that you can execute in a workflow engine.

Another advantage to this approach is that we still can present views optimized for our targeted groups of users:

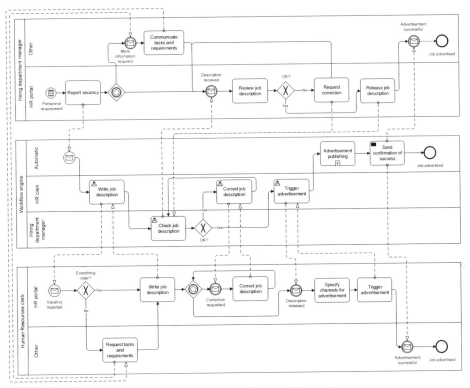

FIGURE 4.13 Representing the job advertisement in a workflow engine.

- The process analyst can see the entire collaboration diagram.
- The process engineer can see only the workflow engine's pool.
- The process participants can see their own pools only. Not only are these pools less complex than the whole collaboration diagram, but they also contain additional information not part of the workflow engine's pool: that inquiries are made in case of discrepancies, for instance.

Our judgment is that this approach is the only practical way to align business and IT in a BPMN process model.

4.4.3 Further requirements

Could our process engineer implement the process from the diagram as shown? Probably, but there are issues still to be settled, such as the templates to be displayed and the exact tasks in a vacancy notification or a job description. These are typical kinds of requirements for any software project, however, and they do not affect the process logic. We don't recommend documenting these requirements directly in BPMN; instead, we suggest linking them to the process at appropriate points. That way, the process represents a central starting point for requirements documentation. Of course, your BPMN tool must support linking.

We have categorized typical requirements as they occur in projects for the development of process applications in figure 4.14. Besides BPMN, we use graphic screen designs, class diagrams, decision tables, and text to document requirements. In integration-intensive projects, we use, among other tools, diagrams to describe system landscapes.

Type	Explanation	Examples	Notations	BPD link
Functional	Functions to be provided by the solution	- Process logic - Features - Use cases - Interfaces - Business logic	- BPMN - UML (use cases) - User stories - Acceptance tests - General text	- Task
Non-functional	Properties to be met by the software	- Service level Agreements (SLA) - Response time - Capacity - Maintainability - Platform compatibility	- Text	- Pool
User interface	Channels through which the user interacts with the software	- Masks - Dialog work flows - Mobile devices - E-mail roles	- BPMN - Mask sketches - User stories - Acceptance tests	- Task
Data	Data to be processed by the software	- Contents - Restrictions - Formats - Channels - Mappings	- ER diagrams - UML (class diagrams) - Spreadsheets	- Pool - Data objects
Rules	Specifications according to which the software is to decide	- Validations - Checks - Calculations - Control points	- Spreadsheets - Trees - Text	- Task

FIGURE 4.14 Typical requirements for implementing an executable process.

You can see drafts of screens and confirmation emails for the job advertisement process and how they link to the process model in figure 4.15 on the facing page. Sometimes you can derive the control elements to be provided on the screens from participants' pools. We know, for example, that Falko can release a job description or request a correction. That may imply the need for option buttons (also known as radio buttons) on the form Falko sees. Options representing advertising channels may be needed for Christine.

4.4.4 Technical implementation beyond the workflow engine

In your BPM projects, you often will find that you have to implement certain software components beyond the workflow engine. For us, this happens most often with:
- Business logic and rules
- Screens and screen flows
- Data transformations

Business logic and rules

Business logic is, for example, a calculation to be programmed. It is appropriate to package the calculations as services so that the workflow engine can call them through service tasks. This builds direct reference to the paradigm of service-oriented architecture (SOA).

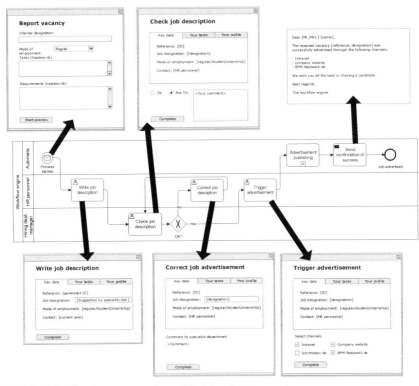

FIGURE 4.15 Drafts of screens and email for job advertisement.

Business decisions can be represented in a decision engine, and they can be called from the workflow engine through custom-developed, business-rule tasks. We deal with this subject in section 4.5.4 on page 141 and section 7.2.5 on page 195.

In either case, it usually makes sense not to model the respective requirements fully in BPMN. A better solution is simply to reference business logic or rules in the process diagram through service or business rule tasks.

Screen flows

Screen flows are a borderline case because, from the process automation perspective, they serve only to execute a single task. It also is difficult to do if the sequence of screens varies with the entries a user makes or with the data established between screens. Screen flows, however, are also processes. UML activity diagrams have been used often to model them, which suggests that BPMN can as well.

Clean BPM architecture strictly separates screen flows from the process model. In other words, a workflow engine is only loosely coupled to a screen flow application by means of clearly defined interfaces. To be consistent about this, you have to define a separate pool for the screen flow application and link it to the workflow engine and to the user with message flows. From the application's perspective, each screen flow is an isolated process.

If your process contains several screen flows, you must create a separate pool for each one, even though the same screen flow application controls them all.

If that seems too complicated, or if your workflow engine combines the screen flow control with the executable process model, you can set it aside and model the screen flow as a collaboration between user and workflow engine. We can't recommend doing so, however, because it leads to process models that are less serviceable and more error-prone. It may be a good compromise to package screen flows in an embedded subprocess.

Data transformations

Data transformations are required primarily in integration-intensive processes. A clean BPM architecture requires that the process model be decoupled from the details of the interface calls. At this point, the Enterprise Service Bus (ESB) comes in, and you should represent it as a separate pool and handle it as you would a screen-flow application. You can likewise integrate these steps directly in the process model of the workflow engine by working with script tasks.

Script tasks represent internal steps of the workflow engine. Data transformations are an example. You could wrap the data transformation in a service and call it through a service task. The difference is that the transformation engine (an XSLT processor that transforms XML data, for instance) would be a component internal to the workflow engine if it were a script task. It would be provided by an external component —that is, from the perspective of the workflow engine —if it were a service task.

4.4.5 Technical implementation without workflow engine

Perhaps you don't use a workflow engine to execute the technical process flows. Perhaps you program it in Java, C#, or another classic programming language. This doesn't matter for the transition from the strategic level to the operational; your compiler or interpreter equates to the workflow engine. Doing without a workflow engine may mean that you cannot execute the process logic directly from an operational process model. Another specification —called requirements specification, or detailed technical specification —will be required instead before the implementation. The process diagrams developed at the operational level can be integrated in this IT specification to form the basis of the technical design.

In conventional software development, requirements are often established without an end-to-end perspective of a process. Instead, they provide a compilation of functions that a user executes in a specified order, depending on the process to be carried out. These functions can be defined as applications or *use cases* in the design phase, which brings us to the classic domain of the Unified Modeling Language (UML).

You can apply BPM and our framework to such projects, but remember that each use case represents an independent process. You have to define a separate pool for each use case. Compared to implementing in a workflow engine, the user has responsibility for linking the use cases into a process that could be represented in a single pool.

Occasionally, the same use case can apply to different scenarios. We recommend modeling the respective roles as simple processes that package the use cases as subprocesses. Figure 4.16 shows two examples of that procedure. Between the pools, you see a UML use case diagram that joins the use cases. This is an example that shows UML and BPMN working well together. Figure 4.17 on the following page shows the fully modeled *login* use case.

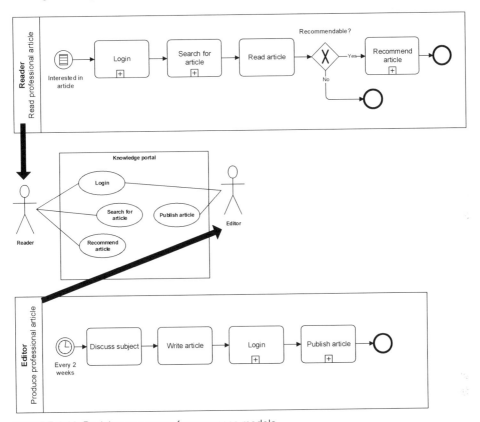

FIGURE 4.16 Deriving use cases from process models.

We can state as a principle that BPMN can benefit conventional IT projects compared to other process notations. As we pointed out earlier, however, BPMN was not developed for that purpose but rather to support projects with a workflow engine in mind. Perhaps the more important point is that it makes little sense to do process-intensive IT projects without a workflow engine.

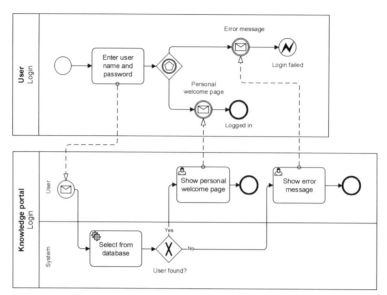

FIGURE 4.17 The *login* use case as a fully modeled collaboration of user and software.

■ 4.5 Hands-on tips for the operational level

4.5.1 From the happy path to the bitter truth

The First Pass Yield and BPMN

The field of organizational process management defines First Pass Yield (FPY) as the "percentage of units that meet specifications in the first process run without need of rework or repair."

You can well imagine that a major goal of process optimization involves maximizing FPY. Traditional organizational process consultants have applied various analytical methods successfully for years, but these methods are based on key figures such as error rates or processing times. Such measures have to be either estimated or manually established in organizational process management, methods that are laborious and error-prone.

Wouldn't it be exciting to integrate the FPY concept into the world of modern BPM (and BPMN)? After all, key figures can be measured with comparative ease, precisely, and in real time by a workflow engine.

To accomplish this integration, first understand how the FPY approach works in traditional sequence notations. Look at the sequence plan process model in figure 4.18 on the next page, which is suitable for FPY analysis, and which we compare to BPMN in section 2.12.3 on page 91).

Notice that there is a main path running from the top left straight down to the result. Anything that needs a change follows the correction path. We can assume that the main path is the path that the process manager desires; it is also referred to as the *happy path*. The probability that a result is not okay and needs correction is 30% in this model. Conversely, 70% of the results do not need correction —that's the FPY. We can analyze key figures recorded

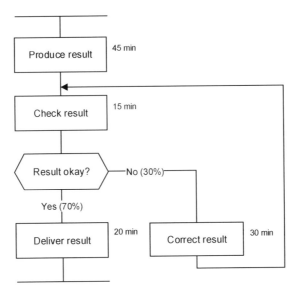

FIGURE 4.18 A process as a sequence plan with a correction branch.

with the tasks, such as processing time, by various analytical methods to assess Key Performance Indicators (KPI). In this simple example, we could state three things about the running time of the process:

Variant	Time
First Pass Yield	80 minutes
Worst Case	110 minutes
Average	89 minutes

The average here results from the calculation: (FPY * 0.7) + (worst case * 0.3) = 56 + 33 = 89 minutes. This is also called *variational calculation*, for which a non-iterative procedure is applied for simplicity. The assumption is that the result must be corrected only once, if at all, per instance.

Could we apply the FPY approach in BPMN? Generally, yes. We showed in section 2.12.4 on page 91 how to store calculated key figures and average running times in process diagrams. Our *job advertisement* case has two possible correction loops:

1. When the vacancy report is not sufficient for Christine's purposes, she has to ask Falko for clarification. We assume in the process model that this is required only once.
2. When Falko does not like the job description, he asks Christine to correct it. According to the process model, this loop could repeat infinitely. We would apply a non-iterative method to assess the key figures.

We modeled the job-advertising process at the operational level from three perspectives, so we should apply the FPY methodology to three different pools for Falko, Christine, and the workflow engine. If we show the process from end to end in the workflow engine, it will be enough to examine its pool to apply the FPY approach.

The collaboration diagram (figure 4.13 on page 129) shows clearly which parts of the process are directly captured by the workflow engine's measurements and which are not. We derive this knowledge from the process modeled in its pool:

1. The workflow engine can measure the running time of these tasks: *write job description*, *check job description*, *correct job description*, and *trigger advertisement*; and of the *advertisement publishing* subprocess.

2. It can also measure the number of times the job description needs to be corrected.

You can analyze these key figures with an appropriate reporting engine. (Or, when in doubt, just use Microsoft Excel for a defined number of process instances, average them, and create colorful diagrams to make your top managers happy.) But we also see which steps the workflow engine cannot measure. It doesn't see the times that Christine has to repeat her request for clarification to Falko. It therefore can't record the rate of occurrence for these necessary correction loops nor can it store that information for analysis. It also does not know how long a clarification takes. From the engine's point of view, all this is part of the *write job description* task, which it assigned to Christine. This may lead to distorted measurements. You need to be aware of distorted measurements, and of the three ways to handle them:

1. Accept the distortion. After all, you know it is limited to the *write job description* task only.

2. Estimate the rate of necessary clarifications and their average time. Enter these estimates by hand into the database. (Of course, now you have adopted the same practice and the same disadvantage as conventional organizational process management.)

3. Represent Christine's inquiries as a human workflow in the workflow engine. Then you can measure and analyze the respective rates and times in a differentiated manner. The risk is that neither Christine nor Falko will be thrilled by this idea, and they may simply bypass the workflow engine and settle their questions with a more efficient phone call.

As you can see, process automation is a powerful instrument for process control, but you should be wary of overusing it. We hope you'll also see that BPMN helps us to recognize these limits in time and to prepare for them.

On the other hand, we have to understand that BPMN in its raw form does not provide sufficient support for process analysis based on key figures. You can only do this with a powerful BPMN tool that takes in the key figures—ideally from the workflow engine—and aggregates them for functional analysis. It can do this usefully because you are a master at producing consistent process models.

Explicit modeling of errors

Unlike other notations, BPMN explicitly models errors with event types (section 2.6.4 on page 51). It is only a question of when to use them. In the last section, we discussed correction loops that apply only in case of errors. You would not want to use error events in those cases, because you want to reserve error events for representing activities that *cannot* complete successfully. If an activity can complete, but the *result* differs from what was expected, that's different. It isn't always clear what every situation calls for, and there can be gray areas. Let's look at a simple example.

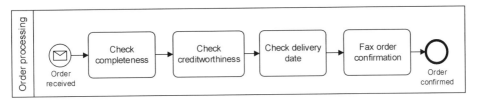

FIGURE 4.19 Happy path order processing.

Figure 4.19 shows the happy path for order processing. There are four steps: For a new order, the order processor checks the order form for completeness, then he or she checks the customer's credit. The date of delivery is checked, and finally, the processor faxes a confirmation.

Now we imagine what can go wrong, what the response is going to be in each case, and how to represent these possibilities in the process model. To think it through, we start at the end and work backwards. The happy path result was that the order was confirmed, so what could lead to the order *not* being confirmed? Yes, theoretically, anything can happen —even an earthquake —but practicality suggests that we deal in events with higher levels of probability. We decide on the following:

1. The order details are incomplete.
2. The order details are illegible.
3. The customer ID is wrong.
4. The customer has insufficient credit.
5. The ordered item is not available.
6. When faxing the order confirmation, someone answers the phone and asks our fax machine if the call is supposed to be a bad joke.

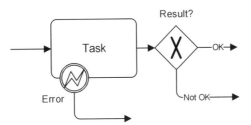

FIGURE 4.20 Representing possible (and probable) problems in the process.

How would we model these contingencies in the process? As shown in abstract in figure 4.20, a task either provides us with a result, that is, information that we can assess as OK or not OK, or there is no result, and the task can't complete at all. If we have the information to assess, we can model an XOR split after the task. If the task can't complete, this is the time for an error event. For each of the possible problems we've defined, we can now construct error-handling solutions. See the fully modeled process in figure 4.21 on the following page.

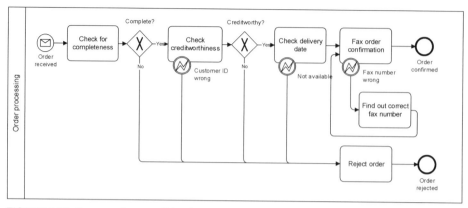

FIGURE 4.21 Representing possible alternatives to the happy path.

- **The order details are incomplete.**

  This is simple: The check for completeness succeeded, but the result is that the order is incomplete, so processing follows the XOR split after the task to *reject order*.

- **The order details are illegible.**

  How can you check for completeness when the order is illegible? This isn't as obvious as when the order details are plainly incomplete, but the result is the same. If we cannot read the details, they don't exist for us. The order is still incomplete. (Though may be helpful to explain to the customer *why* his or her order was rejected.)

- **The customer ID is wrong.**

  Unless we can validate that the customer has the correct customer ID, we can't make much more progress on the order. This is a clear case for an attached error event.

- **The customer has insufficient credit.**

  If our process successfully checks credit, but the result is unfavorable, the result prevents the order confirmation. The XOR split after the task sends the order to *reject order*.

- **The ordered item is not available.**

  This is not so easy, which is why you need to be pedantic. If the item is not available, no delivery date can be established, so no check of the delivery date can succeed if the item is not available. We have to attach an error event.

- **When faxing the order confirmation, someone answers the phone and asks our fax machine if the call is supposed to be a bad joke.**

  You can probably guess how to represent this.

You may be asking yourself why it's necessary to differentiate between error events and XOR gateways at all. Why not just show all error cases by means of XOR gateways as other process notations do? BPMN cannot keep you from doing that, but we recommend the differentiation because:

- Most people who design processes in the target state consider only some of the possible problems. They model these in check tasks and downstream XOR gateways. But when it comes time to implement the process, the IT people come back with questions no one has taken into account, very often concerning situations that keep the check tasks from completing successfully. As part of the required ping-pong between business and IT, we document these questions with attached error events, and then we answer them specifically. Frequently, when obtaining the answer to such a question, new check tasks develop upstream, along with additional XOR gateways. If you placed a *check availability* task before the *check delivery date* task, for example, you could make the error event at *check delivery date* obsolete.

- Can you ensure processes with error events in case *anything* goes wrong? Yes. You can define this kind of extra safety net with an attached error event for a section within a process, or for an entire process.
- In general, XOR gateways differentiate between cases. They can differentiate between error conditions, and they can differentiate also between or among positive outcomes. An example would be the different steps to determine correct size depending on if the customer has ordered trousers versus a hat. So a happy path may not exist without XOR gateways, but positive XOR gateways cannot be differentiated visually or syntactically from the error XOR gateways. Error events are visually less ambiguous. Provided you have the appropriate tooling, you can even use them to switch between a simplified, happy path view and the complete view of the process.

The bottom line: Error events can be a good aid when modeling processes, and you should make use of them.

4.5.2 The true benefit of subprocesses

By now, you know the several levels of our BPMN framework, and how the levels use models with different amounts of detail. At the operational level, we also work with different views of the same process to show only the aspect of the model that is most useful to the people affected.

Have you wondered what role the BPMN symbol for subprocess plays in this framework? We show in section 2.8 on page 66 that subprocesses have three main purposes in BPMN:

- To hide the complexity of detailed sequences. Collapsed subprocesses make diagrams more clear.
- To make sequences modular, and thus reusable.
- To define a scope within a process and then define how the process reacts to catching events for the scope by attaching the events.

You can benefit from all these advantages for both strategic and operational process models. For instance, in the process model for *Job advertisement*, we defined the *publish advertisement* subprocess in the technical flow, that is, in the workflow engine's pool. This avoided overloading the diagram with interface calls (figure 4.13 on page 129). Another option would be to define error processing for the entire subprocess by attaching an error event. Because we likely won't need this subprocess later, we should not define it as global in our BPMN tool. Because the subprocess is embedded, and no longer an independent module, it can be collapsed for clarity.

In BPMN, subprocesses are seldom used to indicate organizational refinements of a process. This is why we often mix tasks and subprocesses in the same diagram. Some process modelers who've trained in other methods may see this mix as an improper or unattractive mixing of granular levels. They may prefer to reserve subprocesses for refining content, or they want to organize their process models by making all subprocesses equally complex. As far as BPMN is concerned, we say forget that! These other views of subprocesses make sense, if at all, only at the level of process landscapes, and that is removed from the examination of individual processes. In your process maps, you can make wonderful process groups or clusters. You can even organize them hierarchically —but don't do that when dealing with an individual end-to-end process.

To be effective with BPMN, it is important to understand that subprocesses are a purely technical construct. They cannot be assigned any content-related degree of complexity. You can define a *sales* subprocess as easily as one called *tie shoelaces*. Collapse both subprocess within the same diagram —it's all good.

While it is highly probable that more subprocesses are defined at the strategic level than at the operational level in our framework, this isn't obligatory. You can apply both these levels of our framework to finely granular processes of any type. The framework merely facilitates transition from a general, result-oriented process representation (organizational implementation) to the actual technical implementation. Just like tasks, subprocesses can help at every level.

4.5.3 The limits of formalization

BPMN is based on the assumption that we can define the course of a process as an unambiguous control flow. The more precisely we model the desired process in BPMN, the more narrowly we define the range of people's action within the process. A total application of this paradigm would be, to put it bluntly, to turn any process into the equivalent of an industrial assembly line in which the work of people is planned down to the most minute detail and which leaves no room for them to maneuver. This approach is not always popular. Various Internet forums discuss this topic in ideological terms, with people opposing the paradigm on humanist grounds, standing up against the increased technocratization of society.

We will not engage with that discussion in this book, but we will make one pragmatic point: In many of the BPM projects in which we have been involved, we have had to leave white spots in the process models. White spots are what we call sections in a process or subprocesses that cannot be clarified unambiguously. There is a negative and a positive aspect to this:

- On the negative side, there is often uncertainty about exactly how the subprocess is or should be carried out. The knowledge is just not (yet) available for various reasons. This is something we are seeking to change.
- On the positive side, the subprocess may be carried out perfectly well, but the knowledge related to it resides in the heads of the people carrying out the subprocess —and is therefore of an implicit nature —which we can accept.

In the first, negative, case of a white spot, we are left with the need to document an undesired intermediate state when modeling the process. In the second, positive, instance, it is our place to document the desired final state. In either case, you have already seen a BPMN design in section 2.8.4 on page 72 that can help us; the ad hoc subprocess as shown in figure 4.22 on the facing page.

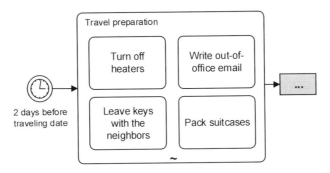

FIGURE 4.22 Preparing a trip can consist of these task, although it does not have to.

Ad hoc subprocesses are a sort of carte blanche for the process analyst. They capture the tasks that can be carried out in a non-binding fashion while they are being worked through. How often this occurs, in what order, and whether they are executed at all is completely up to the participant. An ad hoc subprocess also lets you draw a boundary around an area that remains unclear while you continue to specify the remaining process around it. The ad hoc subprocess is a tool we have often been grateful to have during our BPM projects.

Ad hoc subprocesses, however, can only rarely be executed in an engine. You have to take into account that they were designed several years ago to represent activities that fall more properly into the category of case management. The possibilities for modeling ad hoc processes are rudimentary, which was one of the reasons that the CMMN standard (which we address in section 5 on page 145) was developed.

That is why our recommendation (revised from previous editions of this book) is to evaluate if situations that formerly required an ad hoc subprocess may be addressed better by generating a CMMN model and then by using a call activity to reference it in your BPMN process model as shown in section 5.3 on page 165.

4.5.4 Taking business decisions out of processes

In section 4.5.1 on page 136, we looked at the *receiving order* process, and discussed what mistakes could occur while working through it. We ask a further question now: Under what circumstances should a customer's creditworthiness be examined? If we assume that this question depends on certain facts about the customer and on the total order value, then we define the first step in the process as being *check order data*. After that, we can decide if a credit check is necessary. (See figure 4.23.)

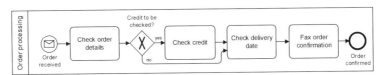

FIGURE 4.23 Receiving an order and examining the customer's credit under certain circumstances.

Now we have to deal with the specific conditions in which we carry out a customer credit check. Let us assume the following:

- Credit has to be checked if the order value exceeds 300,000 EUR.
- If the customer is new to our company, credit must be checked if the order value exceeds 50,000 EUR.
- If the customer is categorized as a *Class A* customer, there is no need for a credit check.

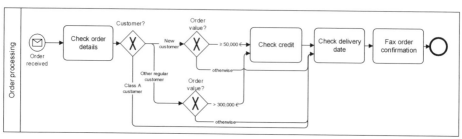

FIGURE 4.24 Conditions which lead to checking a customer's credit.

Of course we can model these conditions completely in the process diagram. We have done so in figure 4.24. What do you think of this diagram? Can you imagine adding further conditions that only apply to certain customers? Sure, but perhaps you're also thinking of the problems those extra conditions imply:

- Every additional condition further inflates the diagram with more gateways and additional sequence flows.
- This inflation problem becomes even more pronounced if the additional conditions are interlinked (for example, both more customer types *and* more levels of order value).
- The process diagram quickly becomes excessively confusing.
- If conditions change—new ones are added or old ones are removed—the diagram has to be adapted accordingly. That will be a time-consuming mess while rearranging symbols and sequence flows.
- If the customer's credit also has to be checked as part of other processes (within a non-binding request, for example), the conditions will have to be modeled redundantly—and then maintained.

This way of dealing with complex decisions is absolutely not best practice; rather, it is a classic mistake in process modeling. To avoid it, we need to understand such conditions as *business decisions* and to separate them from the *routing decisions* implemented by gateways.

Dealing with business decisions is a discipline in its own right. As the name implies, it's about making (often complex) decisions. The conditions on which the decisions are based determine which tasks we carry out and which tasks we omit. Being able to manage conditions centrally, simply, and flexibly is absolutely vital to the success of process management. For process modeling, we therefore have to find a way to separate business decisions from routing decisions.

To do this, we should first select a suitable medium for modeling decisions. This is where (you guessed it) the DMN standard comes in. We detail DMN in section 6 on page 167, so we'll only discuss one element here: the decision table.

4.5 Hands-on tips for the operational level

A decision table for the question of whether the customer's credit should be checked could look like the one in figure 4.25.

Conditions		Decision
Customer type	Order value	Check credit?
Class A customer	Irrelevant	NO
Other regular customer	> $ 300,000	YES
	≤ $ 300,000	NO
New customer	≥ $ 50,000	YES
	< $ 50,000	NO

FIGURE 4.25 Decision table for the question of checking credit.

How can we now link the decision table with the process model? To do so, we can use the business rule task as shown in figure 4.26:

* We introduce a business rule task *Apply set of rules* in front of the XOR gateway. We do so only so we can apply the modeled decision table.
* The result of the business rule task is the decision to check or not to check credit.
* The XOR gateway refers only to this decision, and it leads to the corresponding process flow.
* The link to the decision table is carried out directly in the task and at the attribute level.

Tooling

The link displayed between the business rule task and the decision table is not part of the standard notation. It is something that has to be supported by your BPMN tool. At the time the BPMN standard was created, no DMN standard yet existed, so OMG deliberately left open the question of the link. It is becoming apparent, however, that software vendors offering combined solutions for BPMN and DMN see the business rule task as the preferred way of referencing DMN models from BPMN models.

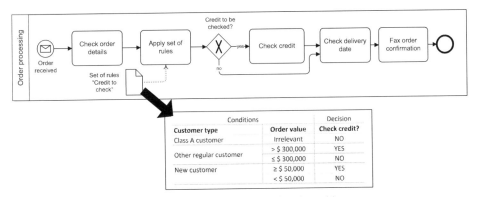

FIGURE 4.26 Receiving an order with reference to the decision table.

Let's take a moment to contemplate the difference between the two decision types:

- **Routing decisions** are carried out by XOR gateways, OR gateways, or conditional sequence flows. They are simple in principle and represent exactly as many possible conditions as there are outgoing flows. The process model therefore stores routing conditions directly.
- **Business decisions** can be extremely complex, and they are routinely managed outside of the process model. A modeled decision, however, can serve to determine relevant conditions for routing. For example, the business decision to check credit is based on the type of customer and the order amount. It has to check a total of five combinations of conditions. It can only generate two possible results: *Yes* or *No*. These are precisely the two possibilities to which the corresponding routing decision in the XOR gateway of the process model refers.

Theoretically, the condition event can be linked to business decisions. Unfortunately, the BPMN specification has little to say about this. From a technical point of view, it can be interpreted as a decision engine constantly checking if a condition stored with the event is taking place. Then, if it takes place, the decision engine reports it to the workflow engine, and the workflow engine evaluates the event as having occurred. The workflow engine either launches or continues the process accordingly (see figure 4.27).

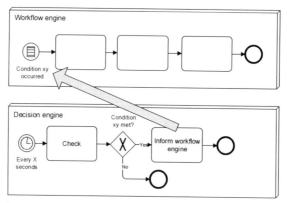

FIGURE 4.27 Condition event and decision engine.

For business-IT alignment, it is important that you understand the basic principle behind this structure because it is in no way limited to technical implementations! We have the same problem when we think of the purely organizational implementation of the process. In our company, we have to abide by certain rules —legal requirements or safety regulations, for instance. Someone has to be alert to situations to which the rules may apply. If they occur, something has to be done —a process has to be launched. Conversely, the process may be launched or continued only once a pre-defined condition has occurred.

From our point of view, the systematic management of decisions, the so-called Business Decision Management (BDM), is an elementary building block of Business Process Management (BPM). In BPM, we ask ourselves the most fundamental questions, such as "What does our company need to do to succeed?" The answer may be many different things, but surely one of those things is to make the best possible decisions as effectively as possible.

5 CMMN - Introduction and overview

5.1 Understanding CMMN

BPMN has been spreading rapidly, and we have taken on an incredible number of processes, many of which have been automated as workflows. There is always the exciting moment when it finally becomes clear to everybody that the order of tasks must be followed strictly. That is an outcome that isn't obvious at first to people who are new to BPMN. Even so, there remains a class of problems that don't submit to strict sequencing because there is a human being in the process who has to decide something according to conditions, and he or she wants to maintain all possible freedom to do so. For this situation, BPMN offers the following approaches:

- Ad hoc subprocess: All tasks contained in an ad hoc subprocess can be carried out optionally and in any given order. Parallelization is also possible here.
- Non-interrupting attached event: If we wish to show that a person can start additional activities during the processing of a certain task, non-interrupting attached events as shown in figure 5.1 can provide good service.
- Event-based subprocess: If the activities are possible throughout a process phase, you can use the event subprocess.

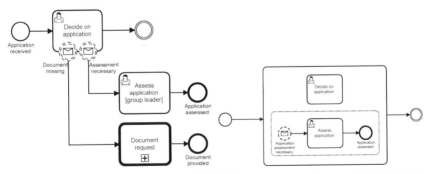

FIGURE 5.1 Launching additional tasks with BPMN during a user task is possible, but it can quickly become confusing.

These approaches in BPMN are not necessarily easy to understand. They also quickly reach their limits when, for instance, knowledge workers seem to have lots of freedom during case processing but those freedoms are constrained by rules.

This is why Case Management Model and Notation (CMMN) was created. OMG published version 1.1 of this sister standard to BPMN in 2016.

CMMN has a basic paradigm different from that of BPMN. CMMN has no sequenced process flow; it instead models a case in a certain state. Depending on the state, some things are possible for processing the case and some things are not, as the case may be. Control is exercised predominantly by people. CMMN is *declarative*, and the model states *what* is to be applied but not *how* to implement it. In contrast, BPMN states *imperatively* exactly how certain steps in a process have to be worked on. Declarative modeling is more complex and less intuitive for most people. As a consequence, CMMN models are more difficult to understand. You can't simply trace a path with your finger!

CMMN models possible activities and the limits on activities. It models when the activities *may* take place, when they *must* take place, and when they *must not* take place. CMMN likewise limits the scope of actions available to people in the process. Case models must be thoroughly considered beforehand. It is important to bring this up to counter the frequent misconception that people can do whatever they want when it comes to case management. That's just not true.

The readability of CMMN notation for business and end users is currently much debated. You should form your own opinion on that, but we are aware of no better notation. Also, let us not forget that CMMN is like BPMN in that it defines exactly how an engine is supposed to act.

We provide an introduction to CMMN in this book only so that you can judge its relevance to your endeavors. Because we're still learning a lot of lessons, and we're collecting lots of examples from experience, it is worth keeping an eye on our blog at http://bpm-guide.de/.

5.1.1 CMMN or BPMN?

CMMN and BPMN both describe activities in a business process. The main differences between the standards are:

- BPMN takes a binding approach. It provides exact sequences for activities. It is harder to provide degrees of freedom.
- CMMN takes a non-binding approach and then adds limitations. It is harder to establish sequencing.

In other words, you can in principle express most problems in either notation. Depending on the type of problem, however, modeling will work better in BPMN or CMMN, and one of these standards is likelier to produce a tidy and effective model.

Strong indicators for using CMMN include:

- No sequence required: If sequence matters little, and tasks can be carried out in any order, this will produce too many connections —spaghetti modeling— in BPMN. Maybe using an ad hoc subprocess *may* avoid the mess.

5.1 Understanding CMMN

- Activities depend on conditions: Defining conditions is CMMN's great strength. Many tasks may be defined, but they can only come into play in certain situations. The situation, for instance, may be that an order exceeds a certain volume or the client has VIP status; other completed tasks can also affect conditions. This combining of the *optional* and *data dependent* factors cannot be reflected in BPMN.
- Dedicated planning phase: Because of its ability to handle discretionary tasks, CMMN can accommodate a planning phase during which one worker plans a case and the tasks to be enabled. Other workers will have to stick to the plan. BPMN can do nothing like this.

If you feel you are reaching the limits of BPMN, it might be worth looking into CMMN. Many projects we know of operate according to the following principle: "We will use BPMN as much possible because we know and understand it. As soon as we notice a situation that can only be expressed poorly or not at all with BPMN, however, we'll pull CMMN out of the tool box and use it instead."

In section 1.2.4 on page 10 we mentioned that unstructured business processes (in CMMN) are more difficult to scale than are structured processes (in BPMN). You should always ask yourself therefore if a request for flexibility is actually an attempt to evade some issue. Perhaps the organization can't agree on a structured process. You can apply CMMN, but are you sacrificing potential improvement or efficiency in the longer term? Perhaps you can use CMMN as a first step toward more structure that can be modeled in BPMN. At least then you can record activities and introduce a BPM environment. Later, perhaps you can demonstrate from an engine's log data that an order exists after all, and you can gently prod the reluctant toward BPMN.

You see, even though we are happy to add CMMN to our tool kit, we still remain huge fans of BPMN. In our projects, our motto is: *As much BPMN as possible and as much CMMN as necessary.*

5.1.2 Introduction example

Let's use the insurance example from the introduction. That's the one involving your application for car insurance and the knowledge worker who has to decide about approving it. (To review the entire example see section 1.2.4 on page 10.)

In CMMN, this could look like figure 5.2 on the next page. Notice:

- The *case*, symbolized by a file folder.
- Several *tasks*. Things are taking place here just as in BPMN.
- A *stage*, which provides additional structuring within the case.
- The achievable *milestones*, represented by the obround shapes, for intermediate and end results.
- Several *sentries* represented as diamonds. These decide which milestones are reached, but they also control when an additional approval step is needed.

Before we go any further into this example we have to lay out a few basics and explain the life cycle in CMMN.

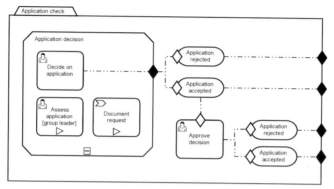

FIGURE 5.2 Case example in CMMN: *Assessing a new application.*

5.1.3 Life cycle in CMMN

Unlike BPMN, CMMN has no token concept. Instead, all elements follow a life cycle. Understanding this is critical to the correct use of CMMN.

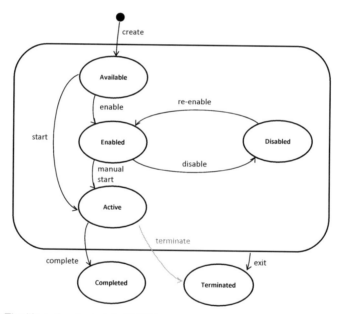

FIGURE 5.3 The life cycle of a task in CMMN.

In figure 5.3, we show an example of a task life cycle. It is simplified, as cases also can be paused. When a new case is generated, the following generally happens:

1. All tasks or stages directly contained in the case are *created*, and this means that they are *available*. Tasks in stages not yet started are not created and thus not available.
2. All available tasks are checked to see if their pre-conditions have been met. Pre-conditions are expressed by small diamonds which represent sentries. If a condition is met, then the task becomes either *enabled* or directly *active*.

3. This enabling or activation is defined through an *activation rule*. *Active* tasks end up on a task list; *enabled* tasks require the case manager to state that he or she wishes to do a *manual start*.

4. A task can be *completed* (or *terminated* if you exit the case processing prematurely).

In figure 5.2 on the preceding page, the *application decision* stage and the *decide on application* task are automatically *started*. Those tasks without sentries but which have a manual activation rule —note the *play* symbols— become *enabled*. The states that individual elements are in after the case has been generated are represented in figure 5.4.

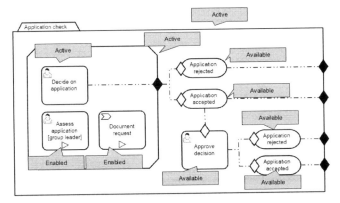

FIGURE 5.4 State of the individual elements after creating a new case.

As soon as the *decide on application* task completes, the state changes as shown in figure 5.5. This is because the *application decision* stage terminates because of the exit criterion. We will explain how this works exactly in the following sections.

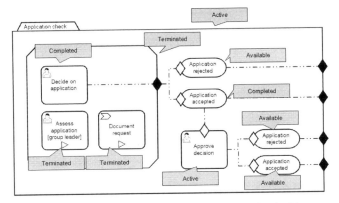

FIGURE 5.5 State of the individual elements upon completion of the *decide on application* task.

5.1.4 User interfaces of case management systems

CMMN models and their life cycles can be difficult to understand. In our experience, it helps to think about CMMN as software for controlling case processing. In actual projects, we create clickable prototypes as early as we can to run through the CMMN models and to validate certain scenarios.

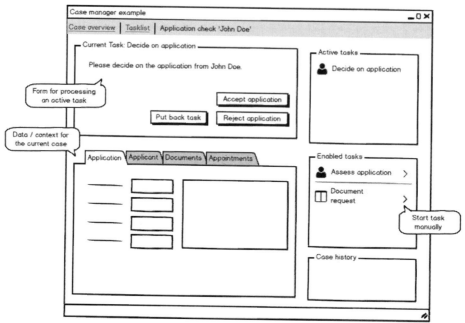

FIGURE 5.6 A possible interface for case management.

Figure 5.6 shows a sketch of a user interface for our imagined software. We have seen similar interfaces in real-life projects. The screen is divided into these primary elements:

- Task area: If the user is working through a user task, he or she may need a form, for example, to document the decision on a prospective customer's application and the reasons for that decision.
- Context: To make a reasonable decision, the user requires access to as much information as possible on the customer, the customer's rating and history, information about the car, regional statistics, documents, and so on.
- Case status: The user can see what has already taken place in the current case and perhaps also what may happen in future. Above all, the user needs the ability to launch enabled tasks.

If you use an engine that works with CMMN, then most of this information can be loaded from the engine and displayed in the interface. In doing so, the CMMN life cycle plays a central role. Figure 5.7 on the next page shows the display of tasks in a certain state. The technical possibilities, of course, depend on the needs and possibilities of actual users in actual situations.

Figure 1.7 on page 13 also shows an example of a simple implementation on the Camunda BPM platform. This version is available for free on the internet as a working example.

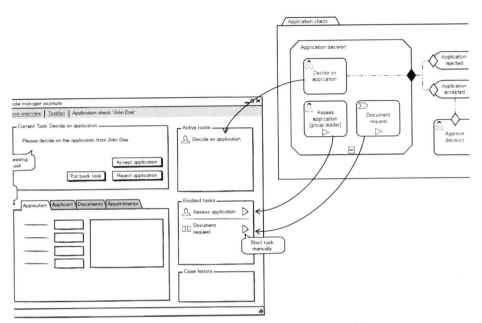

FIGURE 5.7 The interface shows tasks according to their life cycle condition.

■ 5.2 Notation elements

Following this brief introduction, we'll detail the elements of CMMN's notation. We will focus on the symbols we think are the most relevant. The goal is for you to get an overview and to be able to assess how powerful they are.

In other CMMN literature, you may come across the terms *plan model* and *plan item*. While these elements are surely important to the CMMN metamodel, they do not play a role for you as a modeler. At this point, we will spare you such details.

5.2.1 Cases and tasks

A CMMN case is depicted as a folder. The folder contains the entire case, just as paper file folders used to contain cases. Unlike BPMN, in which there is no absolute need to surround a process in a pool, CMMN must have the folder.

Figure 5.8 on the next page shows a support request modeled as a case with four tasks. Within the tasks, something has to be done to process the case.

The tasks in CMMN have no order, thus there are no sequence flows as in BPMN. Instead, tasks can be configured as shown in the introductory example to indicate when they are possible and how they are activated. We will come back to this.

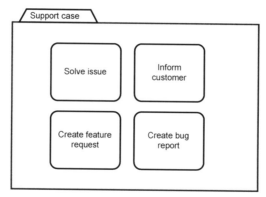

FIGURE 5.8 A case model with simple tasks.

 Our modeling etiquette

When naming tasks, we adhere to the object-oriented design principle of using the [verb] + [object] pattern. We say *create feature request*, for example, not *deal with creating a feature request*.

5.2.2 Types of tasks

The task types shown in figure 5.9 can be used. As with BPMN, you can dispense with these particular types and model tasks with undefined types. Assigning a type to each task, however, becomes absolutely necessary to automate the model. We also recommend assigning types because they contribute to understanding.

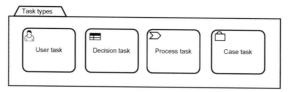

FIGURE 5.9 Types of tasks in CMMN.

Human task: A human task is carried out by a person. It may be assigned by an engine, which may place the task on the user's task list, for instance. Once the person completes the task, the engine expects confirmation —at the least —and usually certain data or a button click in a dialog box. It is therefore the exact equivalent to the user task in BPMN, and it uses the same symbol.

Typical examples are:
- Checking an invoice
- Approving a request for vacation
- Processing a support request

Decision tasks:

A decision task includes a decision. This is usually defined in DMN.

Process task: In a process task, an engine calls a business process; it's comparable to call activity in BPMN. This is how we can integrate structured workflows with CMMN. In practice, it is common to alternate between BPMN processes and CMMN cases because business processes often have phases that have a clear order and can be well represented with BPMN, and they have phases that require greater flexibility and work well with CMMN. Workflows are typically defined in BPMN.

In CMMN, whether the case should wait for the process to conclude can be defined by means of hidden attributes. This is not visible in the graphic model.

Case tasks:

A case task includes a further case. This makes it possible to encapsulate complexity in a subcase and still maintain an overview. Cases can be re-used in different contexts.

At this point, you should note that the subcase has to be defined in a separate model. Here again, hidden attributes can define if the case should wait for the conclusion of the subcase.

5.2.3 Sentries

A sentry decides if a given task can be carried out. This may depend on the following factors:

- Completion of previous tasks: A sentry can prevent one task from beginning until a different task has been carried out. In modeling, we express this with an interrupted line. In figure 5.10, the customer may be informed only after the issue has been solved. CMMN refers to this as an *on part*.
- Data: Sentries can also check conditions for content. For instance, creating feature requests could be reserved for Gold customers only. Data such as the customer's status needs to be known within the case. CMMN refers to this as an *if part*.

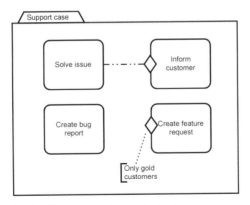

FIGURE 5.10 A sentry decides if a task can be carried out.

Figure 5.11 on the following page shows multiple sentries on one task. This means that only one sentry has to apply before the task can begin, and this is therefore an *or-link* between

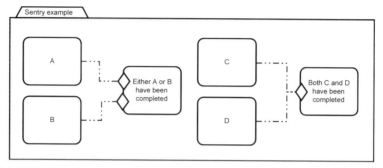

FIGURE 5.11 Several sentries are or-linked, one sentry with multiple triggers is and-linked.

the sentries. To express the need for multiple tasks all to complete first, use a sentry with several triggers (interrupted lines). This is an *and-link*.

Sentries can guard stages as well as tasks. This will be shown later.

5.2.4 Manual activation rule

The *manual activation rule* defines if a task is automatically launched or if a person has to launch it. To understand this better, look again at the life cycle in figure 5.3 on page 148. Normally, each task should switch to active status automatically unless a sentry prevents it, but if manual activation is configured, then the task merely switches to *enabled*, and then it waits for a manual start. As was shown in figure 5.6 on page 150, the manual start typically occurs when triggered through a graphical user interface. Imagine a task list in a workflow management application —the task only appears on the list once it is active.

To summarize, there is a distinction between tasks that result from a person's decisions during case processing and those tasks decided by the engine.

The manual activation rule is represented by a small play symbol as shown in figure 5.12. If the play symbol is present, then it needs to be manually activated. It's familiar and thus easy to remember: The user just has to press play.

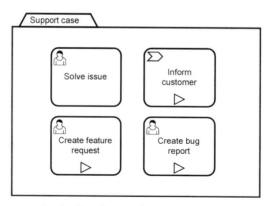

FIGURE 5.12 During manual activation, the user has to press play.

In the case shown in figure 5.12 on the facing page, solving an issue is automatically launched, and it goes onto the task list of a support employee. Because they need to be launched manually, the other tasks do not yet appear in a task list, nor will they appear there until the support employee launches them through the interface —and then only if he or she considers those tasks necessary.

Unfortunately, there was an error while drafting the specification, and the standard case (meaning the task without the play symbol) was wrongly defined as manually activated. That's inverse to the way we've been describing it. The error is both counter-intuitive and counter to the specification intention, and it will be corrected in the future. Meanwhile, if you encounter models in which the meaning of the missing play symbol is the opposite of what was intended, don't be misled. Even we published such examples before we and other leading CMMN manufacturers agreed to follow the approach we describe in this book.

5.2.5 Repetition rule

Every task in a CMMN model can be carried out only once. Should you wish to change this, you can add a *repetition rule*. This is represented by a hashtag (#). In the model in figure 5.13, several bug reports and feature requests now can be set up.

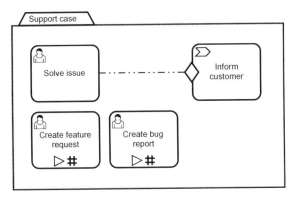

FIGURE 5.13 To make a task repeatable, mark it with a #.

5.2.6 Required rule

Tasks in CMMN are not necessarily required. This means that a case manager can complete a case while tasks are still active. Imagine the support employee clicking *support case completed* on the user interface. In CMMN, exactly when this takes place is up to the employee.

If you want to prevent a case from being closed before certain tasks have been completed, you'll need the *required rule*. In the model, required tasks are marked with an exclamation mark (!). These tasks must be completed if they are created according to the life cycle.

In figure 5.14, the case cannot be completed if no solution has yet been found and the client has not yet been informed. On the other hand, closing the case is possible even if no bug reports have been set up. That task simply would be interrupted.

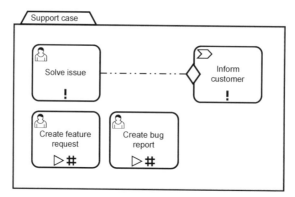

FIGURE 5.14 The case cannot be closed unless the necessary tasks complete.

5.2.7 Auto complete

We already pointed out that a person is always in a position to complete a case as long as no required tasks remain active. Completion, however, can occur automatically. To mark a case as *auto complete*, use a stop symbol as shown in figure 5.15. If all necessary tasks have been carried out and no other tasks are active, the case will complete without further ado.

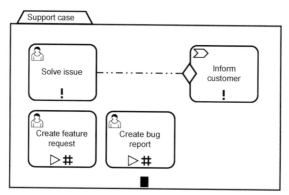

FIGURE 5.15 Once all active tasks have been carried out, a case marked with a stop symbol will complete automatically.

In this example, closing the case requires no further human interaction after the the customer has been informed. If, however, a *create feature request* task is still active, the case will wait —and this could be interrupted if the employee chooses to close the case manually. After all, *create feature request* still is not a required task.

The different possibilities for intervening in the life cycle of a case make the notation powerful but also tricky. When using auto complete, for instance, you should make sure that your case model contains either required or automatically activated tasks. Otherwise, the preconditions for auto complete are immediately met and the case closes immediately. Should you feed the case in figure 5.16 to a CMMN engine, you will never receive an active case!

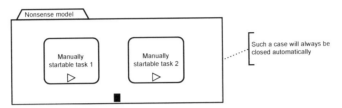

FIGURE 5.16 Careful: This case always completes automatically because it has no automatically activated tasks.

 Hint: Business-IT-alignment

We realize that the description of the manual activation and auto complete may sound excessively technical and implementation related. If it seems too complex for your current modeling project, you may wish to forego these markers during the first stage. If you do use them, use them as intended. We have seen plenty of models in which the play symbol was used incorrectly simply because it looked nice. Please don't do that. ∎

5.2.8 Milestones

As you may expect, a milestone symbol represents something to be achieved. It could be a result, an intermediate result, or some other important outcome.

Milestones must always have at least one sentry because without sentries, results would be immediate. Usually, milestones depend on certain tasks completing; you can see this in figure 5.17. If milestones are reached, then that information can be used by other sentries.

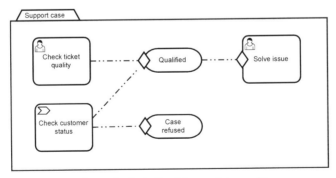

FIGURE 5.17 Milestones mark results, including intermediate results.

5.2.9 Stages

So far, we have situated all tasks within the case without additional containment. Case management, however, is often divided into different stages or phases, and different tasks are possible in each stage or phase. In CMMN this can be depicted by *stages* as shown in figure 5.18.

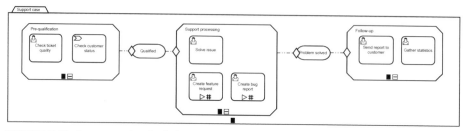

FIGURE 5.18 A case can be divided into several stages.

A stage acts much as a task does; you can use the same life cycle and the same markers. This means that a stage can have a sentry, it can be activated manually or automatically, it can be completed manually or automatically, and it can be be marked as required or repeating.

Tasks within a stage are created only once the stage has been started. In figure 5.19, the stage *further check* only starts under certain conditions. An interesting detail here is the necessary task to *raise at the board meeting*, though that only becomes required if the stage actually starts.

Stages do not have to follow a chronological order. A stage can be nested within another stage. This is why the specification chose the term *stage* over the word *phase*.

 Hint: Business-IT-alignment

In CMMN, stages do not have to be carried out in order, nor is it a problem to be located in several stages at once. That is why we avoid the term *phase*. Should you have several phases in a clear order, then it may be worth modeling the order in BPMN, pulling out individual cases selectively.

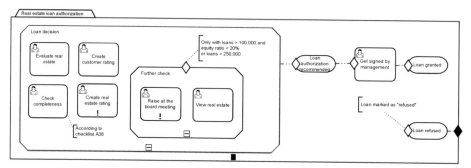

FIGURE 5.19 Stages can be nested within one another.

5.2.10 Exit criterion

We represent an *exit criterion* with a black diamond. As with sentries, an exit criterion can depend on the completion of tasks or stages, or the reaching of milestones. This is shown in figure 5.19 on the facing page.

As soon as an exit criterion applies, then the stage or case to which it is attached terminates. Unlike normal completion, required tasks do not have to conclude. This condition therefore terminates the case, although it can have other business meanings. In the model in figure 5.20, management can end the *loan decision* stage through independent authorization at any time. If they do so, the case reaches a separate milestone, which in turn leads to the termination of the case. Management's authorization takes place at a data level, which we'll take a closer look at shortly.

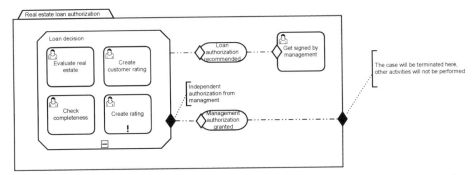

FIGURE 5.20 The exit criterion means that the case can be closed even if some tasks are still active.

Figure 5.21 re-examines support processing, but now with the addition of an exit criterion. What difference does it make? Now the whole case closes once the *solve issue* task completes, and any open *create feature request* tasks are abandoned. Without the exit criterion, we would have to wait for the open task(s) to finish.

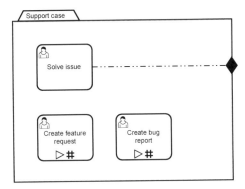

FIGURE 5.21 By completing the *solve issue* task, the case terminates regardless of other open tasks.

5.2.11 Modeling without do-it tasks

At this point, it is worth asking a fundamental question that arises when working with CMMN: Shall I or shall I not use a *do-it task*? That's our nickname for a task that is essential to a stage.

In figure 5.22, we show the *support processing* stage again, as well as its do-it task —in this case, the *solve issue* task, which is key to the stage. There are advantages to this way of modeling:

- We can save additional configuration with the task, for instance, to specify who carries out the task and what user interface will be needed.
- We can use an existing task list (maybe introduced with BPMN) to trigger a person.

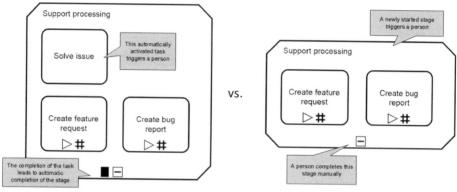

FIGURE 5.22 Modeling with or without the do-it task.

But now consider the alternative: Having an employee carry out the stage or even the whole case. Employees can end stages once they have terminated the support processing. They don't require a task, and instead they just need to view *unread* or *open* cases or stages. Also, cases and stages have to be assigned to an employee or group just as do-it tasks. This variant offers some advantages:

- You can omit the do-it task during modeling and the model becomes more compact.
- Thinking in terms of an employee being responsible for a case as well as for a list of *open cases* is intuitive for people with little experience with workflow management and task lists.

You have to choose the path you want to take when modeling, but if your CMMN model is destined for use in an engine, then you need to know the engine's features. In our projects, for instance, we use a joint task list fed from BPMN and CMMN, and we usually rely on a do-it task. That's the approach we lean toward in this book.

5.2.12 Events

Events can be modeled in CMMN to react to certain occurrences. Typically, these events link to sentries that subsequently activate tasks or stages. A more elegant way to express the management authorization from our previous loan example is in figure 5.23 on the facing page.

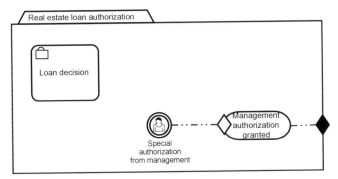

FIGURE 5.23 User and time events can be modeled this way.

Two types of events are possible:
- User event: A person triggers an event —by clicking a button on a graphical user interface, perhaps.
- Timer event: This event takes place at a defined time. Either a date or a duration can be defined. Figure 5.24 shows some examples.

Of course events can be used in stages, and they only become available when the stage becomes active.

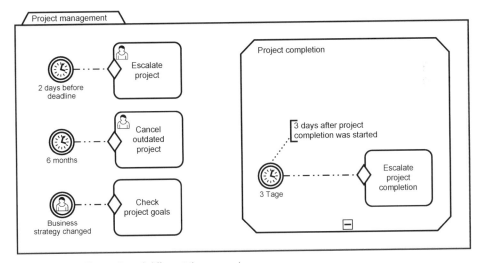

FIGURE 5.24 Examples of different timer events.

5.2.13 Case file items

A person needs information to manage a case well. In CMMN this can be modeled precisely with *case file items*. As with data objects in BPMN, case file items represent all possible information independent of its physical state (paper documents, abstracts, or electronic data sets).

Figure 5.25 shows an example, and in it, we can see that sentries or exit criteria can relate to the content of a case file item. Imagine further that case file items change during processing, and that new information influences the behavior of the case. The entire case will terminate if ticket status switches to *completed*. Only Class A customers are allowed feature requests, but should customer status change during case processing, this will be dealt with correctly.

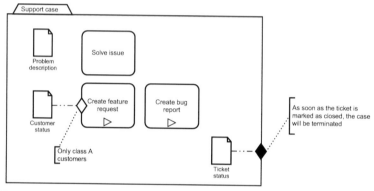

FIGURE 5.25 Data can be modeled with case file items.

5.2.14 Conditions

In CMMN, by the way, all the following rules as well as sentries can relate to data in case file items:

- Manual activation rule: Data can determine if a task activates manually or automatically. For instance, a loan valued more than a specified amount can trigger a review by two different workers.
- Required rule: Data can determine if a task is required. The review by two different workers could be required for loans over a specified amount.
- Repetition rule: Data can determine if a task can (continue to) repeat. For instance, you may phone a customer until she withdraws her consent to be contacted that way.

 Hint: Business-IT-alignment

The representation in the model does not distinguish between a simple rule evaluation of *true* or *not true*, for instance, or something far more complex. We recommend that as soon as conditions become hidden behind rules, you create some transparency by means of text annotations. Without the annotations, the model may become difficult to understand.

5.2.15 Non-blocking tasks

User tasks, process tasks, and case tasks are usually blocking tasks. This means that case processing has to wait until the task, process, or case has been carried out. You can mark tasks as non-blocking, however, so that the case will launch the task but not wait for its completion.

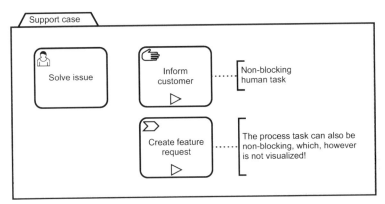

FIGURE 5.26 Only user tasks have a symbol to show that they are non-blocking.

- Non-blocking user task: The task is created and, where relevant, displayed in the task list. The CMMN case, however, won't wait for the task to be carried out; it won't even check for task completion or interruption. As an example, think of the task of notifying people and how there may be no real need to keep the case from closing based on that task alone. Non-blocking user tasks have their own symbol in CMMN; see figure 5.26.
- Non-blocking process task: The process, in BPMN, let's say, launches and then is left to its own devices. The case does not care how or when it is processed after that. The case can only see that the process task completed and that a process instance started.
- Non-blocking case task: This is much like the process task.

5.2.16 Discretionary tasks

Recognize discretionary tasks by their dotted frames, as you can see in figure 5.27 on the following page. You can add them during the runtime of a case. But wait, haven't those tasks been modeled previously? They have, but imagine taking your car to be inspected, for example. You probably recognize this kind of conversation about the work that *may* need to be done: "We may have to replace the brake fluid, which will cost more. Should we go ahead with it, if it needs doing?" The *car inspection* case is being planned at this point, and the employee writing-up the order is adding discretionary tasks to the case. The mechanics in the repair shop then have the task available. Whether they actually replace the brake fluid is something they will decide autonomously while carrying out the work. Suppose that you are not eager to spend money on brake fluid right now, however, and you specify that the shop supervisor should call you before proceeding. That call, if it comes, and the supervisor convinces you of the need for new brake fluid, will modify the planning and then add this task to the case.

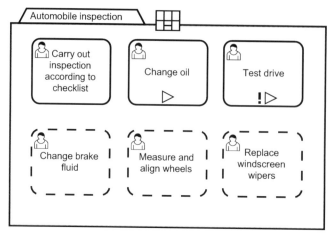

FIGURE 5.27 Discretionary tasks are added to a case during the planning phase.

Discretionary tasks are available to the case only once they have been included in the planning. Only then are they generated and follow the normal life cycle. An interesting detail at this point is that a task marked as required (remember the !) is only mandatory for a case once it has been included in the planning.

Discretionary tasks are popular for two-level processes: First, someone has to plan the case, adding the discretionary tasks or not. Only second is the case truly processed. Perhaps the person doing the planning is more experienced or better trained in making certain decisions, and thus he or she is relied upon to define the framework of the case manager's subsequent work. The goal of planning sometimes may be to enlarge the options open to the case manager; sometimes the goal may be to reduce the case manager's workload by restricting the number of tasks to only those needed most badly.

When discretionary tasks appear in a case or a stage, a small planning table symbol appears in the upper corner of the element. CMMN makes it possible to hide discretionary tasks with a small plus or minus sign next to the planning table. Similar to embedded sub-processes in BPMN, this functionality is not supported in all tools. It raises questions about how exactly the layout can be modified.

Discretionary tasks make possible new variations to our support case. See figure 5.28 on the next page. Additional tasks such as *create feature request* are now up to the discretion of the planner. Here, planning is part of the *solve issue* task and it is depicted with connectors. Discretionary tasks launch automatically and immediately in this process, which means that the two levels previously described no longer apply. This way of modeling is an alternative to the variety we already introduced. So just know that you can represent the same technical situation using either an *automatically started discretionary task* or a *manually started normal task*.

In our projects, we currently stick to this rule of thumb: If there is a two-level planning phase, then we use discretionary tasks. Otherwise, we tend toward using manual activation rules.

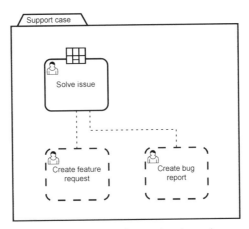

FIGURE 5.28 While finding a solution, other tasks can be planned.

5.3 Linking BPMN and CMMN

BPMN and CMMN can be used together. Actually, it is both typical and desirable to represent structured workflows in BPMN and unstructured cases in CMMN. You can switch notations depending on which tool will work best for each part of a problem.

Evaluating new insurance applications is a realistic example. As a modeler, you try to represent business processes in the most structured and automated way using BPMN. At the same time, you define exit points where a person has to intervene in a case, and you model that in CMMN. You don't have to model all kinds of exceptions, yet you aren't neglecting exceptions either. You end up with a truer model by blending your uses of BPMN and CMMN.

CMMN is sensitive to the activation of BPMN's process tasks, as you can see in figure 5.29. If the task is a blocking type, the case will wait for the process to terminate.

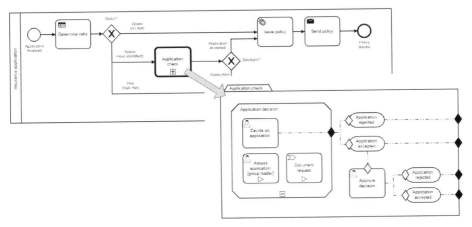

FIGURE 5.29 A CMMN case can launch a BPMN process.

BPMN is quite a bit older than CMMN, so the BPMN standard does not yet recognize links to CMMN. This does not pose a real problem in practice, however, since the path is typically made possible with vendor extensions —and there is an ongoing discussion about standardization. See figure 5.30 for an example.

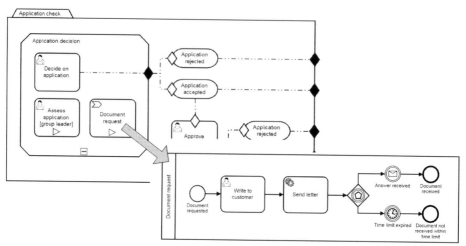

FIGURE 5.30 The CMMN case can be invoked by a superior BPMN process.

Hint: Business-IT-alignment

In an emancipated BPM marriage, it does not matter if the case or the process leads! Depending on the problem, the business process may start as a structured BPMN process (because a document was received that can be processed automatically) or as unstructured CMMN (because a call came in, and an employee wants to start a case directly).

6 DMN - Introduction and overview

■ 6.1 Understanding DMN

DMN is short for *Decision Model and Notation*. Like BPMN and CMMN, the DMN standard is managed by OMG. Unlike BPMN and CMMN, DMN is not about activities or processes. It does, however, work along the same lines: Decisions can be modeled by the business user, and the modeled decisions can be implemented in a decision engine. Just as with BPMN and CMMN, the DMN standard specification contains both a verbal description of the notation as well as an XML-based, formal metamodel. We refer to DMN version 1.1, the version current as we wrote this book.

A decision according to the DMN definition means deriving a result (*output*) from given facts (*input*) on the basis of a defined *decision logic*.

The topic of modeling and automating decisions is not new. When it was known as *Business Rules Management* and *Rule Engine*, it never took off. We think this was because the tools were both proprietary and fairly bulky. These hindrances are being lifted by a new generation of tools as well as the agreement on the DMN standard. This is providing new impetus toward systematic decision-management or *Business Decision Management* (BDM). We expect DMN and the corresponding decision engines to spread rapidly.

BDM can be broadly applied. Sometimes, compliance rules make careful analysis and documentation of the decision-making process necessary. More often, however, the main focus of the work is about automating operational decisions using a decision engine. We'll take a closer look at that in section 7.2.1 on page 191.

DMN deliberately focuses on operational decisions and not strategic ones. It is about the many routine decisions that need to be made repeatedly every day. The big issues, such as if your company should introduce BPMN, CMMN, or DMN, are unique and often do not follow set rules; that's why modeling them is not worthwhile.

Typical examples of operational decisions are:

- Feasibility check or authorization, such as if a customer qualifies for a certain product or if a claim can be regulated automatically.
- Validation, to check, for instance, if an application or a notification of a claim is complete and its content is valid.
- Fraud detection, for example, if a credit-card payment or notification of claim is suspicious.

- Risk assessment, as in if a credit limit is exceeded or an invoice amount can be authorized.
- Calculation. Examples include estimating shipping charges and determining discounts.
- Assigning. Think of skills-based routing.
- Maximization, to evaluate the business value of an assignment, for instance, to determine the correct priority or most appropriate customer classification.
- Addressing target groups, an example of which is determining products or advertising banners that may be of interest for a certain user.

In this book, we use the following terms in keeping with the DMN specification. *Decisions* depend on *decision logic*, which is defined by a number of *rules*, and these often are listed in a *decision table*. The rows in a decision table as well as *conditions* —we will detail Friendly Enough Expression Language (FEEL) expressions later —are therefore rules, and a decision table is a *set of rules*.

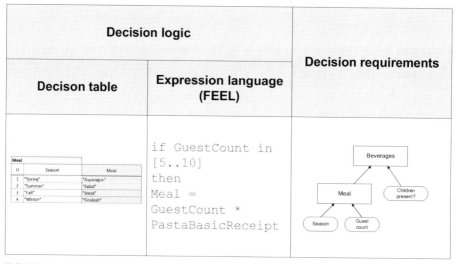

FIGURE 6.1 Elements of the DMN standard.

Figure 6.1 gives an overview of the content of the DMN specification. In this book, we offer an introduction to DMN, but we focus on those elements that, from our point of view, are most relevant to its practical application. We believe this will be sufficient to get you started.

■ 6.2 Notation elements

6.2.1 Decision tables

Decision tables are the central element of the DMN specification. They are *the* means for achieving business-IT alignment. They are fairly intuitive: The left-hand columns contain the conditions and the input values (input), and the right-hand columns contain the results (output). Each row corresponds to a single rule. When the condition on the left-hand side is met, then the result on the right-hand side is passed back.

Decision tables should always remain readable for the business. Technical terms, such as mapping against certain types of data, are hidden in the background. Conditions can be expressed in the FEEL expression language.

 Hint: Business-IT-alignment

Decision tables have the great advantage of being easily understood by most business users, yet suitable decision engines can execute the tables directly. Business-IT alignment in this area is therefore fairly easy to achieve. Make the most of it! ∎

Let's look at an example. Assume that you want to make an extremely important decision: what meal you're going to cook. The selected meal is therefore the desired result. What are the inputs? Well, that could depend on the time of year, and it could lead to a decision table such as in figure 6.2. (Yes, eating asparagus all spring could get tedious, but we're only just getting started with DMN.)

Meal		
U	Season	Meal
1	"Spring"	"Asparagus"
2	"Summer"	"Salad"
3	"Fall"	"Steak"
4	"Winter"	"Goulash"

FIGURE 6.2 A simple decision table.

Even if you're willing to accept a monotonous meal plan, it's simply not possible to entertain guests with six months of meat dishes, particularly as some of them may be vegetarian. We'll add another input column to our decision table. Multiple columns are always linked by AND, so all conditions have to be met; although if you leave a cell empty, that condition will not be taken into account. So in the example in figure 6.3, there will always be asparagus in spring. Hooray!

Meal			
U	Season	Vegetarian guests?	Meal
1	"Spring"	-	"Asparagus"
2	"Summer"	-	"Salad"
3	"Fall"	false	"Steak"
4	"Winter"	false	"Goulash"
5	"Fall"	true	"Pasta"
6	"Winter"	true	"Pasta"

FIGURE 6.3 Decision tables can contain multiple input columns. The conditions are linked by AND.

Look more closely at the table. Two new rules provide pasta as a result. The only difference between these rules is the season. This works well, but we can compact it by using a comma separator. The comma expresses OR within a cell. The table in figure 6.4 therefore has the same content but is easier to grasp.

Meal				
U	Season	Vegetarian guests?		Meal
1	"Spring"	-		"Asparagus"
2	"Summer"	-		"Salad"
3	"Fall"	false		"Steak"
4	"Winter"	false		"Goulash"
5	"Fall", "Winter"	true		"Pasta"

FIGURE 6.4 Within a single cell, different conditions can be separated by a comma. The conditions are thus linked by OR.

We have limited ourselves to equality (=) in our comparisons so far. Other arithmetic comparison operations can also be used, and we can use them explicitly in the table. Let's assume you would like to offer dry-aged steak, but you can only afford it for a limited number of guests. Figure 6.5 shows the corresponding decision table. Dry-aged steak is only served for a maximum of three guests, while larger groups get less-expensive steak.

Meal				
U	Season	Vegetarian guests?	Number of guests	Meal
1	"Spring"	-	-	"Asparagus"
2	"Summer"	-	-	"Salad"
3	"Fall"	false	< 4	"Dry-aged gourmet steak"
3	"Fall"	false	>= 4	"Steak"
4	"Winter"	false	-	"Goulash"
5	"Fall", "Winter"	true	-	"Pasta"

FIGURE 6.5 Comparisons are not limited to equality.

There is a further way of making the table easier to read. DMN makes it possible to link cells, and all cells that are linked have the same condition, so figure 6.6 presents a tidier version. The difference may seem slight here, but in larger tables it can make quite a contribution to readability.

Meal				
U	Season	Vegetarian guests?	Number of guests	Meal
1	"Spring"	-	-	"Asparagus"
2	"Summer"	-	-	"Salad"
3	"Fall"	false	< 4	"Dry-aged gourmet steak"
3			>= 4	"Steak"
4	"Winter"	false	-	"Goulash"
5	"Fall", "Winter"	true	-	"Pasta"

FIGURE 6.6 Cells can be linked for better readability.

Do you want to define appropriate side dishes? It's simple to do because DMN allows as many result columns as desired. Figure 6.7 displays the decision table.

Meal				
U	Season	Vegetarian guests?	Meal	Side dish
1	"Spring"	-	"Asparagus"	"Potatoes"
2	"Summer"	-	"Salad"	"Bread"
3	"Fall"	false	"Steak"	"Fried potatoes"
4	"Winter"	false	"Goulash"	"Rice"
5	"Fall", "Winter"	true	"Pasta"	"Salad"

FIGURE 6.7 Several result columns are possible.

You've probably spent the last few examples wondering why we constantly write *true* and *false* in the table instead of *yes* or *no*, or why we put seasons and meals in quotes. It is to accommodate the FEEL expression language; it always has to be possible to translate a decision table into a valid FEEL. Let's take a closer look at this.

Tooling

As DMN decision tables can potentially be executed, they therefore have to be translated into correct FEEL, so tables need to contain valid expressions. Tools can help a lot with this by offering views that, for instance, hide certain FEEL characteristics in the interests of business-IT alignment. So it may serve you to find a tool that will display *yes* and *no* while still storing *true* and *false* in the background. ∎

6.2.2 Expressions in decision tables

We use FEEL to express conditions in tables. To be more precise, tables are translated into FEEL in the background as exemplified in figure 6.8 on the following page. The following elements of the decision table exist:

* The **input expression** is defined in the column header. During automation, at the latest, variables are referenced here or complex expressions (calculations) are used. You can hide the technical expressions so that the column header remains technically readable.
* An **input entry** is an individual cell. Usually, you enter concrete values (literals) there. According to the standard, you cannot use calculations or function calls in cells, though manufacturer extensions may make it possible.
* The **output expression** is the column header of a result. Typically, this is the name of the result variable.
* An **output entry** is a result cell. It usually contains a specific value (literal), but in principle, it also can be an expression. Calculations or function calls are therefore allowed.

It may be best next to look at some more examples, and to focus on common constructions within decision tables. Further details on FEEL (which by the way can also be applied outside of decision tables), will follow in section 6.2.4 on page 177.

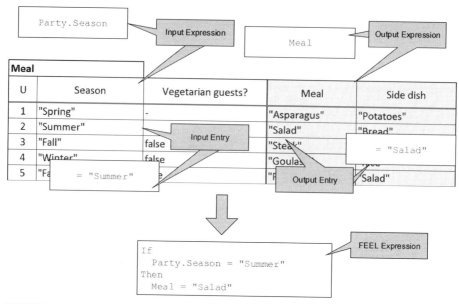

FIGURE 6.8 Decision tables are translated into FEEL expressions.

In the previous section, we got familiar with simple comparisons, but what happens if you want to cook a spinach dish for exactly 6, 7, or 8 guests? You could use the comma (6, 7, 8), although that would be annoying when dealing with larger value ranges. This is why FEEL recognizes ranges, which makes the table in figure 6.9 possible.

Meal			
U	Season	Number of guests	Meal
1	"Spring"	<= 4	"Green asparagus"
2		5	"White asparagus"
3		[6..8]	"Spinach"
4		>= 9	"Pasta"
5	not("Spring")	-	"Lasagne"

FIGURE 6.9 Using [..] to express ranges.

We've actually hidden a bit more FEEL here. The NOT function negates a condition, meaning that we only eat lasagna when it's not spring.

We said that the comma acts as an OR link; it can be used with as many conditions as you wish. A superstitious mathematician could even eat green asparagus only with a prime number of guests during spring, as shown in figure 6.10 on the next page.

You should pay particular attention to the possibilities provided by logical links. There are limits on what can be expressed in a decision table —and to be honest, we've encountered them all. For instance, you may not link conditions in one cell by AND. Instead, you would have to split conditions across columns. Figure 6.11 on the facing page shows how the range [6..8] would have to be split. It also shows a further example of the NOT function.

Meal			
U	Season	Number of guests	Meal
1	"Spring"	<= 3, 5, 7, 13, 17	"Green asparagus"
2	"Spring"	4, 6, [8..12], [14..16], >17	"White asparagus"
5	not("Spring")	-	"Lasagne"

FIGURE 6.10 Complex OR links between conditions are possible with commas.

Meal				
U	Season	Number of guests	Number of guests	Meal
1		<= 4	-	"Green asparagus"
2	"Spring", "Summer"	5	-	"White asparagus"
3		>=6	<=8	"Spinach"
4		>= 9	-	"Pasta"
5	not("Spring", "Summer")	-	-	"Lasagne"

FIGURE 6.11 An AND link between two conditions is only possible by using two columns.

If you want to carve out exclusions, they need to appear within brackets. In other words, you cannot write:

`not("spring"), not("summer")`

Because it is *always* either not spring *or* not summer.

Finally, we want to mention that FEEL also recognizes other types of data such as time, date, and duration. This means that you can easily express the fact that you want fondue on New Year's Eve. This is shown in figure 6.12.

Meal			
U	Season	Date	Meal
1	-	date("2016-12-31")	"Fondue"
2	"Spring"	-	"Asparagus"
3	"Summer"	-	"Salad"
4	"Fall"	-	"Steak"
5	"Winter"	not(date("2016-12-31"))	"Goulash"

FIGURE 6.12 Thanks to the date data type, we can count on fondue on New Year's Eve!

As you can see, we need to check the rule for winter to exempt New Year's Eve. This has to do with the *hit policy*. We are currently using the *unique* hit policy, which is indicated by the *U* in the header of the left-most column of the table. Exactly one rule (that is, one row) of the table has to correspond. We cannot eat fondue *and* goulash; it simply isn't allowed. That may seem unfair, but it is clearly what the table expresses. Let's take a closer look.

6.2.3 Hit policy

The hit policy determines how many rules may apply and what happens if several rules apply at once. The first letter of the hit policy appears as the header of the left-most column of the table. All our examples so far show *U* for the hit policy *unique*.

Unique (U): Unique hit

The *unique* hit policy means that exactly one rule (in other words, one row of the table) will apply. This hit policy is standard, and it is the default if no hit policy is specified. You could leave out the *U*, but we recommend including the hit policy designation to avoid misunderstandings.

Typical applications for the *unique* hit policy are:

- Determining discounts
- Determining the employee responsible for a task

As we saw in figure 6.12 on the preceding page, *unique* is not always the best hit policy to rely on to arrive at a clear table of rules.

First (F): The first hit

The hit policy *first* (*F*) makes the example table much clearer, as shown in figure 6.13. Only the first matching row determines the result, all other rows are irrelevant, and the order goes from top to bottom. Now we can write very simple rules to ensure that our exceptions are dealt with higher up, and we can define standard outcomes lower down. Having fondue on New Year's Eve is a clear exception, and if it doesn't apply, then there is no need to ensure that it is *not* New Year's Eve, although it may still be winter.

Meal			
F	Season	Date	Meal
1	-	date("2016-12-31")	"Fondue"
2	"Spring"	-	"Asparagus"
3	"Summer"	-	"Salad"
4	"Fall"	-	"Steak"
5	"Winter"	-	"Goulash"

FIGURE 6.13 The first matching row determines the result when using the *first* hit policy.

One consequence of the *first* hit policy is that the order of the rows must be taken into account while maintaining rules. Large sets of rules make this more difficult, and of course, the author must know what the *F* means.

Typical applications for the *first* hit policy are:

- Determining credit worthiness. By putting them at or near the top, clear rules can be established for black sheep or existing customers. Rules for new customers can then be evaluated using a more comprehensive table.
- Assessing risk or detecting fraud. It is possible that various risks may apply, although it is often sufficient to determine the first risk.

Priority (P): The most important hit policy

Another variety is the *priority (P)* hit policy. In DMN, priority is defined by the result columns. We can now tell you something we left out earlier: In columns, you can enumerate the applicable values. These values then apply in the precise order in which they are enumerated. The priority in figure 6.14 is therefore:

1. Exception
2. Normal

Meal					
P	Season	Date	Relevance *Exception, Normal*		Meal
2	"Spring"	-	Normal		"Asparagus"
3	"Summer"	-	Normal		"Salad"
4	"Fall"	-	Normal		"Steak"
1	-	date("2016-12-31")	Exception		"Fondue"
5	"Winter"	-	Normal		"Goulash"

FIGURE 6.14 The results column can define a priority that determines the result.

To determine the priority of a rule, we look first at the left-most *results* column (not the left-most column in the table). All applicable rules with result values in this column are then sorted by priority, and the result with the highest priority becomes the one selected. In our example, it is essential for the *relevance* column to be the first results column, and that the entries in the cells are empty. If several results with the highest priority exist, then the next results column to the right becomes determinative among them.

One advantage of the *priority* hit policy is that the order of rows makes no difference. That may mean easier maintenance, but it also may mean greater difficulty in recognizing when one rule trumps another or how conflicts are resolved.

Typical applications for the *priority* hit policy are:

- Assessing risk when different levels of risk exist, and we're only interested in the highest level detected.

Collect (C): All hits

Up until now, only one row (or rule) has determined our result. That doesn't necessarily have to be the case. Let's assume that you want to decide what drinks to serve at your dinner party as well. You'll offer beer, wine, soft drinks, and water.

We need the *collect (C)* hit policy. This policy collects the results of *all* matching rows. The result of the decision is therefore a list of results.

Figure 6.15 on the next page shows a decision table for various combinations of drinks. If we decide on asparagus, then white wine is offered. If children are present, we'll offer soft drinks. And no matter what food we serve, there will always be water.

Typical applications for the *collect* hit policy are:

- Assessing risk where all risks must be collected
- Detecting fraud or validating where all anomalies must be collected

Drinks			
C	Meal	Children present?	Drink
1	"Asparagus"	-	"White wine"
2	not("Asparagus")	-	"Beer"
3	-	true	"Soft drinks"
4	-	-	"Water"

FIGURE 6.15 A list of appropriate drinks is the result of a decision table that applies the *collect* hit policy.

Collect with aggregation: The sum of the hits

Suppose your party is to be a costume party, and you want to assess the guests' outfits. Of course, this too can be handled by a decision table. Basically, it is like your bank assessing your credit rating using a scoring model. We attribute a certain number of points to various factors; the sum of points determines a score for each costume.

This situation may lead to a decision table like the one in figure 6.16. Note that we can *punish* factors by attributing negative points for a boring costume, for instance. By applying this decision table to each guest in costume, we can receive a corresponding assessment, and DMN will even tally the score results. How did that become possible? Notice the small C+ in the header of the left-most column of the table.

Costume scoring					
C+	Manufacturing method	Make-up	Creativity factor	Realistic?	Score
1	"Self-sewn"	-	-	-	20
2	"Made out of other costumes"	-	-	-	10
3	"Bought"	-	-	-	0
4	-	"None"	-	-	-10
5	-	"A little"	-	-	10
6	-	"Serious"	-	-	20
7	-	-	"Boring"	-	-20
8	-	-	"Very creative"	-	20
9	-	-	-	true	5
10	-	-	-	false	0

FIGURE 6.16 The aggregation function calculates a total score as a result in the decision table.

DMN recognizes aggregation functions in connection with the *collect* hit policy. The aggregation functions available are:

- C+: Adds the values.
- C<: Applies the smallest value.
- C>: Applies the largest value.
- C#: Counts the hits.

Of course, you could take a different approach and decide that the factor with the highest number of points is determinative. In that case, you simply enter C>, since you are now interested in the maximum.

A typical application for the collect hit policy is:
* Scoring.

Hit policies - an overview

We have described the hit policies we consider relevant. For the sake of completeness, however, here is a list all the hit policies made possible by the standard. First, the *single hit* policies, which allow for exactly one unambiguous result:

* **U**nique: Exactly one row has to match.
* **F**irst: The first row that matches determines the result.
* **A**ny: As many rows as desired may match, all of which then have to provide the same result.
* **P**riority: The row with the highest priority matches.

Second, these *multiple hit* policies allow several results to be passed back:

* **C**ollect: The result is a list of all results without a defined order. Optionally, one of the following aggregate functions can be added: + (total), < (minimum), > (maximum), # (count). The use of aggregate functions of course means that only one result is passed back, so strictly speaking, the Collect hit policy behaves more as a single-hit policy.
* **R**ule order: A list of results in the same order as the table rows.
* **O**utput order: A list of results in order of priority.

Most situations can be addressed by using a combination of different hit policies, as we saw with the meal-planning example. In that case, the hit policy will have an effect on the readability and maintainability of the table. It is often worth trying different varieties until you have a feel for what will work best. We also recommend real-world testing as early as possible. In practice, we often use simulator for testing decision tables. We provide a free simulator online at https://camunda.org/dmn/simulator/.

6.2.4 Advanced FEEL

We have mentioned FEEL several times. This is the Friendly Enough Expression Language, and we have applied it in decision tables. In this book we focus on S-FEEL. The *S* stands for *simple*. S-FEEL is a subset of FEEL for simple conditions. It is generally sufficient for most purposes.

When standardizing FEEL, the aim was to achieve an expression language understandable to business users but also formally precise so that it can be executed directly by engines. If you were to say that that goal is simply not possible, then we would disagree. Consider Excel. We have seen clients using Excel formulas written by business users that would severely test people with IT degrees. In any event, though, most of the formulas needed are easy enough for most users to read and understand.

Besides decision tables, FEEL can be used in simple decision logic without tables. This may seem a bit confusing at first, but there are indeed some decisions in which it makes little sense to invest effort in a table. If you recall assessing the fancy costumes in our earlier example, a sensible rule would have been: The costume with the highest number of points wins. Should there be equal points, then a final result is decided alphabetically by surname. You could now describe this as a FEEL expression.

One step at a time, however. Let's start with a simple FEEL expression you already know from figure 6.8 on page 172.

```
if
   Party.Season = "Summer"
then
   Meal = "Salad"
```

This is a rule that can be applied. It doesn't have to be expressed in a decision table (although a table still may be a better choice in terms of business-IT alignment).

We'll go deeper into the nature of FEEL in the rest of the chapter. If the examples given so far have been sufficient for you to make your decision tables, you can skip the following details. But if you are defining rules to be executed or just want to understand certain expressions better, you will find these details helpful.

Types of data

You can provide specific values as literals in FEEL. The following data types are permitted:

- Text (string): Surround with quotes. Example: *"Summer"*
- Numbers (number): Write without quotes. Example: *42*
- Yes/no (Boolean): Write *true* or *false*
- Time and date (time, date): Write as functions using the patterns HH:MM:SS and YYYY-MM-DD. Example: *date("1980-01-01")*
- Duration (in days, months, or years): Example: *"P1DT2H"* for 1 day and 2 hours

Besides specific values, you can reference variables to be provided by an engine at the moment of execution. Write the names of variables without quotes. Be careful! The following two lines, for instance, do not express the same thing:

```
Season = "Summer"
Season = Summer
```

The first expression compares the text string *Summer* as a literal. The second expression compares the value of a variable named Summer. So you have to pay close attention to the type of data.

By the way, complex objects can be used as variables, so the party itself could be an object with several attributes:

```
Party.Season = "Summer"
Party.NumberOfGuests > 17
```

Values for dates always have to be generated by the *date* function, otherwise they will not be treated as a date but instead as text. If you wanted to verify that the party is only taking place after BPMCon 2016, you would write:

```
Party.Date > date("2016-09-16")
```

The DMN specification allows text strings to be displayed in italics *instead of in quotes*, and for date values likewise to be displayed in bold and italics. This helps with the display, but correct values still have to be generated in the background. Since these details can easily be overlooked, we are not great fans of these alternative representations.

Operators

The most important operators are:

- Comparisons: =, !=, >, >=, <, <=.
- Ranges: [1..10],]0..11[, (0..11). All of these ranges mean 1 to 10, inclusive, because][or () do *not* include the limit values, whereas [] does. We recommend using only one construction per project if possible. So far, [1..10] has proven to be the best solution, at least for whole numbers.
- Negation: not().
- Calculations: You can use basic arithmetic operators to carry out mathematical calculations.

The following examples show a few operators in action. For these, we use the logical AND operator, which is only available in FEEL and not in S-FEEL:

```
if
    Party.Date = date("2016-09-16") and
    Party.NumberOfGuests in [25..100] and
    Party.CoolnessFactor > 5 and
    not( Party.FocusZeroCode )
then
    Recommendation = "Party at same time as BPMCon! But not enough
        participants. Ignore."

if
    Party.NumberOfGuests + Party.NumberOfPrebookings > 500
then
    Recommendation = "Find new venue"
```

6.2.5 Decision requirements

Some decisions cannot be expressed in a simple table. Often, one decision depends on another one. These situations can be modeled using the *decision requirements graph* (DRG) and visualized as a *decision requirements diagram* (DRD).

At your dinner party, you want to decide which drinks to serve. This of course depends on the meal. After all, you would like to serve a good white wine to accompany the delicious asparagus, right?

The DRD in figure 6.17 on the following page shows the decisions that need to be taken, what the necessary inputs are, and how decisions relate to one another. This is how you use the result of the meal decision as an input value for a drinks decision.

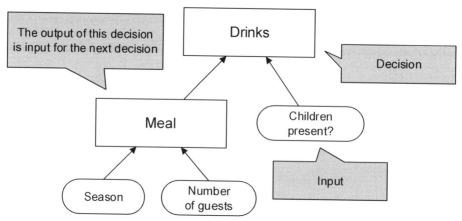

FIGURE 6.17 The decision requirements diagram (DRD) displays decisions, input values, and relationships between decisions.

DRD is a good tool for discussing decision structures, so you might do a workshop with your spouse. During the workshop, he or she points out that some guests will prefer non-alcoholic beverages. On the basis of the DRD, you may decide to outsource this decision to avoid over-complicating the drink decision table. You change the DRD as shown in figure 6.18.

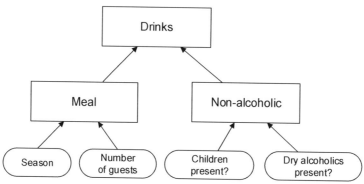

FIGURE 6.18 This DRD has outsourced the decision on whether or not alcohol is okay.

This has a further advantage: In the future, you will be able to introduce additional reasons for not serving alcohol without having to modify the drink decision. Furthermore, the logic is re-usable. That will be an advantage if you need make sure your desserts are alcohol-free as well.

A decision node in a DRD is linked to decision logic. This means that FEEL or a decision table can be linked in the background. When discussing DRDs in a working session, by the way, it can be extremely helpful to set up example decision tables, as they make a situation a lot easier to grasp. Figure 6.19 on the facing page shows an example of this. It is probably exactly what you and your spouse drew on the kitchen whiteboard while planning the party.

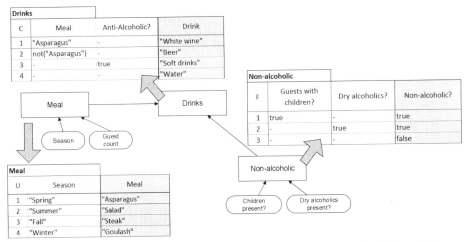

FIGURE 6.19 Decision nodes in a DRD are linked to decision logic —usually decision tables.

Not all inputs contained in the table necessarily have to be represented graphically. On the contrary, in practice, it sometimes may be desirable to select your own granularity. You may wish to see only the *party* as an object in the DRD, but to use the table to go into details such as the date or the number of guests.

DMN makes it possible to diagram a complex *decision requirement graph* (DRG) through various diagrams (DRD). This means that each diagram may show only fragments to explain a particular situation. This is comparable to BPMN, in which you can, in theory, also draw several business process diagrams for a single collaboration. This is rare in practice —and we haven't yet actually experienced it with DMN. For the sake of simplicity, you can usually assume that a DRG equals a DRD.

■ 6.3 Practical tips

6.3.1 Linking BPMN and DMN

For processes, decisions need to be made regularly. In section 4.5.4 on page 141, we explained when and why these decisions should not be modeled with gateways in process models. Instead, BPMN offers its own type of task to link sets of rules: the *business rule task*. (At the time BPMN was being standardized, we spoke of *business rules management* instead of *decision management* as we do today.)

The approach is simple: As soon as a BPMN process arrives in the Business Rule Task, the set of rules is evaluated. Then the result of the decision is present in the process, and it can be evaluated, for instance, by a gateway. In section 7.2.6 on page 195 we look more closely at the technical integration of workflows and decision engines; they are often integrated into one engine. The specific link to DMN has not yet been standardized because BPMN is significantly older than DMN, although this reality is cushioned by vendor extensions.

Figure 6.20 recalls an example from earlier in the book. During a risk assessment, the DMN set of rules applies, and the result triggers a routing decision in the process. You may wish to review section 4.5.4 on page 141 and think again about the difference between business decisions and routing decisions.

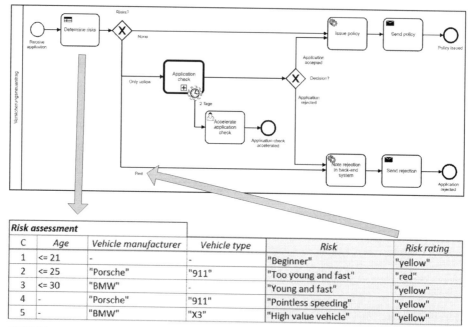

Risk assessment

C	Age	Vehicle manufacturer	Vehicle type	Risk	Risk rating
1	<= 21	-	-	"Beginner"	"yellow"
2	<= 25	"Porsche"	"911"	"Too young and fast"	"red"
3	<= 30	"BMW"	-	"Young and fast"	"yellow"
4	-	"Porsche"	"911"	"Pointless speeding"	"yellow"
5	-	"BMW"	"X3"	"High value vehicle"	"yellow"

FIGURE 6.20 Logic for business decisions in DMN can be called from BPMN processes. The result is often used for routing decisions in the process.

6.3.2 Decisions with a decision flow

Let's assume you want to decide on a place and date for your party. That shouldn't be too difficult. Back in the workshop with your spouse, you sketch the diagram in figure 6.21 on the next page on the kitchen whiteboard.

This seem straightforward enough, but it doesn't quite work out once you start working on a decision table.

- You really can't generate a decision table to evaluate all possible dates. First, you would determine all relevant days, let's say Saturdays in May or June. Second, you evaluate those dates to find the most appropriate one.
- You want to decide on a date, the one with the highest evaluation. This decision is not suitable for a table, but it can be rendered as a simple expression.
- With the date in hand, you can decide on a venue. You'll need more information first, such as the weather forecast.

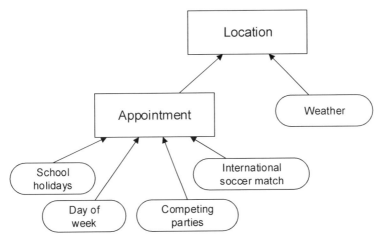

FIGURE 6.21 A simple decision?

As you can see, the decision is complicated, and it requires that a certain order be maintained at certain stages. The DMN standard is entirely mute on this topic, but in practice it has proved useful to model a *decision flow* in such cases. Naturally, we use BPMN.

Figure 6.22 shows the decision flow for our party. As you can see, we first collected all dates of interest. We did it here as a script task but it could also have been a service task. The business rule task is then carried out once for each date, and it scores them. With a score for each date, it's easy to determine the most suitable one. Then, for this date only, we have to pull up a weather report —and that can truly be a service call. Now we can decide on the venue.

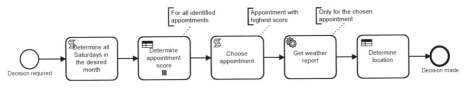

FIGURE 6.22 The decision flow provides order for complex decisions.

To have a full set of rules for our decision, we have to implement the two necessary decision tables. See the examples in figure 6.23.

Appointment score

C+	School holidays?	Distance from competing party (in km)	International soccer match?	Score
1	true	-	-	-5
2	-	<20	-	-50
3	-	[20..50]	-	-20
4	-	-	true	-10

Location			
U	Season	Weather	Venue
1	"Winter", "Fall"	-	"Hire restaurant"
2	-	"Rain"	"Dining room"
3	"Spring", "Summer"	"Changeable"	"Balcony"
4	-	"Sun"	"Garden"

FIGURE 6.23 Decision tables to be used in the decision flow.

This example shows a typical pattern when trying to pick out something from a large number of values. We call it the *decision funnel*. Typically, it consists of the steps depicted in figure 6.24:

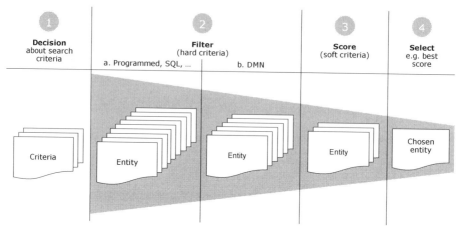

FIGURE 6.24 To select a value, you often go through the decision funnel.

1. You decide on certain search criteria such as *all Saturdays in May and June*. In this case, it is an informal decision reached by gut feeling. This also could be modeled by DMN, however, by assessing the correct months and possible weekdays according to the requirements of the party.
2. From a large volume of data, you seek the elements that match your criteria. For performance reasons, this is typically not done with DMN but with programmed services or SQL queries to a database.
3. You may filter the results again with DMN to apply rules that exclude certain results. (Our example does not show this.)
4. You evaluate all elements in the current list, usually with a DMN scoring table.
5. You select exactly one element, usually the one with the highest score, although this doesn't always have to be the case. In tenders, for instance, sometimes the second-cheapest option is selected.

Decision flows are a powerful tool and we enjoy using them. A word of warning, however: Even if the decision flow is also modeled in BPMN, it should remain strictly separated from the actual business processes. Always create a separate BPMN model for a decision flow, which is then called up in one node of the business process —just as with a decision table. Otherwise you will end up mixing the process flow with business decisions and, as we've already said, we do not believe that to be a good idea.

Technically, a decision flow can be automated using a normal workflow engine as can any other BPMN process.

6.3.3 Linking CMMN and DMN

Like BPMN, the CMMN standard defines its own type of task for decisions. In CMMN, it is called a *decision task*, and it can be linked to a DMN decision table. Even though CMMN does not dictate the use of DMN, it is recommended.

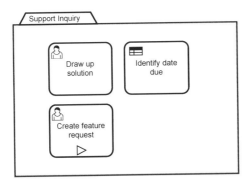

FIGURE 6.25 For the decision task in CMMN, decisions can be called up in DMN.

Figure 6.25 shows an example of a support inquiry. In support, the task is to determine the SLA (service level agreement) of the ticket, so a decision table is brought up. If you look closely, you'll see that the decision task has no play symbol here. It is carried out automatically when a case is created.

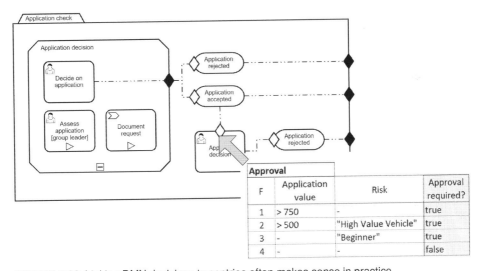

FIGURE 6.26 Linking DMN decisions to sentries often makes sense in practice.

In CMMN, sentries in particular often contain complex conditions, as shown in figure 6.26. These conditions can often be well expressed through DMN, which is why we highly recommend linking sentries to DMN decisions, even if this is not defined in the standard. In practice, this is usually possible through vendor extensions or technical tricks.

6.3.4 The life cycle of decisions

When we started working with DMN, a decision life cycle emerged. It is similar to Camunda's BPM life cycle from figure 1.1.3 on page 2. Again, we tried to compromise between overly-correct complexity and simplified presentation. You see our compromise in figure 6.27.

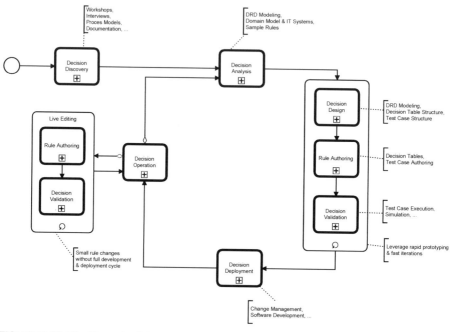

FIGURE 6.27 The life cycle of decisions.

The life cycle assumes that you need to implement one decision. For this decision, you should collect as much information as possible during a first *discovery*. Using that information, you can start your *analysis*. During the analysis, DRDs like the ones introduced in section 6.2.5 on page 179 are useful tools. You also should start drafting tables early so that you can render the rules as specifically as possible for all concerned.

Once you finish this preliminary work, you can verify if all necessary input data is truly available —and where it came from. We often find that during this early phase wishful thinking collides with reality. You realize that desired rules cannot be implemented because necessary information is either missing or painfully difficult to obtain. It is good to catch these problems early, however, as you can still take countermeasures. Perhaps you can change the rules, for instance, or make the additional effort to acquire the required information. Costs and benefits are easy to see at this point.

Once agreement has been reached about the early phases, you can begin to *design*. First, create the structure (the columns) of the decision table. Provide some sample rules (a few rows). This work may be done by specialists or the IT department if the table is to be automated later on. Second, record the rules fully. The business may do this part, or it should at least review the table and take over ownership. They should not delegate this responsibility.

If the project is headed toward an automated outcome, define test cases during design. This is always important later when it is time to validate the set of rules. Also ensure that the test cases are recorded in a form understandable to the business that will be maintaining them. Common worksheets in Microsoft Excel have proved useful for this, but there are specialized test frameworks available as well.

Rules should be validated once they are complete. For the simplest cases, it can be enough just to run the table through a free online simulator such as https://camunda.org/dmn/simulator/. You also can simulate decisions using historic data. In the best-case scenario, you may have access to automated tests based on test cases previously defined.

The *deployment* of a decision varies with the type of decision. It can range from comprehensive change-management procedures and software releases to simple working instructions by email.

Once the decisions are in production, the desire is often expressed to *live edit* them. Remember this rule of thumb: It is comparatively easy to adapt the rows in a table, but it is less easy to change columns —in other words, the structure.

Decision engines offer the possibility of changing the tables by a push of a button during runtime. In production. Immediately. This sounds great, and it usually makes clients' eyes light up ...but after that flash of enthusiasm, the eyes narrow with skepticism. It doesn't take long for someone to ask: "But who's going to push this button? What actually happens if something goes wrong? Does the change then really go live immediately? That's a bit scary, isn't it?"

Those are exactly the right questions. Unfortunately, there are no universal answers. The best thing to do is to think about your organization and your plans. One thing remains true: The are no technical hurdles to having a rule change go live in real time without involving IT.

7   Automation

■ 7.1   Purpose and benefit

This chapter is about automating business processes and decisions with software. Of course, this can be done using traditional software development, but it is much more interesting —especially in the context of business-IT alignment —to use an engine. We introduce this possibility in this chapter, and we detail the advantages it offers.

Since engines can operate with all three of the standards presented in this book (BPMN, CMMN, and DMN), we use *model execution engine* as an umbrella term for:

- Workflow engines. These carry out structured processes in BPMN. They are also known as process engines.
- Case engines, which carry our unstructured cases in CMMN.
- Decision engines, which make decisions on the basis of DMN. These are also known as rule engines or business rule engines.

Products exist that integrate all three standards.

A model execution engine reads models as XML files, and it executes the models directly. The models, acting as source code of a software solution, must be precisely defined and detailed. That's important. After all, the engine cannot interpret things that aren't defined. That models equate to source code also is a huge opportunity; the models always represent reality! To make a change, you adapt the model.

With process models in BPMN, we have the freedom that only the automated parts end up in an engine. This brings us to a second important aspect of our framework, which we explain more in section 7.3 on page 197: If human and technological process flows are sensibly connected, you stand a good chance of keeping the documented work organization up to date. Suitable tools can project technical modifications into the human flows and, in the context of process monitoring, show what has been executed by the engine in ways easy for non-technical users to understand.

7.2 Basics

7.2.1 Model execution with model execution engines

The model execution engine (or just *engine*) is a software component for executing BPMN, CMMN, or DMN models.

Workflow or case engine

For workflow or process automation, the workflow engine needs the business process to be in a BPMN model that contains all technical details required for execution. While running, process instances are generated for each process run. The workflow engine calculates the control flow and always knows what has to be done next. This actualizes the token concept introduced in section 2.1.4 on page 26. To be precise, it is not the business process that is automated but rather the control over that process.

Case management in CMMN is automated similarly except that the engine controls the life cycles of tasks (see section 5.1.3 on page 148).

An engine recognizes two fundamentally different types of activities: those that require human interaction and all others that run automatically. The latter may be service calls, but they also may be evaluations of gateways, events, or sentries. For human interaction, user or human tasks are used. Usually, engines contain a list of tasks comparable to an email inbox in that they let the user know which tasks still have to be completed. If you open a task, you get a preconfigured screen mask that makes it possible to view and process data or make decisions. See the overview of how the workflow engine functions in figure 7.1.

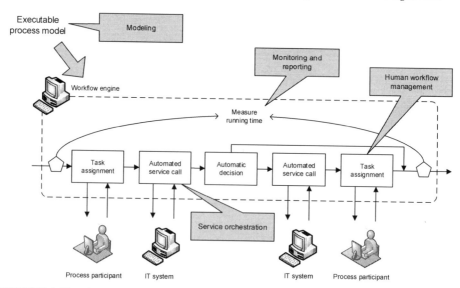

FIGURE 7.1 How the workflow engine works.

As you can see, the engine has to do more than simply manage the control flow because it is necessary to also account for the data flow in the process. This means that during one process instance, data can be added which the engine then manages together with the state. Usually, this data is also stored in a database so that it can be restored after a system failure.

Decision engine

Making decisions based on a DMN model has somewhat different requirements. A decision engine is software that can make decisions automatically based on business rules. No state needs to be maintained. The primary aim is to distinguish business logic from program or process logic, which means you can make fundamental changes to business rules without having to change program code or redesign the business process.

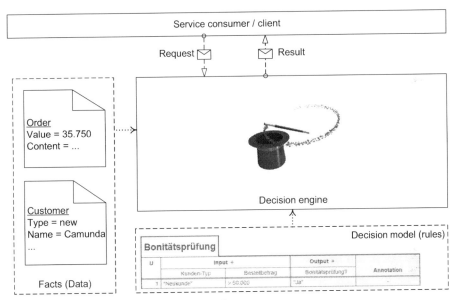

FIGURE 7.2 An overview of the decision engine.

You can picture the decision engine as a black box (see figure 7.2). The engine responds to a request according to the rules it knows. To evaluate the rules, the engine uses data —so called facts. Typically, the facts are contained within the request. They may also be provided from an external source such as a database.

Advantages of model execution engines

Besides managing the control and data flow, a typical model execution engine provides many additional functions:

- **Versioning of models**: Business processes are long-running by nature. An order process, for instance, may take from a few days to several months. This means that when you modify a process, some instances still may be running. Engines can process different versions of a model simultaneously, thus making a transition to a new process possible by phasing out the old version.

- **Data collection, key performance indicators, and reports**: The engine can collect data automatically while managing processes, cases, or decision instances. For an order, for instance, it can collect when authorization has been occurred, when shipping has been initiated or completed, and so on. This data can be aggregated and reported on, providing a good overview of efficiency and potential bottlenecks within the process. Once it has been well aggregated, it also provides an overview of the process landscape. A further possibility is *business activity monitoring* (BAM), an approach meant to recognize patterns in real time and issue warnings or to intervene autonomously.
- **Technical monitoring and administration**: The engine offers the chance to view current status of the process or case instances. This opens various possibilities for intervention such as aborting or restarting a faulty instance.

7.2.2 Executing the BPMN, CMMN, and DMN standards

Models in BPMN, CMMN, and DMN can be stored as XML files. Each standard defines a precise XML schema. The information relevant for execution is stored in XML, as are the coordinates and other details for graphical representation called *diagram interchange*. This makes it possible to use models in different tools without losing the layout. The configurations needed for the graphical layout and for execution are stored in the same XML file.

All three standards also define execution semantics, which means that for each notation element, there is a precise definition for how the engine should act. Precise definition makes it possible for models to be carried out in any standards-compatible engine without proprietary extensions. In section 7.4.2 on page 202, we outline everything that needs to be taken into account in this context.

In this book, we do not delve into the complete execution semantics nor the details on the XML schema. We deliberately avoid XML source code —and we even removed some code that was in earlier editions —because it should to be transparent to you as a user. Of course, you are welcome to pore over further examples at http://camunda.org, for instance, or in the official example documents.

7.2.3 Alternative automation languages

Web Services Business Process Execution Language (WS-BPEL) is an XML-based language that combines web services into more powerful services. Services are combined as processes; this is called orchestration. WS-BPEL was introduced in 2002 by major IT companies including IBM and Microsoft.

The acceptance and use of BPEL peaked around 2010. After BPMN 2.0 was released, BPEL started to decline, although some experts still maintain that it provides some functions that are missing in BPMN. Either way, from what we are seeing, it is obvious that few BPEL projects are left, and only a few workflow engines still support it.

We don't think it makes much sense for you to occupy yourself with BPEL now. We do, however, offer respect to the authors of the standard; it was an important milestone on the road to BPMN 2.0.

For those interested in the history, here is why we think BPMN prevailed over BPEL:

- **Control flow as graph**: In contrast to BPELs' block structure, BPMN processes are graph-oriented. Functionally modeled processes can thus be executed without problems. This challenged the vendors of workflow engines, but they found practical solutions even for complicated gateway designs. Those solutions may not satisfy theorists in certain esoteric special cases, but for practitioners, they represent a useful compromise.
- **No close binding to web services and XML**: BPMN, in contrast to BPEL, deliberately leaves open the question of applying Web Services and XML in a workflow engine. These technologies may be the defaults, but we have seen that it is often better to use other technologies. If a project focuses entirely on a Java architecture, for instance, it makes sense to apply a Java workflow engine to avoid the lengthy trip through web services. So far, this has required proprietary tools, but BPMN 2.0 enables such engines to be integrated through the standard as well.
- **Graphical notation**: Most BPEL tools provide a graphical view of a process, but this is not standardized. Also, the resulting block-oriented diagrams are dissimilar to the functional model. In contrast, BPMN processes have a well-defined appearance that is entirely aligned with the concepts and ideas of the functional models. This is a big step toward aligning business and IT.

We published a summary evaluation on the future of BPEL at http://BPEL.de.

Besides the BPMN and BPEL standards, there is also the *XML Process Definition Language* (XPDL) from the Workflow Management Coalition. Like BPEL, XPDL is no longer relevant. There are, obviously, manufacturers and related service providers who claim otherwise. There are also many language-proprietary workflow engines with a wide variety of architectural approaches. We can't provide an overview of products with proprietary languages. We note, however, that these are increasingly adapting to BPMN as they issue new releases.

7.2.4 When is it worth using a workflow or case engine?

Why should you even use a workflow or case engine in your projects? Can't you just implement the process diagrams and case models you've generated in your preferred programming language?

Surely, this question is justified. As is so often the case, however, the answer is: It depends. Let's step back and look at automation in its entirety. The rule of thumb is that process automation is worth it especially for business processes that exhibit the following:

- **High number of repetitions**: The work put into automation is worthwhile only if many instances can be executed. Otherwise, the cost of development may exceed the savings in process costs.
- **Standardization**: If processes are barely structured, and they run differently all the time, then an engine is not appropriate. Even case management with CMMN requires that the possible tasks be thought through in advance; the majority of instances therefore should follow the same pattern.
- **Rich in information**: Basically, processes that carry a lot of information are better suited to automation because computers handle information very well. If physical objects have to be moved often, automation is more difficult and less exciting.

- **High potential degree of automation**: Of course, task automation can increase the efficiency of a process. Some tasks, such as booking in an ERP system, are well suited to automating with an engine. The data no longer has to be entered manually into the mask. Some manual tasks are not suitable for automation —calling up clients, for instance.

Would you like to automate your business processes? Let's return to the question of why you *should* use an engine:

- **Visibility**: A main advantage of using an engine is that the process is not only available as source code (XML, Java, and so on), but also as a diagram. This means that the execution of the process is not buried deep in the software; it is rendered visible. This advantage is essential because it makes it easy to discover how the process is implemented. Truth, as we know, lies in the source code, and suddenly it becomes accessible and understandable for everyone. What an advantage when it comes to discussing weak points, possible improvements, and modifications! Without the engine, IT specialists have to embark on a quasi-archaeological search to unearth how the process was actually implemented. Process automation provides the transparency necessary to make sensible re-engineering possible. Being able to ensure that an automated process is truly being carried out as described —and being able to prove it with log data afterward —is also immensely helpful for meeting compliance requirements.

- **Agility**: Often, BPM and SOA are compared to Lego. You simply construct your new process from existing services as if the services were Lego building blocks. A customer once said to us: "Take a look at Lego kits nowadays. You get highly complex and specialized building blocks that you cannot easily reuse at other points." And he's right —that's exactly what happens in IT today. If we want to obtain a complex end product such as a cool Lego spaceship, then we can't work with simple building blocks. This also means that we can't just place the blocks wherever we choose. Does that mean no agility? We don't think so, because we think the agility comes from increased transparency that makes changing processes feasible in the first place. It doesn't work at the push of a button, but at least we can estimate what consequences a process change will have and where we'll have to intervene. The visibility of the process also leads to services of suitable granularity, and it supports the sensible modularization of IT systems.

- **Quality**: Imagine a mail-order firm of your choosing. If you call them to find out where your order is, there are two possible answers: "Let me find out for you; please wait a minute," or the immediate: "Your order is currently waiting at xy." A mail-order firm that can offer the second answer probably uses an engine that offers a more precise look at the process definitions and process instances. Escalations in the case of excessive waiting times don't have to come from frustrated customers but rather from the engine itself.

In theory, you can achieve these advantages by building your own engine. Perhaps you could also build your own database, but would you? Probably not. Instead you would trust reliable products. If they were available free of charge, so much the better!

7.2.5 When is it worth using a decision engine?

When it comes to decisions and their underlying rules, there are two basic possibilities for execution:

- Programming as source code
- Decision engine

Even today, it is common to program decisions in a classic programming language. As an approach, this has some disadvantages that need to be weighed:

- **Translation**: Rules always have to be translated from the specification into program code by a software developer. This is true both for the initial development and for subsequent modifications. Even developers regularly fail to find the implemented decision logic in the source code that was generated, making subsequent modifications laborious and prone to mistakes.
- **Release cycles**: Because they are programmed into software, decisions are subject to the same release cycles as other software components. Comprehensive test and approval cycles can take a long time, and that can be a problem when business rules change frequently. That is why there is a call for a more agile approach in this area in particular.
- **Readability**: Rules hidden in program code cannot be understood by the business departments. This makes validation difficult. Determining the implemented business rules from looking at evolved systems is extremely difficult and furthermore, the logic often is spread across the entire system.
- **Traceability**: If a decision is made, it is desirable to record why, for example, a credit check was not necessary—be it for legal reasons, internal traceability, or even to be able to show this information directly to the customer. This means that the customer even could be given the names of the rules that resulted in his or her declined application. Emulating this in source code is extremely cumbersome.

According to our assessment, the tools of the past that were a great obstacle to the universal spread of rule engines. Platforms known as *business rule management systems* (BRMS) were typically expensive, proprietary, and bulky. With DMN, however, a new generation of engines and tools have entered the market, and this will lead to an expansion of decision engines and DMN. Already, there are some open-source projects in this area. Gone are the days when decision (or rule) engines were outmoded or too expensive. The integration of modern decision engines has become easy, and it explains their increased popularity.

To sum up, we point out that from a business-IT alignment perspective, decision engines represent low hanging fruit that you should not overlook.

7.2.6 Decision and workflow engines in interaction

If you want to use a workflow engine and a decision engine together, you should decide first if you want to use an integrated product or two separate engines. From an architectural point of view, we recommend keeping the two *concepts* clearly separated, but that does not mean you can't use an integrated product.

The decision engine intervenes in the process intermittently. It is explicitly called to do so, as shown in figure 7.3 on the next page. A big advantage of this is that you can provide

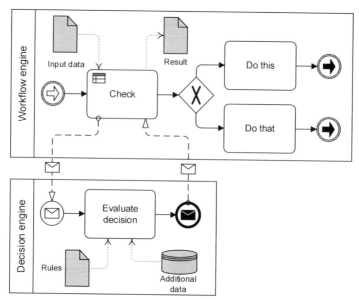

FIGURE 7.3 The decision engine interacting with the workflow engine.

decisions as a service that components outside of the process can also use. Our credit check, for instance, will surely be used at other points in the process. Ideally, from the point of view of the process, it shouldn't matter if a decision engine or a conventionally developed software component is working behind the scenes as long as the result is correct.

 Our modeling etiquette

Rules for a decision should be written independently of their current use in the process. Try to imagine a second use case in a different process or even in a different context. If you can apply the rule in the second situation without having to modify it, you end up with better rules —and ones that may be reusable even outside of the current process. ∎

By the way, the technical connection plays a more subordinate role here, and it mainly depends on the technology of the workflow engine. BPMN defines three connection possibilities for the business rule task: business rule web service, generic web service, or other technologies. Of course, manufacturers prefer to offer the decision engines within their own portfolios, but we know from experience that it is usually okay to use other engines and to connect them through web services, REST, or Java. From a design point of view, the use of other engines doesn't really matter. Direct integration into a product, however, often has an advantage when it comes to monitoring.

7.3 Automating technical process flows

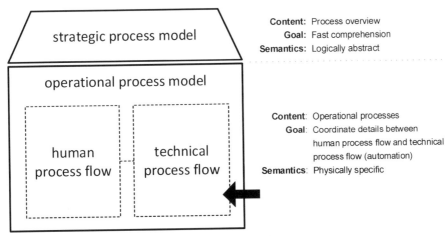

FIGURE 7.4 Technical process flows in the Camunda house.

7.3.1 Model requirements

Technical process flows must be syntactically and semantically correct, but they must also contain all the technical details necessary for automation with the workflow engine. The model must be precisely built, leave no room for interpretation, and all cases of technical error or exceptions have to be dealt with. After all, this is the source code for a software solution!

This is also the main difference between the framework described in this book and previous approaches. The precise modeling, however, also poses a huge challenge for the process analyst. Many tool vendors have tried to hide this complexity in their own technical models, and those models have never worked. From experience, we know that an operational process model with human and technical flows can make business-IT alignment possible while meeting the same kinds of requirements you would expect of software —provided that the necessary tooling exists. (We go into this again in section 8.4.2 on page 224.)

7.3.2 Procedure

The success of a technical flow when implemented depends on the procedure for developing the flow. This is where business collides with IT. In our experience, prospects for success depend not only on the process analyst's skill, but also on his or her collaboration and communication with the process engineer.

Development typically has these steps:

1. Clarify the target-state process at the organizational level. These are the human flows we discussed in section 4 on page 117.
2. Decide on the technology, language, and the workflow engine.
3. If you apply a BPMN engine (see section 7.2.2 on page 192), all you need to do is refine the definition of the technical flows. If you use another technology, you need to map the technical flows to the language of that technology.
4. Iteratively refine and specify the operational process model as new questions arise.
5. Test and execute the process with established methods of software development.

We have only examined the workflow aspect of process control so far. For technical implementation, it is essential to reconcile other aspects of software technology. (See figure 4.14 on page 130 especially.) In the next section, we examine some technical aspects still missing from the operational process model such as:

- Specifying data in the desired technology such as XML or Java.
- Defining service calls in the desired technology, for example, web services.
- Detailing human tasks such as assigning users to groups or determining the forms to display.

7.3.3 The executable process model

Starting with the previously defined process model, we use it as input for the technical flow (see figure 4.13 on page 129), but we only consider the workflow engine's pool. Figure 7.5 represents this process. Before, we did not show that the job advertisement was executed on different platforms. Instead, we extracted it as subprocesses. For simplicity, we now embed it.

To illustrate this, we also show *MajorJobs.com* as a separate pool, mainly to show the message flow. We will specify the exact content of the message later.

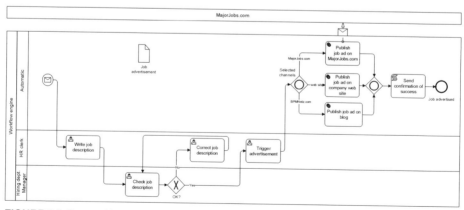

FIGURE 7.5 Executable process model of the job advertisement.

So far, the process doesn't look all that technical, does it? Many of the details necessary for automation are hidden in the underlying model, and that's available as an XML file. For now, we want to examine several aspects step-by-step. We do not cover the whole process here to save space, but you can see the full example at http://www.bpm-guide.de/bpm-java/.

From a merely visual point of view, the technical flow in this example corresponds to the technical flow defined in the last chapter. Isn't that brilliant? For those concerned with details, note that we changed two more things:

- We added the *job advertisement* data object because we have to store certain data in running process instances.
- We changed *send confirmation of success* from a send task to a script task. Why? While the confirmation could be sent by different means, it will probably be by email, and the email could come through an automated service or some built-in capability of the workflow engine. In our example, we assumed the latter, and this leads to the use of a script task in the process.

The displayed process still doesn't look too technical, does it? The crux of the matter is that the many details necessary for automation are hidden under the hood. As we said, they are buried in the underlying model, which exists as an XML file. In particular, these are:

- Specifying data in the desired technology such as XML or Java
- Executing the gateway with *expression language*
- Defining the service calls in the desired technology such as REST, Java, or web services
- Human task details such as assignment to user groups or forms to be displayed

Let's take a closer look.

Data modeling and expressions

In the process diagram, the job advertisement is represented as a data object. BPMN refrains from implementing detailed technical data modeling. Instead, it provides expansion points to accommodate diverse technologies. The default setting for this is the XML schema, although we could use Java or .NET data types just as well. By the way, data in the process does not necessarily have to be visualized in the graphical model.

The specification also recognizes formal languages for representing conditions, which are called *expressions*. The formal language therefore is called *expression language*.

Expressions can glean new information from existing data and, in the easiest case, a simple true-or-false assessment takes place. A good application example is the data-based exclusive gateway: depending on the process, at the time of execution, the token will leave the gateway through a given sequence flow.

In BPMN, the standard setting is to use the XPath expression language. XPath is a query language that works directly on XML data and therefore makes sense in combination with the XML schema for data types. This language also can be exchanged. In connection with Java data type, for instance, *Java Unified Expression Language* (JUEL) could be used.

This ability to configure a data type and the expression language to match it offers great flexibility. It also means that vendors can develop lightweight engines that are close to programming languages. This is what we have done with Camunda BPM. On the other hand, it should be noted that proprietary developments like this can lead to processes that can't run on different engines. We come back to this topic in section 7.4.2 on page 202.

Service calls

You can call IT systems from a BPMN process. You can use various elements:

- Service task: Synchronous communication, during which you obtain a response straight away, is represented by a service task. The BPMN process remains in the service task until it receives the response.
- Send and receive task: In the case of asynchronous communication, the send task sends a message or calls a service, acknowledging receipt of the request. The actual response takes place asynchronously and is then modeled by a receive task or a corresponding event.

In both cases, we use logic to extend the task to call the service. If the call is a SOAP web service, the call can be carried out in a completely standardized fashion. To do so, we have to define data objects and messages as well as incoming and outgoing data mappings. BPMN, however, is not firmly tied to SOAP, meaning that other technologies such as Java or REST-based services can be connected directly.

In section 8.4.3 on page 224 we go into our own platform, Camunda BPM, which we have used extensively in practice. This takes a different approach to service calls in that it provides extensions so that you can link a service task directly to Java code or corresponding expressions. While this is a deliberate *deviation* from the standard, we are not *violating* it because the standard permits extensions. Overall, we find that the extensions make it much easier for Java developers to deal with process definition. Success depends on the individual customer's situation. Most of our clients seem to think it is a worthwhile trade-off.

User tasks

Human interaction takes place in the form of a user task. The existence of user tasks in the process leads to tasks being placed in task management and tasks ending up on a user's task list. Only after the user completes the task does the process continue.

The exact technological connection is often a detail in the implementation of the particular workflow engine, making seamless integration possible. If it is essential for you to be independent of a specific engine, there is generally a standardized way using web services: *WS-HumanTask* (WS-HT). This comprehensive specification defines user tasks in a detailed and powerful way. Aspects such as responsibilities, delegation, escalation, or even meta information for the display can be defined. In real life, however, WS-HT is often too complex to be used easily.

Forms for tasks or other interface components, by the way, are completely left out by BPMN. This is where workflow engine vendors go off in different directions.

7.4 Practical tips

7.4.1 The zero code trap

Once people get familiar with the idea of a workflow engine, we often run into a problem: the expectation that the magical BPM suite will solve everything. Ideally, we feed the suite on models developed by the business before IT systems are automatically integrated and human workflow management just works magically. Finally, we create a dashboard of key performance indicators. These enable the business to recognize process problems in real time and to resolve problems for themselves.

This scenario sounds too good to be true, and in practice, it is. Developing process applications is always a form of software development. The promise that this can be taken on by business users in the future is appealing, but it is a promise that cannot be kept. We have seen this over and over. At the end of the day, you need comprehensive wizards and forms to develop process applications in a model-driven way, and the wizards and forms are so complex that they overwhelm the average business user.

What happens then? The company's own IT department is called in to take over development. Unfortunately, the first thing the company's software engineers have to do is figure out the BPM suite. After all, they can't just apply their prior knowledge of programming languages because the technology has been hidden behind the wizards and forms. Ironically, the aim of making development faster and easier is completely thwarted.

During our many years of BPM project experience, we have come to realize that this is exactly where the core problem with the classic BPM suite lies. It is especially pronounced in companies that already have been carrying out software development —in Java, for instance. The following disadvantages arise:

- **High programming effort**: Because software development is vendor specific, in-house developers need to learn and practice the vendor's specific platform. The related expense is not a one-off but instead continuous, with retraining required to maintain knowledge. Existing knowledge (in Java, for example) cannot be applied. In addition, existing tools, techniques, and best practices of software development (unit testing, for example) can be applied partially or not at all. This severely limits the developers' productivity, and as a result, technical implementation is much more complex than it at first appears.

- **Inability to model distinctive parts of a process**: Because the development approach is model-driven, the possibilities for technical implementation are limited. Compare this to a painter: On a blank canvas, an artist can paint a picture exactly the way she imagines. Another artist paints by numbers. He can create stunning images, but only by daubing predetermined colors onto predetermined places. This second artist can create only what was predesigned.

  Painting by numbers in BPM suites is like using off-the-shelf application software. Often it is sufficiently flexible for standard support processes (vacation requests, for example, or invoicing), but the limited possibilities for technical implementation remain insufficient for capturing and implementing core business processes.

- **Inability to integrate into existing IT**: On an operational level, the drawbacks of off-the-shelf applications also apply to traditional BPM suites: they cannot be incorporated easily into existing IT structures.

- **Specialized developers needed**: As we mentioned, a model-driven development approach is inevitably vendor specific, so there's no escaping the fact that you will need developers trained in a particular BPM suite. Such developers are scarce, and if they are not available, it is much easier to find developers for popular programming languages such as Java.
- **Vendor lock-in**: Consequently, there is a strong vendor dependency as the vendor and its partners are usually the only ones with developers with the required level of expertise. This is acceptable in the context of support processes (invoicing, vacation requests, and so on), but it represents unacceptable risk when capturing and implementing core business processes.

To us, it seems that traditional BPM suites are...stuck in the middle...neither fish nor fowl. They are as unsuitable, compared to existing software development, as off-the-shelf application products, and they don't even offer an out-of-the-box solution for process automation. This dilemma has resulted from an unsuccessful search for compromise between the two extremes and also, to a large extent, to a more academic flow during the last decade: model-driven software development. The modest growth of BPM suite vendors during the same decade seems to confirm our assessment.

Does this mean that using BPM software for process automation is a bad idea? Of course not, but it does mean that the right approach is not as simple as we might wish. In practice, it is a hybrid approach that proves best, where certain parts —the process itself —are model-driven while other parts —complex user interfaces for instance —are developed through classic programming. You therefore have to accept that software development will require software developers in the future. Sounds fairly logical, doesn't it?

In section 8.4.3 on page 224, we present the Camunda BPM platform as an example that supports the hybrid approach and is available as an open source project.

7.4.2 The myth of engine interchangeability

We have indicated that some aspects may be solved differently in different products. The flexibility of the standards gives vendors latitude in selecting technology. Can a process model then be executable on different engines? Usually not. That is, we have not yet seen a model that covers real requirements and was able to do it completely without vendor extensions.

We think that BPMN engine interchangeability is of limited concern. Consider how much time the SQL standard for databases has had to mature. Still, you often want to fall back on features of a product that you know. We find that legitimate. Any requirement for swapping around the workflow engine without having to touch your process solution should not be given too much weight.

Most projects end up buying a clearly simplified process execution, such as using Java shortcuts, while sacrificing interchangeability. This is further catalyzed by the fact that Webservices are not exactly touted as the technology of the future, and many projects prefer other technologies.

In short: Don't make complete interchangeability a sticking point. Just trust that the notation, meaning the BPMN model structures agreed upon with the business (without execution attributes), can survive a switch in engines.

7.4.3 Modeling or programming

Okay, so you're going to use a BPMN engine. The next questions are which aspects will be expressed through technical process models, and which requirements may it be better to continue addressing with classical software development? As is so often the case, there is no generally applicable answer to this question. Even if some of the following factors sound trivial to you, our experience shows that you will do well not to overlook:

- **Technology and architecture**: Depending on the workflow engine and the overall architecture to be used, it can be either simple or difficult to execute certain requirements within a process. Some engines, for example, make it possible directly to integrate Java code, connectors, or script language. Others restrict the possibilities to web services.
- **Existing infrastructure**: Few projects start from scratch. Existing systems and services should be reused or integrated. Processes can be triggered using an existing scheduler, for example, and not the workflow engine itself. These peripheral conditions need to be taken into account.
- **Roles within the project**: It is important to account for existing roles and know-how within the project. Often, there are developers involved who can implement certain functionalities quickly with classical programming but who will need a long time to do so with the workflow engine. On the other hand, there are also projects involving trained process engineers, and they work better with process models than with programming languages.

We often see that once a workflow engine has been procured, there is impetus to use it come hell or high water, and process models quickly follow that are so detailed that you can't see the forest for all the trees. These models do not help when communicating with the business, and they are no easier to maintain than classical programming code. Besides, the IT department will hate the more detailed models, and that's no good to anyone. Success is all about finding the right granularity. Modeled processes are a piece of the puzzle, but they are only one piece.

Figure 7.6 on the next page shows an example of going too far. The model shows a customer status inquiry explicitly. At the moment, it doesn't matter if we're modeling this process with a signal event (as shown), or with a condition event, or perhaps even with a terminating end event; you can see how complicated the process becomes. It probably isn't such a good idea to integrate the inquiry into the actual order process. It would be better to model it in its own process or to use a simple service to query the state of the workflow engine's instance. The only requirement on the engine is that the status must be retrievable. Now look at the modeling in figure 7.7 on the following page. Whether the inquiry is carried out as a process or as a simple service depends on the architecture.

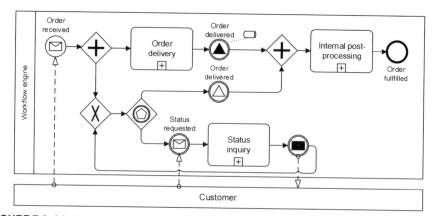

FIGURE 7.6 A bad example of modeling. It models too many aspects of the process.

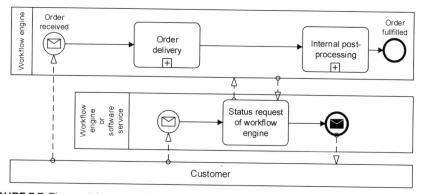

FIGURE 7.7 The model improved by removing status inquiry from the process.

 Hint: Business-IT-alignment

Business-IT alignment doesn't mean that software can no longer be developed conventionally. It does mean introducing the workflow engine and graphical views of technical processes as additional tools. But beware of process models that are too finely granular! Use diagrams in a way that enables business users to understand the technically executable models.

7.4.4 Overcoming technical challenges

In automation projects based around BPMN, CMMN, and DMN, there are some patterns and pitfalls that we would call typical. They depend on the technical environments and the tools used. Vendors address many problems with their features and extensions, so it is hardly worth going into too much detail in this book. Instead, let us give you some examples that will support your understanding of the kinds of problems you may encounter.

Data in the process

An exciting discussion always takes place in a project: How much data do we want to store in the process or case? Surely we'll need all order data for an order process, won't we? Our recommendation would be the opposite: Store as little as possible —but as much as necessary. It is usually a good idea to store order data in the preceding system for orders. Then, for the process itself, just reference the order number. If the process needs more information to support a decision at a gateway, for example, it can load the order data using a service call. This has advantages:

- The data is always up-to-date and there is no risk of divergence.
- You do not need to store data redundantly in the process where it may persist in different versions —meaning multiple times.

Exceptions confirm the rule, however, and our experience shows that there are times to keep data in the process:

- The preceding system is too slow. Constant loading leads to a performance issue. In this case, you could use a cache, or you could abuse the engine as a cache.
- You want to keep a copy of the data as it existed at a particular moment in the process and to use it for the duration of the process run.
- Your BPM platform does not make it possible to load data in the background. If this means you have to model a service task over and over just to load the order, your model quickly will become unreadable. As we said, it's about finding the right balance between graphical modeling and programming behind the scene.
- You only store data needed for controlling the process flow, for example, decisions in user tasks not available from other systems.
- Often it may be desirable to store messages in an as transmitted form. This can make it easier to repeat service calls or to identify errors.

Being *ready-to-receive* to receive events

From an automation point of view, intermediate events deserve a closer look. First, consider the semantics of the *ready-to-receive* state we mentioned in section 2.6 on page 43. Remember that, strictly speaking, incoming events are lost if no process instance is ready to receive them. Looking at the example in the upper part of figure 7.8 on the following page, a delivery order is sent to route planning, then the invoice goes out. If *send invoice* is a human task, it may take some time. The *delivery sent* message may come in before the invoice is ready, but we don't want to lose the message.

In technical modeling, pragmatism usually gains the upper hand —and modeling that is completely correct can seem unclear. In principle, workflow engines can solve the issue of an out-of-sequence message by buffering the message. This is an extension of the BPMN standard. If you have this functionality at your disposal, we recommend that you make your approach visible in the model with an annotation.

By the way, buffering a message in an engine usually raises an immediate question: What happens if a process never pulls the event out of the queue? The message sender can't be informed. This means that sophisticated error handling needs to recognize when a process instance terminates the correlated event. As you can already tell, this is no mean feat.

You may have no choice but to restructure the model. You can wait for the event in parallel. As figure 7.8 shows in the lower part, a working alternative is not difficult. This restructuring shouldn't cause a problem for IT, should it? At the very least, the diagram has become more complicated, and that's a problem in terms of business-IT alignment. Even this modeling does not always have to be consistent because in some technical environments the answer may arrive before the process moves toward the receive event. Here, again, the devil is in the details.

Testing processes

Testing processes, cases, and decisions is crucial. Executable models equate to source code, after all. They need testing in the same way and, as is now common in software development, the tests should be automated. Automated testing has the great advantage of being repeatable at any time at no additional cost. If you change the process, you can repeat the testing to confirm that you haven't broken anything. Of course this approach means that when you change the model sufficiently, you also have to adapt the test cases. It may seem at first that testing comes at the price of agility, but our experience suggests that you have to take a longer view. Agility is preserved over time because otherwise, at some point, no changes will be possible. You will have become too worried about breaking something.

There are now exciting frameworks for automating tests that make the writing of tests easy to read or that allow test cases to use tables or languages readable by normal people. In addition, *mocks* make it possible for process tests that are not necessarily integration tests. In other words, during a test, services from the surrounding systems are not called up. This then makes *unit tests* possible that can be automated easily and without placing a burden on the environment —as long as the engine supports them.

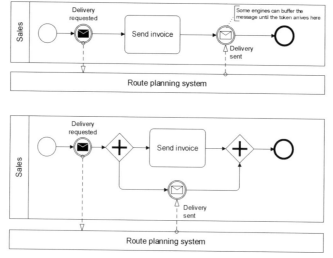

FIGURE 7.8 Never miss a message, even if the process is not ready to receive. A feature of the workflow engine or explicit modeling?

Processes or cases are typically tested with specific scenarios that illustrate a run-through of the BPMN model or a specific case in CMMN.

7.4.5 Acceptance criteria when introducing a BPM platform

If you want to introduce a BPM platform, there are more than technological challenges to overcome. Some aspects we have already addressed:

* The relevance of business-IT alignment through a suitable methodology as suggested in this book.
* The roundtrip, so that all stakeholders understand the executed models that represent the truth.
* The right granularity of models, so that they contain only business-motivated issues.

The approach taken when introducing a BPM platform also is important, in particular the *choice of tool* and the *first steps* undertaken with the platform. In our experience with projects, the approach shown in figure 7.9 has proved itself.

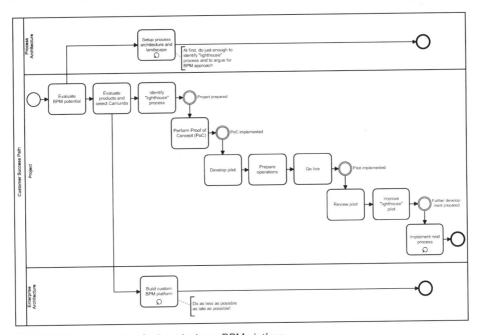

FIGURE 7.9 Best practice for introducing a BPM platform.

It's hard to carry out a sensible evaluation. We regularly see long tables with feature wishes sent to vendors of BPM platforms. The expected answers are *yes, no, maybe* —so that a score can be easily tallied. Of course, the following happens: The vendor who wants to obtain a high number of points replies *yes* as often as possible. That's how he expects to get his foot in the door during an early evaluation phase. Features may hurriedly be introduced just to be able to have more *yes* answers. Whether or not the feature is really a good solution for the fundamental requirements is sometimes secondary. We had a revealing experience of this when an employee of a potential client called us up secretly and said: "You said no at some places where your competitors said yes. I *know* that your software is better than the competition's in this area. Please don't be too honest, otherwise we will end up having to choose the wrong tool!"

As we keep saying, process automation projects are always software development projects. If you accept this, then you can see it is not necessary for *every* requirement to be covered by a zero-code tool. You will remain able to solve many requirements with conventional software development, and you won't necessarily need to hear yes to every item on your wish list. A *maybe* may suffice when it means *it can be implemented in the project*.

What is appropriately decisive? We would ask: Does the platform offer extensions so that you can implement requirements yourself if needed? Questions of implementation effort remain, of course, and of course, prefabrication by the vendor remains desirable. But the worst thing is a boarded-up platform that leaves you at a dead end. Too rarely do prospective clients inspect the BPM vendor's *philosophy* or *vision* deeply enough to understand if there is consonance with their own.

Once you have determined a suitable candidate, we recommend a *proof of concept* (POC) that implements one of your processes in the planned target environment. By all means, let the vendor assist with this; it will be quicker. In any event, make certain you are present to truly experience how process applications are generated, what effort goes into them, and what kind of know-how is required. Also be alert to tricks that the vendor's consultants may have up their sleeves, tricks they may be applying secretly to hide shortcomings in their own products.

Prior to the POC, you have to be absolutely clear about your goals. Are you seeking to verify if the tool will fit into your architecture and is able, for example, to call up your specific services correctly? Do you have a whole catalog of questions you are seeking to put to the vendor? Are you looking to showcase a wide variety of choices as a way of selling BPM or a particular tool to decision makers within your own company? The POC will be designed differently for different goals. It's therefore essential for all parties to be clear on what the goal is.

Once you decide on a tool, you should move quickly to implement a suitable process. Put this process into live operation! Suitable processes should be:

- Relevant, preferably close to the core processes of the business.
- Not too small, otherwise it will seem too easy, and it will make it difficult to show off the project as a BPM success story.
- Not too big, or you risk taking too long to deliver results.
- Not a political minefield. Unfortunately, this often is the case with business processes.
- Suitable for displaying the advantages of BPM. Remember that the first project will be used to decide on how to proceed.
- Not too demanding on organizational change. Suggesting too much change only generates resistance that can be overcome only with a lot of willpower and endurance. It isn't helpful to expect much change while also introducing a new technological platform. On the other hand, organizational change cannot be completely avoided —and a desire for change is usually what triggers the introduction of the BPM platform in the first place.

In the context of that final point, by the way, it may be a good idea to keep an existing task list and to enter tasks for the new BPM platform into it. This implies that end users (process participants) do not need to use either a new interface nor two different task lists. If you are replacing an existing workflow management tool, the change could be transparent to end users.

In your first project, you should move forward as quickly as possible and not spend too much time on conventions, patterns, or setting up your own process-application blueprint. You will learn so much during the first project that you will be better off to plan time *after* the project for analysis and documentation of lessons learned and best practices. Best of all will be to review your process once more after the fact. It will surely have a spotlight on it, and you can hope that many others will seek to copy what you did. To summarize: Revising your first project afterwards will cost you a lot less than trying to get it completely right the first time. In principle, this is us recommending an agile approach.

Armed with this, you can venture out confidently to meet your next projects. We hope you have lots of fun automating your business processes! Further information on BPM tools can be found in section 8.4.1 on page 222.

8 Introducing BPMN on a broad base

■ 8.1 Goals

Over the last several years, we have helped many organizations introduce BPMN, and not just for a few people or for a few processes. Our work was intended to introduce BPMN broadly, and to model processes in a standardized way throughout an entire division or even a whole company.

"At our company, one person draws processes using Visio, another describes them in Word or PowerPoint, and a third uses Excel. Somebody also introduced a BPM tool at some point, but that has its own notation. Now we have an excess of different process models, and that complicates our work considerably!"

We hear this type of statement often as we prepare to introduce BPMN. It is a mistake simply to buy a new BPMN tool and then to expect instant improvement. Even if all a company's modelers start using BPMN as a common language, its complexity can still result in widely divergent models. Even worse, it can result in modelers who become overwhelmed, and then frustrated, and who then give up. It doesn't help that process modeling and modelers are generally underrated. Have you heard anything like the following?

"Most importantly, the tool must be easy to operate. That way, we can find an inexpensive student trainee to interview the staff to find out how they work, and then the trainee simply draws the diagrams. Can't be that hard!"

But it *is* hard. We believe that most of the infamously unhandy process wallpapers from the nineties continue to gather dust in office cabinets because of this misunderstanding. Those who think of process modeling as merely a laborious task produce much paper and little benefit.

In contrast, a successful introduction starts with clarifying and prioritizing concrete goals. This is harder in practice than it may seem because, too often, goals are expressed in a vague manner. A few examples:

- We want to make our processes transparent.
- We want to maximize customer orientation.
- We want to optimize the process efficiency.

All those goals sound plausible, don't they? If you, as a project manager, were given these as directives by management, you wouldn't question them. Our advice though, is to do exactly that, and as quickly as possible! Why? Because these goals are not S.M.A.R.T. (S.M.A.R.T. is

FIGURE 8.1 Clarifying goals is critical.

an acronym for Specific, Measurable, Attainable, Relevant, and Timely. See the Wikipedia entry at http://en.wikipedia.org/wiki/SMART_criteria.)

- **Specific:** Clear, precisely expressed goals leave little room for interpretation. What exactly is meant by *transparent processes*, for example? Does it mean that they are all documented? To what level? In what form? For which target group? How does one recognize when an appropriate level of transparency has been reached?
- **Measurable:** You have to be able to verify that you've reached a goal. So how will you know if customer orientation has improved, much less been maximized? Besides, how does that goal connect to your BPM or BPMN project?
- **Acceptable:** The people responsible for executing against the goal must accept it as adequate and attainable. If you expect your team of three people to optimize all processes in a 1,000-person company within six months, don't be surprised if the project fails.
- **Relevant:** Do your goals matter to the people your work will affect? Are they in keeping with your organization's purpose and suitable for the environment in which it operates?
- **Timely:** Without expressing clearly when the goal should be attained, expect resources to be pulled off-task constantly to deal with more urgent, short-term issues. Your project fizzles out.

Almost as important as clearly defined goals is unambiguous priorities. Perhaps your project team can't really achieve all the stated goals. Without clear priorities, however, the team may try to achieve all goals equally —and it may fail to achieve them equally too! Process documentation is a frequent victim of this: Somehow or other, you get it done as quickly as possible. You check it off officially without blowing the budget or the schedule. The result is a sad excuse for documentation, and it ends up gathering dust next to the process wallpaper. It's a waste of time and energy from the outset.

With clearly defined goals and unambiguous priorities, you can discern what roles, methods, tools, and meta processes will be required to apply BPMN successfully. These are the four topics to keep constantly in mind while preparing to introduce BPMN, and while introducing BPMN. We will explain each in detail in the following sections.

In the end, success depends on recognizing what your goals imply. If all the processes within a company, for example, are to be documented to achieve ISO 9001:2000 certification, then the roles, methods, tools, and meta processes you define for that goal will be different from what you define to automate certain core processes with a technical BPM platform. It is also important to take the goals of the BPM or BPMN project seriously, and to carry the project through in all its details.

8.2 Roles

8.2.1 Of gurus, followers, and unbelievers

As with so many things, the successful introduction of BPMN depends on the people involved. It is false to believe that BPMN or process modeling can be learned along the way. They're too complicated for that, and both things require a lot of practice and experience before modeling processes in BPMN becomes second nature. Consequently, an organization must recognize that BPMN cannot be rolled out widely or quickly. First, create kind of an epicenter —a group of top-notch experts in methods —BPMN *gurus*. These people should possess certain attributes:

- They really understand BPMN completely.
- Even if they don't have years of experience in BPMN, they can build it quickly, practicing its implementation as often as possible.
- They are highly interested in BPMN, certainly, but also in Business Process Management in general, and they support and inspire their fellow workers with their passion and competence.
- They are accepted and appreciated as the authoritative BPMN experts within the organization.

We don't claim that gurus like these are enough to ensure success, but we can say applying BPMN on a broad base *without* these gurus is doomed to fail in most cases.

At the opposite end of the know-how scale are the *unbelievers*. Don't worry. It isn't as though you have to convert these people to your way of thinking. The unbelievers are simply all the people in the organization who have no interest in BPMN and who view it, at most, as an instrument for process improvement. They are not keen to deal with the symbols, the syntactical rules, and certainly not the subtleties of token flows. As you've guessed, the unbelievers are the majority of your fellow workers. They are executives like the process owner or process manager, and they are also the process participants who work in the processes.

You shouldn't resent the unbelievers for their attitudes, nor should you think about changing them. Focus instead on how best to involve your colleagues on the front lines in working with BPMN. You can't really expect unbelievers to create meaningful and formally correct BPMN process models; the learning curve is too steep.

If you think of our framework, you can expect unbelievers to model no deeper than the strategic level. Even then, expect that the gurus will have to check the model for quality. It's unreasonable to expect unbelievers to model operational process models, much less technical process flows. *Reading* the models is a different matter: Most unbelievers are able to interpret operational process diagrams after a brief explanation of the symbols (especially if they are shown only their own pools as described in section 4.3 on page 122). So we need not only to distinguish among the levels, but to distinguish also if a given person can create a model him- or herself, or just interpret it (see figure 8.2).

	Gurus		Followers		Unbelievers	
	Model	Read	Model	Read	Model	Read
Strategic model	Yes	Yes	Yes	Yes	Limited	Yes
Operational model Human process flow	Yes	Yes	Limited	Yes	No	Yes
Operational model Technical process flow	Limited	Yes	No	Yes	No	Limited

FIGURE 8.2 Model processes or read models: Who can do what?

In larger organizations, it may not be enough to differentiate between gurus and unbelievers. Just as a religious guru needs followers, a BPMN guru sometimes needs someone else to disseminate the good news, or who can negotiate between the guru and the unbelievers. These BPMN followers, as we call them, find BPMN interesting, but are not as crazy about it as are the gurus. Because they work alongside their unbelieving colleagues, they usually know the daily business well. But they were given the time or had tasks that exposed them to BPMN as supported by the gurus to the extent that they can do process modeling to a certain standard. Followers have become able to transfer the activities of unbeliever colleagues into meaningful process models. They feel comfortable approaching the gurus with questions or problems or to seek advice on how best to model given situations. The followers are, to some extent, the representatives of the respective divisions regarding BPMN issues. As such, they can take some of the workload off gurus and unbelievers alike.

8.2.2 Anchoring in the organization

First of all, organizations should not hire external consultants as BPMN gurus, at least not on a continuing basis. We have been in that situation often, and from a short-term economic point of view, it is not that bad for a management consulting firm. But if a company wants to be successful with BPMN in the long term, the consultant must advise against such a strategy. BPMN gurus within the company are supporters as well as driving forces, and they need to be available every day. It is a decisive role that cannot be filled by external consultants who are in-house sporadically and only for a limited time.

Potential BPMN gurus are likely to pop up in the company's business operations or IT departments. This results in an interesting situation: Guru status comes with a certain control over BPM. If both business operations and IT departments exist, who gets control? Things can get political fast, and they can devolve into unproductive feuding.

There's no single right answer for how to deal with this question. Some project organizers claim BPM (under the label of process management) for themselves. No one can deny that IT plays a much bigger role in BPM than it did in the 1990s, but IT experts don't necessarily understand BPM from the organizational point of view. Similarly, geniuses in operations may lack insight into the technical aspects. Project responsibility belongs in the hands of someone who understands and appreciates both points of view. As a general rule, anyone who is inclined to dismiss the competences and concerns of either party is a poor choice to lead the project. The following two quotes vividly illustrate what we mean:

- Business operations: "We have no idea what the IT guys down there actually do, and basically, we don't care. IT has to function; how they do it is not our problem. We only give specifications. It's not for nothing that they say 'IT follows business!'"
- IT: "We sometimes ask ourselves what those ops guys are actually paid for. Sitting in meetings all day long, drawing arrows and rectangles...that's not really work, is it? And then, when they finally give us their requirements, they are so absurd that we can't do anything with them! Anyway, we understand what's needed better than they do."

The only solution in such a situation is to form a joint committee, a BPM Competence Center (BPM CC). The Center involves the BPMN gurus, who act as the contact persons for the BPM representatives from the various divisions (see figure 8.3).

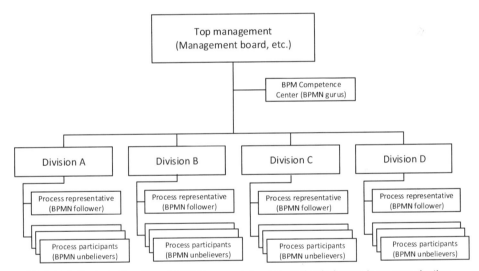

FIGURE 8.3 Typical allocation of BPMN gurus, followers, and unbelievers in an organization.

8.2.3 Training of BPMN gurus

If the success of introducing BPMN depends on the in-house gurus, how can you help your candidates become qualified? Reading this book may not be a bad start, and attending one of our excellent workshops (or one of another provider) also may help. Certainly, humans learn best by doing, so you can't start applying BPMN early enough. Without practical application, gurus-in-training quickly start to lose what they learned in even the best workshops. We have found the following process successful:

1. Read the BPMN book to understand the basics and to be able to assess if BPMN can be helpful to your work.
2. Attend a workshop or hold one in your company.

3. Use BPMN, ideally in your own work, but if that's not practical, try modeling kitchen recipes (seriously!).

4. Optional: Have your modeled processes reviewed and corrected by a BPMN expert, perhaps an external consultant or trainer.

There is another step, not always easy to realize, but it has proved astonishingly fruitful: In initial training, we show typical beginner's mistakes. These nevertheless crop up within a few weeks when we review students' models. For some reason, such mistakes have to occur in your own work before the lesson sinks in. This applies even more to certain best practices that can be applied when modeling processes.

Those most serious about achieving guru status can get official certification from the Object Management Group (OMG). An OMG Certified Expert in BPM (OCEB) is someone who, depending on the stage of certification, has passed the OMG's test. The first test certifies at the fundamental level, that is, in the basic essentials of BPM. About 40% of these questions refer to BPMN and get fairly well to the heart of the matter. You can expect that someone certified at the OCEB Fundamental level to have a good knowledge of BPMN. After Fundamental come Intermediate and Advanced certifications. There are business and technical variants for each level. This depends on where the participant wants to focus his or her competencies. (See figure 8.4.) If you want to know more about OCEB, visit the OMG homepage (www.omg.org/oceb/) or a training at Camunda (http://camunda.com/oceb/).

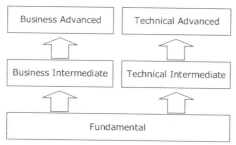

FIGURE 8.4 Stages of certification pursuant to OCEB.

8.3 Methods

BPMN alone will not be sufficient to model the business reality in most projects.

Documenting the process landscape presumably requires something like a process map, that is, a clear representation of all processes in the company. You then refine the process map until you end up with individual BPMN sequence diagrams. You may wish to link these with organizational charts to show the relationships between operational and organizational structure. Perhaps you'll even decide to write operating procedures down to the most detailed level, and then assign these to tasks in the BPMN diagram.

On the other hand, if you want to model processes in the context of IT projects, you will probably need to define data structures as well as describe the pure process, which can be represented in the IT solution. You therefore resort to UML class diagrams, which you have to link reasonably with your BPMN diagrams. The same applies to screen designs, use case diagrams, and so on (see section 4.4.5 on page 132).

The first questions in the methodical cluster are therefore: In what methodical context is BPMN to be applied and how can the BPMN diagrams be combined sensibly with the other modeling notations?

The next question is about modeling conventions, the guidelines for process modeling with BPMN. It almost always makes sense to define BPMN guidelines, because:

- BPMN is a comprehensive modeling language, and it may overtax beginners.
- You can model the same situation in different ways in BPMN, which complicates both standardized modeling and the mutual understanding we hope for when reading models.
- A guideline is a hands-on aid to orientation, which increases the acceptance of the notation, especially for beginners.
- The bottom line is that guidelines make modeling easier and faster while ensuring high quality in the process models.

Which guidelines make sense depends on what you want to achieve with BPMN. If your goal is process documentation, you will need different guidelines from someone whose goal is requirement engineering for IT projects. Think about the Camunda house in this context: The choice of the modeling level and thus the choice of method arise from what you want your modeling to accomplish.

Regardless of the goals, we have established that the following categories make sense in all guidelines.

8.3.1 Range of symbols

For a start, define a subset of available symbols. This helps, especially in the beginning, if everyone isn't familiar with the whole set. For BPMN followers who may not achieve a deep mastery of BPMN, the smaller, clearer palette works.

The range of symbols we use depends on the level at which we are working. In section 3.3 on page 102, we introduced the subset for the strategic level. At the operational level, we normally restrict the palette for human process flows only a little. For technical process flows, the range depends on the BPMN symbols supported by the designated workflow engine. Regrettably, we cannot assume that every officially BPMN-compatible BPM software product actually recognizes all the symbols.

On the other hand, it can make sense to extend the palette with custom artifacts (section 2.11.2 on page 88). That may seem contradictory at first: restrict the range, then extend it? Custom artifacts frequently solve modeling problems that the default BPMN symbol set cannot solve. We know several insurance companies, for instance, which have to document risks in their processes for legal purposes. These BPMN users include a red warning triangle among their symbols, and they use it whenever it makes sense. The important thing here is to observe the syntactical rules for artifacts and never connect the custom symbols directly to the sequence flow —always link them by associations to flow objects.

8.3.2 Naming conventions

Within the scope of the modeling etiquette in section 2 on page 23, we enlarged upon the pattern we use to designate certain symbols. For example, we use the pattern [verb] + [object] for tasks, and the pattern [object] + [state] for events. There are situations in which you cannot follow these conventions, of course, though you should try. Beginners especially tend to make mistakes that can be prevented by following naming conventions. Figure 8.5 shows an extreme example. Do you think it's unlikely even for a beginner to make such an obvious mistake? We have experienced it often. If the modeler follows a naming convention when labeling tasks, the chances are good that he or she will see the mistake and self-correct.

Another example is shown in figure 8.6.

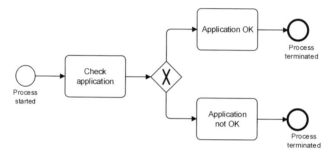

FIGURE 8.5 Wrong: The branching conditions are contained in the tasks.

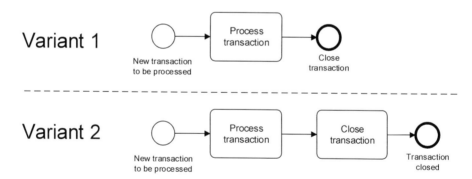

FIGURE 8.6 Variant 1 violates the naming convention for events.

This isn't a mistake, but rather a difference of opinion on whether the *close transaction* activity should be modeled as an event or as a task. You may think that it is clearly a task, but in practice, we find that final activities like this often slip in. This may even be correct for certain end events like the message end event. Particularly in the beginning, however, a mutual understanding on what a none end event symbolizes should be established, and that it means nothing other than setting a status. Without this understanding, some of your co-workers may model the final activity as an end event (as in variant 1), and others may model it explicitly as a task (as in variant 2). In more complex models, this kind of small difference can grow into another hurdle for understanding and acceptance.

When securing naming conventions in a guideline, we use a simple pattern, which we also apply to other guidelines:

- **Specification**: One short, concise sentence specifies the actual guideline.
- **Explanation**: A short explanation helps the modelers to understand the intention and to accept the guideline.
- **Example**: According to experience, most modelers take an immediate look at the sample process model illustrating the implementation of the guideline.
- **Counter-example**: One or more counter-examples also help to drive home what the guideline means.

Other reasonable naming conventions may deal with the labeling of subprocesses, gateways, and pools.

8.3.3 Layout

This category deals with guidelines about the visual appearance of process diagrams. They make diagrams more uniform and somewhat more readable by guiding the sequence flows in ways that do not confuse. For example, a guideline may specify how to represent XOR gateways:

- **Specification**: Always represent the XOR gateway with an X in its middle.
- **Explanation**: The X instantly distinguishes the gateway from other types of gateways, and so it reduces the risk of confusion.
- **Example and counter-example**: See figure 8.7.

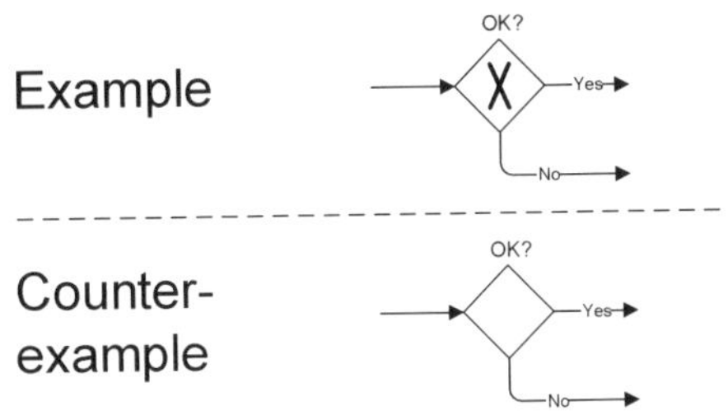

FIGURE 8.7 Example and counter-example for representing an XOR gateway.

8.3.4 Modeling alternatives

While the layout only affects the visual representation, guidelines from this category determine which of the various BPMN options should be used to model certain situations. These situations, however, must be presented as very general and abstract; they should not refer to specific contents of processes or process fragments. That's the case with the design patterns in the next section.

The example refers to applying end events:

- **Specification**: End events with a similar content should be summarized in one symbol. End events differing in content should be modeled separately.
- **Explanation**: This way, the viewer will know faster that different end states are possible, and he or she will recognize the respective state sooner.
- **Example and counter-example**: See figure 8.8.

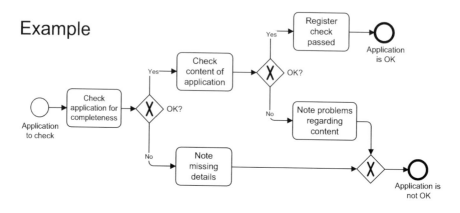

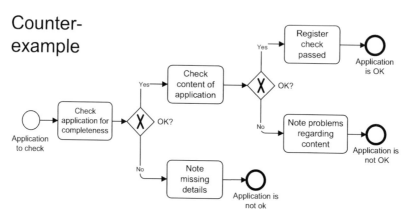

FIGURE 8.8 The positive example has one consolidated end event in case the application is not okay.

8.3.5 Design patterns

We describe design patterns differently than we do guidelines. A design pattern is like a recipe: It can guide you, but it requires some abstraction for the pattern to apply in different situations. Compared to guidelines, design patterns are much more flexible.

- **Requirement**: Describes in what situation the design pattern can be helpful.
- **Recommendation**: Refers to a pattern (from among those that follow), then recommends it. The recommendation may depend on the section of the Camunda house that the model falls into.
- **Available design patterns**: The design patterns suitable for the situation are shown through examples.

For example, here are the design patterns for a two-stage escalation:

Requirement

I want my interaction partner to do something, so I send her a message: an invoice to be paid, an item to be delivered, or an instruction to be executed.

My interaction partner does not react. After a while, I remind her of my request, and I may set a new deadline. If necessary, I can repeat this several times, but eventually I have to escalate the process (by forwarding the invoice to a debt collector, by canceling the order for the item, or by informing a superior of non-performance).

Recommendation

From the following design patterns, we recommend *event-based gateway with loop*. It is clear, easily understood, and formally correct. Because modeling technical process flows depends on the workflow engine, however, if the selected engine cannot interpret the event-based gateway, you can instead use *attached timer events*.

Available design patterns

Figure 8.9 on the following page illustrates the available design patterns using the example of ordering a pizza:

- **Event-based gateway with loop**: If the pizza has not arrived after an hour, we inquire where it is. Before inquiring, however, we see if we've already inquired. This ensures that the inquiry is made only once. Because the process returns to the event-based gateway after the inquiry, the maximum waiting time is two hours. In addition to the clarity, this pattern allows you to exercise extra patience without having to change the model significantly: Just replace the *inquired before* question with *inquired twice already* or even *inquired ten times already*.
- **Chain-link of event-based gateways**: The model behavior is identical to the previous one, otherwise it would not be a valid pattern for this scenario. But now we are chain-linking the event-based gateways. This is less clear and harder to adjust, but you see the number of escalation stages at a glance.
- **Attached timer events**: We can model the required behavior without any event-based gateway by using interrupting and non-interrupting timer events. We would attach these to a receive task (see section 2.7 on page 61).

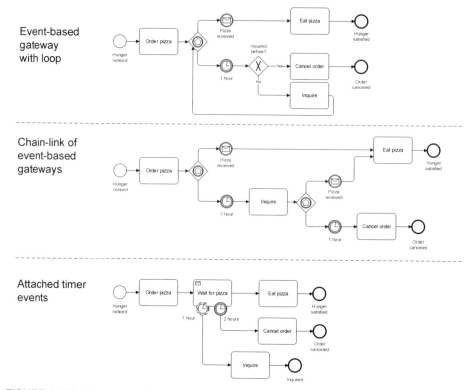

FIGURE 8.9 Design patterns for modeling a two-stage escalation.

8.4 Tools

8.4.1 Definition of your own BPM stack

In the previous chapters, we referred over and over to the typical things required of a BPMN tool, by which we mean a software product used to model processes in BPMN: to show the models to others, to analyze improvements, and to devise new and improved processes. We also mentioned workflow engines, which execute the BPMN process models technically. A third issue is the development environment that process engineers use to enhance a process model devised with the BPMN modeling tool. This is where the engineers combine the model with other technical components such as an Enterprise Service Bus, entity or data models, or user interfaces so that it can be executed in the workflow engine. Because the workflow engine can rarely function independently, it also needs an environment to take care of executing all the peripheral components of the process such as the user interface. An execution environment complements the development environment.

A rough list of the components in an integral BPM stack is therefore:

- The BPMN modeling tool
- The development environment
- The workflow engine

- The other technical components of a process application
- The execution environment

If you don't plan to implement process applications, and your only interest is in the BPMN modeling tool, skip the next section. Otherwise, what approach do you want to use for implementing the BPM stack? There are two strategies:

- Use a product that integrates the entire stack (a *one-product stack*).
- Use a combination of products (a *composite stack*, often referred to as *best of breed*).

This is not an all-or-nothing supplier decision. There are suppliers who offer a complete composite stack. But will you tolerate the troubles of a loosely coupled stack for the freedom to swap products in and out? The components of a one-product stack may be more smoothly integrated, meaning it is easier to handle. Because so many things are prefabricated, you can develop process applications faster.

With a composite stack, you usually have more design freedom, and you can develop process applications that are better and more highly customized. The components in a composite stack are optimized for their respective purposes (for example, the BPMN modeling tool for process modeling), meaning that they can be superior to the corresponding components in a one-product stack. The single product has to be all-in-one. Okay, maybe it does everything, but it does nothing right!

Are you going to get the source code? That's a big factor in the one-product vs. composite stack decision. Source code usually is not available with one-product solutions, whereas source code often is available for the composite stack. And while cost is a factor, you really shouldn't think about saving money on licenses because of open source. (Just because source code is available doesn't make it open source. Depending on the license, software published with an open-source license can be used for free and even embedded in your own products.) There also are products available for a lump sum or monthly fee that include the source code. The advantages of having the source code are not about costs; rather they are about these potential benefits:

- You have less dependence on the manufacturer (vendor lock-in).
- You limit your risk in case the manufacturer is taken over or becomes insolvent.
- You gain a deeper and more nuanced view into the software. It isn't a black box any more.
- You obtain the greatest flexibility in developing applications for your process.
- You secure the capability to integrate the stack with the company infrastructure: test automation, version management, deployment, and so on.

Using a composite, open-source BPM stack may only interest you if you have software developers who can work with it. This usually means those who can program in Java. If you employ Java developers, then a stack such as the one we describe in section 8.4.3 on the following page, should be of particular interest. Otherwise, you may be better off sticking with a one-product stack or looking to Software as a Service (SaaS). SaaS represents the easiest and most economical way to create process applications. You'll need to accept that SaaS platforms, however, create an even higher dependence on the manufacturer and less flexibility in your application development than do other one-platform stacks.

8.4.2 The BPMN modeling tool

"A fool with a tool is still a fool." This worldly wisdom certainly applies to process modeling, but that doesn't make tool choice secondary or even irrelevant, as some people believe. The best craftsman can't do anything without his tools —except maybe MacGyver.

In general, you should choose a tool that can represent all the BPMN symbols. This way, the choice of which symbols you can do without belongs to you and not to the tool manufacturer (see section 8.3.1 on page 217). If you want to tinker with BPMN before committing the entire company to it, consider a lower-cost solution. You can switch later.

Camunda provides a free modeling tool that supports BPMN, CMMN, and DMN. It saves models as standard XML files, meaning that you can execute the models directly in corresponding engines. Camunda Modeler is part of the Camunda BPM Platform; find it at:

https://camunda.org/download/modeler/

Currently, Camunda Modeler is a desktop application. We developed it using components that can be used directly in a web browser. A cloud offering that allows collaborative modeling within teams was in the works at the time we wrote this; it may be available by the time you read it. Check at:

https://modeler.camunda.cloud

Camunda Modeler focuses on creating models to be executed. While it is user friendly and ideally suited for use by business analysts, it doesn't provide extensive functions for documenting processes. For that, we recommend the following products (listed alphabetically):

- BOC Adonis (http://www.boc-group.com/)
- ibo Prometheus (https://www.ibo.de)
- Signavio Process Editor (http://www.signavio.com/)

All three products support the BPMN standard for modeling as well as for documenting processes. For example, you can add additional work instructions or generate handbooks for employees. These products let you export your models in BPMN standard format, which can then be used in a BPMN workflow engine. The tools also enable importing, which makes technologically driven changes accessible to business users.

We have experience with all three tools, and we have used them with our own workflow engine. We present our engine in the next section.

8.4.3 Camunda BPM: An open source BPM platform

After several years of experience in BPM projects and with many BPM software products, we decided in 2011 to develop our own BPM platform for process automation. You can call Camunda BPM a open source, composite BPM stack intended mainly for developing process applications in Java. That is why we call it a BPM platform and not a BPM suite.

The basic components are:

- **Modeler**: The modeling tool supporting BPMN, CMMN, and DMN already mentioned.
- **Engine**: The execution engine that can execute these models.
- **Tasklist**: A web application to process user tasks.

- **Cockpit**: A web application to monitor and administer running processes, view reports, or leverage Business Activity Monitoring (BAM).
- **Cycle**: A web application used for the BPMN roundtrip to synchronize the development environment of the IT department with various business-oriented BPMN modeling tools.
- **Admin**: A web application to administer users, groups, and authorizations.

It may seem unusual —maybe even impertinent —for us to introduce our own product in a general reference book about BPMN. When we released the first edition of this book, Camunda was a consulting company only. Despite the need for really good, all-around technical BPM platforms, however, we discovered that there weren't any. We decided to develop one ourselves. As declared Open Source followers, we made our product freely available, and we financed the entire project with add-on features and support.

The result was so successful that we transformed Camunda into a software vendor in short order. That doesn't mean, however, that we've lost our passion for the methodical questions of the BPMN application. Quite the contrary!

Many notable companies and authorities now work with our platform, and they are well satisfied. We are confident that we are contributing to the successful application of the three standards, and so we think it is useful to readers if we reference our product in this book.

You can find more information about the Camunda BPM platform in the following places:

- http://camunda.com/bpm has a description applicable to management.
- http://camunda.org describes the Open Source project, and it includes downloadable files and documentation.

8.4.4 It can't always be software

In your first group discussions about a process, it can be constructive to avoid any modeling using software tools. Why?

- Only the person at the computer can model. All suggestions by other participants in the workshop have to be filtered through that person. That's a hurdle.
- The person working at the computer may not have mastery of the tool, especially in the beginning. This can mean delays and distraction from the work on the modeling itself.
- Participants often have too much regard for the process model as shown by the software. Even though they all know it is a work in progress, the inherently tidy appearance inhibits spontaneous ideas, criticism, and suggestions.

The alternative is to draw on an office white board, though this can become inconvenient when remodeling or drawing the BPMN symbols. It gets easier if you prepare movable cards in advance of your workshop. They are easy to make:

1. Print symbols for tasks and subprocesses on A6 (4x5-inch) stock. Use A7 (3x4-inch) stock for all other symbols.
2. Laminate the cards.
3. Attach self-adhesive magnetic tape to the backs.

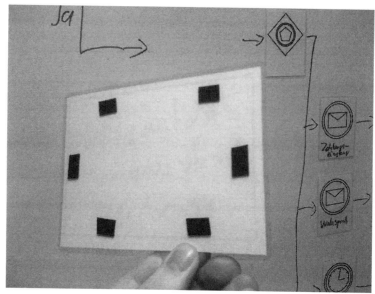
FIGURE 8.10 Card with self-adhesive magnetic tape on the back.

Originally, we used a print shop for the printing and laminating; attaching the magnetic strip involved some cumbersome handiwork (figure 8.10), but it was worthwhile. Participants have used our cards like this:

1. Use a marker to label the small cards.
2. Start laying out the process only by placing and moving the cards around.
3. As you reach agreements, draw lines to connect the cards where that is helpful.

Add lines for flows, pools, lanes, and so on only toward the end of the procedure. Doing this while the picture is still evolving is too cumbersome (see figure 8.11 on the next page).

All this is helpful for exercises, initial surveys, and discussions of simple processes. It also works for roughly representing complex processes or to represent process fragments detail. Everyone can join in, and there is no computer or software to inhibit participation. You can even add custom artifacts. At the end, you transfer this work into the tool.

At the Hasso Plattner Institute in Potsdam, Dr. Alexander Lübbe has developed *tangible bpm (t.bpm)*. The approach uses Plexiglas blocks in the shapes of BPMN activities, events, gateways, and data. Participants use the blocks to model processes on a table (see figure 8.12 on the facing page), demonstrating their ideas by placing and arranging the blocks on the shared work surface. The result is captured in the process model. Alex's research proves that t.bpm strongly motivates participants to contribute, and the process model they design themselves receives a great deal of critical checking during the workshop. Another result of the teamwork is high acceptance for the solution. For more information, see www.t-bpm.de.

FIGURE 8.11 After the lines are drawn, shifting them is a little impractical.

FIGURE 8.12 Tangible BPM in use.

8.5 Meta-processes

In section 1.1.3 on page 2, we introduced the Camunda BPM life cycle for business processes and its stages:

- Survey
- Documentation
- Analysis
- Design
- Implementation
- Controlling

These stages can be themselves seen as processes; they form meta-processes, and we have to clarify exactly how these meta-processes are to be handled, at least if BPMN is to be applied in more than one project or across teams of varying composition. This responsibility lies reasonably with the BPMN gurus. By describing meta-processes, the issues of roles, methods, and tools grow together. We can examine this with the example of a typical process to survey and document business processes (figure 8.13):

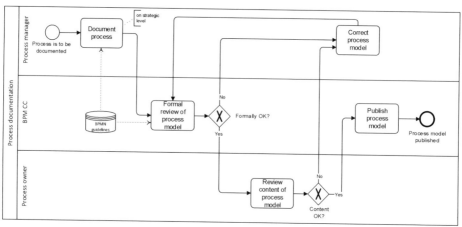

FIGURE 8.13 The meta-process of process documentation as it is lived in many companies.

The background of this meta-process is the documentation of a large number of business processes. The managers of the respective processes, who could be BPMN followers in competence, carry out this documentation in a decentralized manner. They are only supposed to document their processes at the strategic level, because doing so at the operational level across the whole organization is too much effort. When the strategic process diagrams are done, the BPM Competence Center (BPM CC), which includes the BPMN gurus, formally reviews them. Among other things, the BPM CC checks to see if the models comply with defined BPMN guidelines. The process managers correct their models as needed, otherwise, the process owner reviews the content and approves the documentation. The BPM CC then takes care of publishing the approved documentation, on the intranet, for instance.

This is just one example of a meta-process, and it may not apply to every kind of company. A completely different process may be better suited to your case. We only wanted to illustrate meta-processes are about and why it is important to clarify them.

8.6 Practical example: Process documentation at Energie Südbayern

8.6.1 Energie Südbayern company profile

Energie Südbayern (ESB) —an energy provider operating all over Germany —supplies about 160,000 residential and business customers as well as municipalities and local energy providers with electrical power and natural gas. The sustainably oriented range of services focuses on integrated energy and climate concepts from energy production and the operation of energy networks through trading to innovative solutions for energy efficiency and eco-mobility. ESB has a headcount of more than 300 and has been successfully for 50 years.

8.6.2 Starting point and assignment

Due to strong growth, ESB decided to advance the systematic management of its business processes. This task was assigned to the company's division for organizational development, which tackled developing and implementing effective BPM governance. We got the job of coaching these activities with emphasis on process documentation in BPMN.

8.6.3 Project development

In the beginning, we discussed BPM generally, as a road map to introduce the subject and also as a template for management instruction that we devised to get management to commit to the initiative. Energie Südbayern adopted the Camunda BPM life cycle as its reference model.

After the core project team completed initial BPMN training, we had to choose a suitable tool. The team compiled a company-specific list of criteria. Because the core project team intended to introduce BPM on a broad basis for the whole company, the process owners of the hiring departments were involved. They helped with the criteria selected, determined which criteria should be emphasized, and assessed prospective tools.

Following the successful selection and procurement of the tool, the core project team received advanced BPMN training. The team also helped define appropriate modeling conventions for the company on the basis of our best practice guidelines. In subsequent training for more than 20 process owners, we explained the relevant subset of BPMN that the conventions defined. This way, we avoided having BPMN hinder the short-term application on a broad basis. At the same time, we laid the groundwork for formally correct models that could be expanded with automation. In addition, we developed and introduced a meta-process for the creation, quality assurance, and release of process documentation.

At the end of this start-up phase, we prepared the core project team members for the OMG Certified Expert in BPM (OCEB) test that would officially certify the BPM competence that they acquired during our six months of coaching.

8.6.4 Conclusion

According to the motto *Helping companies to help themselves*, we supported Energie Südbayern as it introduced BPM successfully. Notably, we helped to get the process documentation done with BPMN in a short time. We succeeded at this because we worked continuously to qualify core team members and empower them to handle the introduction themselves. The success of the project is therefore actually not our success, but that of the committed project team. Their commitment means that BPM will be practiced successfully at ESB, and without depending on us.

9 Tips to get started

■ 9.1 Develop your own style

We have explained BPMN and illustrated its hands-on application based on our framework. Now it's your turn. You have to consider what you want to do with BPMN and develop your own procedures and associated conventions. You can resort to our framework, which —deliberately—allows enough room for creativity. So familiarize yourself with BPMN and then decide when you want to apply which symbols and constructs.

It is best to develop your BPMN style not in an abstract way, but rather by working with it, with actual processes from your company. Start with processes that are relatively straightforward, for example:

- Making a vacation request
- Receiving invoices, including verification and release
- Ordering office supplies

Yes, you could start by jumping on your core processes, trying to survey and document them completely. These are wonderfully suitable as long-term undertakings, and maybe you could benefit from them in your next life. For starting out, however, we cannot recommend these as BPMN projects.

For starting out, you should prefer a compact and easily manageable support process, and you should model it strategically, that is, with a focus on operations and results. When ordering office supplies, for instance, an employee urgently needs something. She reports this need, the purchasing department procures the item, and the employee receives it and is happy. Now proceed to the operational level, where you can go into the detailed operational handling, perhaps taking into account that the purchasing department won't order the items immediately. Instead, purchasing may accumulate all office product requests into a larger order. Then, from your operational process model, you can derive a simple technical process flow and even implement it. Voila, you have just automated a process that is transparent, efficient, and agile. You're ready to tackle a more difficult process, like those invoices.

The devil is always in the details, even with relatively simple processes. And you have to be aware that these processes often do not contain all the possible problems you will encounter in your core processes. The bottom line is still what we explained in the introduction: BPM works best step-by-step, and when you have a map and compass.

9.2 Find fellow sufferers

You are not alone. Many people in many organizations already have experience in BPMN. Find and contact them. Exchange information with them.

One way to find and exchange information with other BPMN users is to use the Camunda BPM network (https://network.camunda.org), which may be one of the largest multilingual online communities that deals with BPM. It's free, and you can find lots of know-how among the 10,000 people who occupy themselves with BPM. In the BPMN forum, you can upload your diagrams, discuss them, and ask questions. You can also participate in meetings that take place in your region —and if you can't find one, start your own! Simply send an e-mail to community@camunda.org to get the necessary support.

If you become a member of a network like the ones listed above, do yourself and everyone else a favor:

Be generous!

A community is not just a chance to extract knowledge from others for free. If all you do is ask questions without providing any answers, or criticize without offering ideas for improvement, eventually no one will want to talk to you. Benefit from the ideas and experience of others, of course, but share your ideas and experience as well. To give is not only more blessed than to receive, it also creates more success. Does that sound esoteric? Maybe, but it works!

9.3 Get started

Thank you for reading our book. We hope it will help you to improve the processes in your organization. Ideally, good processes free everyone to focus on the things that truly create value. If our book helps you to do that, then we have achieved our goal.

Do you have feedback about the book? Do you have ideas for improving our BPMN framework? We are eager to hear from you. Please email us at bpmn@camunda.com. And maybe we'll meet up in some of our BPMN classroom trainings! You find details online: http://www.camunda.com/bpmn/.

We've kept you long enough. Go get started!

Bibliography

[Eur09] EUROPEAN ASSOCIATION OF BPM: *Common Body of Knowledge for BPM.* Schmidt (Götz), Wettenberg, 2009

[Obj09] OBJECT MANAGEMENT GROUP: *Business Process Modeling Notation (BPMN) Version 1.2. http://www.omg.org/spec/BPMN/1.2/PDF*, 2009

Made in the USA
Columbia, SC
04 March 2018